TEACHING ENGLISH

TEACHING ENGLISH
As a Second Language

ROBERT L. POLITZER
FRIEDA N. POLITZER
Stanford University

XEROX COLLEGE PUBLISHING
Lexington, Massachusetts · Toronto

Consulting Editor

Charles N. Staubach

University of Arizona

Preface

This book is a companion volume to *Teaching French*, *Teaching Spanish*, and *Teaching German*. It deals primarily with imparting basic language skills in English to students who are studying English as a foreign language on either the high school, university, or the adult level. The emphasis of the book is on the application of linguistic principles to teaching, rather than on the development of techniques of linguistic analysis.

The aim of the book is not to present a complete analysis of the English language. In the chapters on morphology, syntax, and vocabulary we discuss only selected aspects of English, those most likely to present learning problems to the foreign students. The book is also eclectic in drawing from different linguistic theories. Some of the presentation, especially in the chapter on syntax, makes use of some of the findings of generative transformational grammar; however, no attempt has been made to follow generative grammatical theory completely or to write a transformational grammar of English. We trust, however, that the reader of this book will find it possible to consult some of the recent more technical works on English grammar, which are mentioned in the Selected Bibliography at the end of the text.

Chapter I contains a very brief summary of various linguistic views of language, not only because some of the concepts explained are utilized later in this book, but also because some familiarity with linguistic concepts will enable the student to follow the rapidly expanding literature and professional discussion in the second-language teaching field.

Parts of this book, especially Chapters I, II, III, IV, follow rather closely the presentations of *Teaching French*, *Teaching Spanish*, or *Teaching German*. In Chapters VI and VII, the strictly contrastive approach taken in the companion volumes has been abandoned—partly because there is growing evidence that inconsistency and conflict **within** a language structure may be the cause of at least as many difficulties as the clash between the native and the foreign language; and partly because, in the majority of teaching situations envisaged by this book, the teacher (probably a native speaker of English) either will not know the native language of the pupil or will deal with a class of students of multiple or varied native language backgrounds. In some sections of the book—especially Chapter V—illustrative examples of interference due to native language background are primarily taken from conflicts of English with Spanish, German, or French. The reasons for the choice of those languages are that Spanish is the native language of a very large number (perhaps the majority) of foreigners learning English within the United States, and also that Spanish, French, or German are three languages with which the readers of this book are most likely to have some familiarity.

The authors of this book are most grateful to all their colleagues and friends who read the manuscript of this text and who contributed valuable advice and criticism.

RLP

Stanford University, 1972   FNP

Contents

PART ONE

I. *Linguistics and "Applied Linguistics"*   3

  (A) LINGUISTIC VIEWS OF LANGUAGE   3
  (B) THE MEANING OF "APPLIED
      LINGUISTICS"   18

II. *Some Psychological Aspects of Language Learning*   25

III. *Teaching Procedures*   34

  (A) PATTERN PRACTICE   34
  (B) VISUAL AIDS   43
  (C) THE LANGUAGE LABORATORY   47

PART TWO

IV. *Teaching Pronunciation*   51

  (A) PHONEMICS   51
  (B) THE SOUND SYSTEM OF AMERICAN
      ENGLISH   53
  (C) THE MAIN PRONUNCIATION PROBLEM:
      INTERFERENCE   70
  (D) SPECIAL TEACHING PROCEDURES   86
  (E) A SPECIAL PROBLEM: ORTHOGRAPHIC
      INTERFERENCE   102

V.   *Teaching Morphology*   123

    (A)   MORPHOPHONEMICS: ORTHOGRAPHIC
           INTERFERENCE CONTINUED   123
    (B)   WORD FORMATION   129
    (C)   THE GRAMMATICAL PARADIGMS   140

VI.   *Teaching Syntactical Patterns*   152

    (A)   BASIC STRUCTURES AND GENERAL
           PROBLEMS   152
    (B)   THE NOUN PHRASE   154
    (C)   THE VERB PHRASE   167
    (D)   THE SUBORDINATE CLAUSE   206
    (E)   TRANSFORMATIONS   215

VII. *Teaching Vocabulary Problems*   225

    (A)   IDIOMS; DIFFICULT CONSTRUCTION
           TYPES   225
    (B)   SIGNIFIER INTERFERENCE   226
    (C)   PROBLEMS OF MEANING   232
    (D)   GENERAL PROBLEMS IN TEACHING
           VOCABULARY   236

    Selective Bibliography   240

TEACHING ENGLISH

PART ONE

Linguistics and "Applied Linguistics"

(A) LINGUISTIC VIEWS OF LANGUAGE

All languages are systems used for communication, and while many languages have been reduced to written form, all human languages are primarily systems utilizing the medium of the human voice. The sounds which our vocal organs are capable of producing are the material through which language systems are actualized. The human voice is capable of producing many sounds, but only a few of those many sounds are utilized by any one language.

We may think of a language as a set of building stones out of which we can construct utterances. All speakers of a given language know — implicitly at least — the rules according to which the building stones may be put together into constructions. They all know that certain constructions express certain meanings. The sounds which a given language has chosen are the smallest units, the smallest building stones with which this language operates. All other building stones are created by combining or recombining these smallest building stones, **phonemes**, into different sequences.

Phonemes operate basically according to a very simple principle. The sounds representing each phoneme of a language must be different from those representing any other phoneme of the same language, and the speaker must know how to **perceive** and **produce** these differences. The fact that a native speaker of English can make and hear the difference between the initial sounds of *pit* and *bit* proves that the *p* and *b* sounds represent distinct phonemes of English. (Conventionally linguists express this by writing /p/ and /b/ between slanted lines.)

Sounds that are different from each other and used within the same

3

language system are not necessarily different phonemes. First of all, the human voice is not really capable of producing the same sound in exactly the same way every time. If you repeat the word *pit* ten times, you are likely to vary the pronunciation of each sound. You do not really say the identical sound ten times; but the variation is an accidental one—it is of the type that will be automatically disregarded by the native speaker. These accidental variations occur perhaps even more frequently from one individual to another than within the speech of the same individual, and the non-native may detect these deviations and be confused by them. Other nonsignificant (**nonphonemic**) differences between sounds are predictable and follow distinct patterns. Thus the *p*-sound of English *pit* is not the same *p*-sound used in English *spit*. The sound of *pit* is followed by a slight puff of air (**aspiration**) which is absent in the *p* of *spit*. This absence of the puff of air is predictable from the preceding *s*. Whenever the *s* precedes the sound *p* (as in *spit*, *spot*, *spike*) the puff of air is absent. This is another way of saying that the *p* without the puff of air exists only in positions in which the *p* with the puff of air does not exist. They are in **complementary distribution**, which means that they are only variations of each other and cannot be used to differentiate words. To be able to distinguish between words they would have to occur in exactly the same position (as do /p/ and /b/ in *pit* and *bit*). They would have to be in **contrastive distribution**. All phonetically similar sounds which are not in contrastive distribution are variants of the same phoneme. Such variants are called **allophones**, and they appear similar to each other to the native speaker of the language. To the native speaker of English the *p* of *pit* sounds just like the *p* of *spit*. To the ears of a speaker of a language that utilizes these two sounds as phonemes in contrastive distribution (for example, distinguishing a word *pa*—no puff of air after *p*—from a word *p*ʰ*a*—with puff of air), the two sounds are probably very different. Differences between allophones can be considerable. There are languages (such as Korean) in which the difference between the sounds *p* (as in *pit*) and *f* (as in *fit*) is nonphonemic and in which these two sounds are in complementary rather than in contrastive distribution: *p* occurs only at the beginning of the word, *f* only between vowels. The native speaker of such a language may hear very little difference between *p* and *f* and may therefore experience serious difficulty in differentiating the words *pit* and *fit* in English.

From a purely phonetic point of view the units next in size to the phoneme are the **syllables**. However, syllables are units created by the alternation of sounds in the stream of speech; they are not building stones of the language system. As we speak we alternate sounds produced with a great deal of power with other sounds produced with less power. Typically each sound which represents a peak of voice power (usually a vowel) and the neighboring less powerful sounds form a syllable. Within the linguistic system, however, the units next in size to the phoneme seem to be of slightly different nature. In order to isolate these units let us compare these English sentences:

> *Many foreign students study in American universities.*
> *My friend teaches English to foreigners.*
> *He understands his pupils very well.*

What are the smallest units above the phoneme level into which these sentences can be dissected? As stated above we are not speaking about syllables. Our sentences give examples of units which are smaller than syllables and which are, nevertheless, usable and reusable building stones of English which appear to have the same constant meaning in each of their uses. The *s* at the end of *universities, pupils, foreigners* indicates plurality. The *s* at the end of *understands* (and its variant *es* at the end of *teaches*) indicates third person singular of the verb. The *s* at the end of *understands* or at the end of *students* functions, in a sense, differently from the *s* at the beginning of the words *study* or *students*. The latter is merely a phoneme; it has no special, identifiable meaning of its own. The *s* at the end of *understands* or *foreigners* is more than a phoneme: since it does have an identifiable meaning or function it is at the same time a linguistic unit of a higher level. It is a so-called **morpheme**: the smallest unit used with such an identifiable meaning or function.

If we look at our sample sentences more closely we will see that some of these units may be phonemes (for example, the *s* of *understands*), some may be words or syllables, or units composed of several syllables. For example, *in, be, to* are small one-syllable words and at the same time morphemes. It does not seem possible to decompose them into smaller meaningful units. The word *foreign* is made up of two syllables but represents a single morpheme. The word *foreigners*, however, contains at least three identifiable, reusable units: (1) *foreign*; (2) the suffix *-er* which can be used in the formation of other nouns (for example, *strange/stranger*); and (3) the plural morpheme *s*.

In a similar way we can identify three morphemes in the word *students*: (1) the element *stud-* (reused in the word *study*); (2) a suffix

-ent which can be found in some other nouns (for example, *resident*); and (3) again the plural morpheme *s*.

Just as a phoneme can appear in different forms or variants (allophones), so it is possible for a morpheme to have several shapes or forms (**allomorphs**). All allomorphs of the same morpheme must have the same meaning or function and they must be in complementary distribution. In other words each allomorph can occur only in a specific position where the other ones are not possible. Sometimes the following or preceding sounds determine which allomorph must be used.

We said above that the *s* at the end of *students* or *pupils* represents the plural morpheme. However, the *s* sounds under consideration do not have the same pronunciation. The *-s* of *students* is pronounced as a **voiceless** /s/ while the *-s* of *pupils*, standing after a **voiced** /l/ sound, has a voiced /z/ pronunciation. If an English noun ends in a sound represented by *s*, *sh*, etc., then the plural morpheme becomes *es* (pronounced /əz/) as in *dishes*, *houses*. We can say that /z/ (as in *pupils*), /s/ (as in *students*) and /əz/ (as in *dishes*) are all variants (allomorphs) of the plural morpheme and that the ending of the noun determines which allomorph must be used.

Unfortunately the use of a specific allomorph cannot always be predicted on the basis of the **environment** (that is, the preceding and following sounds with which it occurs). The plural allomorph used with the word *ox* is *-en* (singular *ox*, plural *oxen*) and not the *-es* that we might expect. And in our discussion of morphemic units in the three example sentences above, the statement that the morpheme *stud* appears in *students* as well as in *study* did not include the observation that it appears in those two words with two very different pronunciations — and consequently in two different allomorphs.

Just as a morpheme must contain at least one phoneme but can be made up of several phonemes, so a word must contain at least one morpheme but may be made up of several. As a matter of fact, linguists have difficulty establishing a clear-cut and unambiguous definition of the word as a linguistic unit. However, the concept seems fairly clear in actual usage. One way of defining a word is to say that it is the smallest possible form that could normally be used as an independent utterance. Perhaps more important than the correct definition of **word** is the realization that in many languages words belong to two broad categories: those that carry the lexical meaning (or content) of the utterance, and those which primarily serve the purpose of expressing or denoting grammatical pattern or relationship. Of course words can be combined into an infinite number of constructions, clauses, phrases, etc., which form the highest levels of combinations of building stones of the linguistic system. While the possible number of phrases or clauses that can be said is infinite, many phrases or clauses follow the same blueprint, the same pattern. Let us compare the two sentences:

1. *This brilliant student understands our position very clearly.*
2. *That unusual professor recognizes your problem quite easily.*

These two sentences do not have a single word in common. Neverthe-less we know that they share the same blueprint or pattern. Perhaps the best way of proving this fact consists in showing that Sentence 2 can be derived from 1 by successively substituting the words of Sentence 2 for the words of Sentence 1.

1. *This brilliant student understands our position very clearly.*
   ***That** brilliant student understands our position very clearly.*
   *That **unusual** student understands our position very clearly.*
   *That unusual **professor** understands our position very clearly.*
   *That unusual professor **recognizes** our position very clearly.*
   *That unusual professor recognizes **your** position very clearly.*
   *That unusual professor recognizes your **problem** very clearly.*
   *That unusual professor recognizes your problem **quite** clearly.*
2. *That unusual professor recognizes your problem quite **easily**.*

We shall return to this successive substitution procedure later to discuss it as a possible pedagogical device for teaching grammatical patterns to the student. For the time being the procedure allows us to determine a way in which we can define grammatical patterns in English:

1. Sentences belong to the same pattern if they are made up of strings of words which belong to the same word classes.

2. Whether or not words belong to the same word class is deter-mined by whether or not they are substitutable for each other in the same sentence.

Thus in Sentences 1 and 2 above, *this, that, your, our* belong to the same class of words (we shall call them **determiners**, abbreviated **det**) because they can be substituted for each other. *Very* and *quite* belong to another word class which we shall call **intensifiers** (abbreviated **int**). The **adverbs** (abbreviated **ADV**) *rapidly, easily,* belong to the same class. So do the **adjectives** (**ADJ**) *brilliant, unusual*; the **verbs** (**V**) *understand, recognize*; and the **nouns (N)** *student, professor, position, problem.*

The pattern underlying Sentences 1 and 2 may be represented by the formula

det ADJ N (singular) **V** (present) **det N int ADV.**

Within the above pattern the main lexical meaning or content is conveyed by the nouns, verbs, adjectives and adverbs. The other words may be considered as function words, elements which help keep the structure of the pattern together. They signal grammatical relationships rather than the main content of the sentence, or at least they signal grammatical relation in addition to whatever lexical meaning they may carry. Grammatical relation is also signaled by the morphemes which denote grammatical structure (in our sentences the *-s* at the end of the verb signaling the third person singular present, the *-ly* at the end of the adverb which indicates the adverbial function).

The final element which makes up the signal of the grammatical pattern is the **sequence** of the words themselves. Almost any interchange of word position would result in an incomprehensible sentence: For example, *this understands student brilliant.

One way of showing that (1) **sequence**; (2) **function words**; (3) **grammatical morphemes** combine to convey the grammatical meaning — the underlying pattern — of a sentence is to replace the content words (nouns, adjectives, adverbs, verbs) by nonsense syllables:

This gropy gleep leckons our gluff very bulbedly.

As long as the elements

det _____ _____ _____*s* **det** _____ **int** _____*ly*

are preserved, a native speaker of English can still identify the pattern. If we go on to replace the elements denoting the pattern with nonsense syllables, the entire structure falls apart into a completely meaningless string of nonsense denoting neither **lexical** nor **grammatical meaning**:

Gwa gropy gleep leckont girt gluff dlow bulbeddo.

So far we have used substitutability as the only criterion for classifying words: **words belong to the same class if they can be substituted for each other**. Another criterion that we could use are the grammatical endings with which words can be combined: **words which can take the same grammatical endings belong to the same word class**. As far as

English is concerned, both criteria will furnish approximately the same results: words which can be made plural by the addition of a plural morpheme are nouns: *house/houses*; *cat/cats*; *ox/oxen*, etc. Words which take a third person singular ending (*he writes, he thinks*), form a past tense (*laugh/laughed, buy/bought*), etc., are verbs. Adjectives are usually capable of forming a comparative or a superlative either by the addition of an ending (*-er, -est*) or the equivalent use of *more* or *most* (*happy, happier, happiest,* but *studious, more studious, most studious*). Adverbs are also capable of expressing comparative and superlative and are typically marked by the adverbial suffix *-ly*.

The function words of English also share one important characteristic from the point of view of morphological classification: unlike the words conveying the main lexical meanings (nouns, adjectives, adverbs, verbs) they are generally not capable of combining with grammatical endings or their equivalent; however, occasionally there are some words — usually categorized as function words — which constitute exceptions to the rule (*this, that* have forms *these, those,* expressing plurality).

The main types of function words used in English are the following:

1. **Determiners (det)**: words which can be substituted for the definite article: *the, this, that, some, many, each,* etc.

2. **Intensifiers (int)**: words which can be substituted for *quite, very* — usually before an adjective or adverb: *quite, very, rather, too, more,* etc.

3. **Linking words (lw)**: words which connect other words or sentences and which are usually substitutable for *and*: *and, neither, nor, either, not* (*I know him, **not** her*).

4. **Prepositions (prep)**: words such as and substitutable for *with, without,* etc.: *with, at, on, across,* etc.

5. **Question words (qu)**: words substitutable for *what, which*: *when, how, what, which,* etc.

6. **Subordinators (sub)**: words which introduce subordinate clauses: *after, whenever, as soon as, when,* etc.

7. **Auxiliary verbs** subdivided as follows: (**aux$_1$**): words such as *can, must, shall, will, ought to,* traditionally called **modal auxiliaries**. (**aux$_2$**): *do, be, have.*

If we compare the modal auxiliaries (**aux$_1$**) with general verbs like *write, speak,* etc., we note that they do not share their morphological characteristics; while some auxiliaries can form past tenses (*can/could*) none of them can take the *-s* ending of the third person singular present (*he writes* but not *he *cans write*).

The last consideration brings up the problem of whether the word *do*, which in fact does (note *does*) take the *-s* of the third person singular, should be considered as an auxiliary. A similar question could also be asked about the words *be* and *have* which—though not substitutable for *can* in a sentence such as *he can write*—are commonly considered as auxiliary verbs in many grammars. We shall return to the problems connected with *do*, *be*, *have* later in this text. For the time being we point out that these verbs are perhaps best treated as special individual cases. All three of them do serve specific grammatical functions; for example: (1) *Do* is substitutable for auxiliary verbs: *I can write*, *I do write*; (2) *be* and only *be* can be used with the *-ing* form of the verb in the formation of the progressive tense (*I am writing*, etc.); (3) *have* is used in the formation of the perfect tense: *I have written*. At the same time, however, all three of these verbs often function like and are substitutable for general verbs: (1) *we prepare our homework*, *we do our homework*; (2) *he looks good*, *he is good*; (3) *we own a car*, *we have a car*.

Therefore we may say that there are three verbs, *do*, *be*, *have*, which function as auxiliaries in the formation of the various tenses of the general verbs; and there are three verbs, *do*, *be*, *have*, which are general verbs having a specific lexical meaning. This can be illustrated by sentences such as *did you do your homework?*; *the child is being very quiet*; *he has had a cold all week*. There are also two general verbs: *will* (*he willed his money to his son*) and *can* (*she cans peaches*) which are unrelated to the modal auxiliaries *will* and *can*.

Having described the main word classes of English we can now describe by way of "formulas" the grammatical patterns underlying English sentences. The formula or pattern of a sentence such as *this book looks very interesting* would be **det + N**(sing) **+ V + int + ADJ**. A sentence such as *your boy seems quite intelligent*—though made up of different words—would follow the same pattern. *Who can help these poor children with their homework?* would represent the pattern: **qu + aux + V + det + ADJ + N**(plural) **+ prep + det + N**(sing). *Who can influence these important decisions by his intervention?* represents the same pattern again.

English nouns and verbs can appear in different forms: Nouns can be singular or plural, verbs can appear with the ending *-ing* (*writing*), in the past participle (*written*), in the past tense (*wrote*), or with the ending of the third person singular of the verb. We can include these possible choices of form in our formula—and write the symbol indicating the choice **before**, rather than **after**, the symbol for verb or noun (a procedure normally employed in transformational generative grammars). We can abbreviate noun singular as **sN**, and noun plural as **plN**. For the *-ing* form of the verb we write **ingV**, for the past participle **ppV**, for the past tense **ptV**, for the third person singular of the verb **sV**.

The formula for two sentences such as *these children are working with their parents* or *our friends are helping with our efforts* can be written as $det + plN + aux_2 + ingV + prep + det + plN$. *Can our friend really help?* is represented by: $aux_1 + det + sN + ADV + V?$ *Does our friend really help?* is: $aux_2 + det + sN + ADV + V?$ *My friend has always helped his parents* is: $det + sN + aux_2 + ADV + ppV + det + plN$. *John is preparing his lessons* corresponds to the pattern $sN + aux_2 + ingV + det + plN$.

So far we have explained the pattern of language as formulas derived from strings of words. Sentences may be created from patterns by a process of substituting actual words for the symbols (denoting word classes) used in the formula. According to this approach the main task involved in learning a first as well as a second language would be to learn the formulas and a way to manipulate them correctly. Especially in learning a second language, the view of language which we have just described will lead us to believe that the most useful exercise consists in having students substitute words in a formula (= a pattern) in order to make them aware of the pattern and of the procedure by which they can create new sentences from a pattern that has been learned.

However, there are various shortcomings attached to the description of language as we have presented it so far:

1. Formulas such as $det + sN + sV + prep + det + sN$ (for example, *the teacher works in his office*) may **describe** the sentences of a language, but they do not give us any information about **how** the sentences are constructed. For example, they do not even contain the simple information that in the above sentence the sequence $prep + det + sN$ (*in his office*) could be omitted, leaving the basic structure of the sentence intact, while the omission of the initial sequence $det + sN$ would leave us with a fragment rather than a complete sentence. The strings of symbols which we have used so far do not establish a hierarchy of importance.

2. The formulas used so far tell us nothing about why some sentences

using the formula are perfectly good possible English while others are impossible. For example, the sentence *good American students work hard* corresponds to the formula **ADJ + ADJ + plN + V + ADV** and is a possible sentence. To prove the inadequacy or shortcomings of the formula as such, the best known exponent of generative transformational grammar, Noam Chomsky, quoted the sentence: **Colorless green ideas sleep furiously*. This sentence also follows the formula **ADJ + ADJ + plN + V + ADV**. It is a nonsense sentence which was produced only to illustrate the shortcomings of the formula (the other possibility is perhaps that it could have been produced by a student learning English who went thoughtlessly through the process of substituting words in a pattern).

3. The formulas or patterns described so far do not show the relationship of sentences to each other. We may illustrate this by quoting another example widely used in the literature on transformational grammar: (a) *he is easy to please* and (b) *he is eager to please*. Both represent the formula **N** (or pronoun) **+ sV + ADJ +** *to* **+ V**. The surface identity of structure does not give the information that Sentence (a) can be changed to, and is related to, *it is easy to please him*, while the same change or operation applied to Sentence (b) will furnish a nonsensical **it is eager to please him*. The purely formulistic description of a sentence will assign the sentence *the dog bit the boy* to the formula **det + sN + ptV + det + sN** and *the boy was bitten by the dog* to the formula **det + sN + aux₂ + ppV + prep + det + sN** without explaining the relationship between the two sentences.

In still another often quoted example from transformational grammar literature, the formula alone cannot tell us why a sentence such as *the shooting of the hunters occurred at dawn* (**det + sN + prep + det + plN + ptV + prep + N**) is ambiguous. To explain the ambiguity we must again look at related sentences: the above sentence is ambiguous because it can be related to two possible sentences: (a) *they shoot the hunters*; (b) *the hunters shoot*.

There are various ways in which the description of sentences by formulas can be supplemented in order to give more depth to the formula and to show the relation between the elements of the sentence. One way of approaching the problem is to make successive cuts in a sentence in such a way that each cut separates the elements (**immediate constituents**) which themselves make up the larger units being dissected. The sentence *many foreign students are studying English in* *the United States* can be taken apart into the two immediate constituents: (1) *many foreign students*; and (2) *are studying English in the United States*. *Many foreign students* can in turn be divided into *many* and *foreign students*. The latter can be divided into *foreign* and *students*. Part (2) of our sample sentence comes apart into the constituents: (a) *are studying English* and (b) *in the United States*. Constituent (a) divides into *are studying* and *English*; and (b) is divided into *in* and *the United States*. We can identify the elements arrived at so far as *are studying + English* and *in + the United States*. Finally *are studying* is divided into *are + studying*, *the United States* into *the + United States*.

The structure of the sample sentence may be represented in the following way:

Another way of establishing a hierarchy of importance and a sense of relation among the elements of a sentence is to approach the problem from the point of view that elements which are substitutable for each other, which "fill the same slot," belong to the same grammatical category — they are not merely of the same word class but are also the same grammatical unit or **tagmeme**.

For example, in our sample sentence the first element (*many foreign students*) could simply be replaced by *they*: *they are studying English in the United States*. This replacement tells us not only that *they* and *many foreign students* can function in the same way (are the same tagmeme), it also indicates that *many foreign students* is a unit because it can be replaced by a single word. In the same way, *are studying English in the United States* could be replaced by a single word (for example, *work*: *many foreign students work*). This substitution establishes the fact that *are studying English in the United States* makes up a single unit and that our sample sentence is in fact made up of two grammatical elements (tagmemes). *Many foreign students + are working in the United States* is related to a sentence such as *they + work*, which represents the same basic structure. Other subdivisions in our sample sentence would be established by similar procedure: for example, *in the United States* can be replaced by *here*. So *in the United States* and *here* can function identically and *in the United States* represents a group which must be interpreted as one unit (tagmeme).

Yet neither the cutting into immediate constituents nor the procedure of establishing a hierarchy of importance and of deciding which elements belong together by a process of replacement will answer all the questions concerning the limitations of formulas that we have raised previously. Immediate constituent analysis or tagmemic analysis will not tell us how *the boy is beating the dog* is related to *the dog is being beaten by the boy*, nor will it tell us why *the shooting of the hunters occurred at dawn* is ambiguous.

Concern with questions of this type led to the development of the generative or transformational model of language. Unlike the descriptive or structural approach, the generative approach is not concerned with how to dissect utterances but rather with the formation of rules which describe how these utterances were created in the first place. The ideal generative model of grammar is a set of rules which specifies how all the possible grammatically correct (= acceptable) sentences of a language are created. The model is also transformational in the sense that it shows how certain structures of the language are related to others, how some structures can be derived from others. But we must emphasize that, like most grammars, a generative-transformational only describes the sentences of a language; this is little reason to assume that this grammar has any "psychological reality"—that it describes the processes by which people produce sentences.

The description of language that we have used so far has depicted language as a set of building stones. The smallest building stones are the phonemes. These are combined into larger units (morphemes) which in turn form words and larger utterances.

The generative model of grammar starts at the level exactly opposite to the one that has been our starting point: the first step in developing the grammar is the speaker's desire to make an utterance, a sentence **S**. Once he has made this decision, the facts of English grammar dictate that the sentence be composed of a **noun phrase NP** and a **verb phrase VP**. We can state this in a formula which states that sentence **S** can be rewritten as **NP + VP**:

$$S \rightarrow NP + VP$$

In rewriting the formula for the noun phrase **NP** we can adapt the convention of putting optional elements in parentheses:

$$NP \rightarrow (det) + (ADJ) + N$$

The above formula indicates, therefore, that the noun phrase which corresponds to it may be represented by:

$$\textbf{det} + \textbf{ADJ} + \textbf{N}: \quad \textit{many foreign students}$$
$$\textbf{ADJ} + \textbf{N}: \quad \textit{foreign students}$$
$$\textbf{det} + \textbf{N}: \quad \textit{many students}$$
$$\textbf{N}: \quad \textit{students}$$

The verb phrase **VP** may be rewritten as $\textbf{VP} \rightarrow (\textbf{Aux}) + \textbf{V} + (\textbf{NP}_1) +$ (**Adverbial**).

The above formula indicates that the verb phrase corresponding to it may be

$\textbf{Aux} + \textbf{V} + \textbf{N}_1 + \textbf{Adverbial}$:	*can study English in the United States*
$\textbf{V} \mid \textbf{N}_1 + \textbf{Adverbial}$:	*study English in the United States*
$\textbf{Aux} + \textbf{V} + \textbf{N}_1$:	*can study English*
$\textbf{V} + \textbf{N}_1$:	*study English*
$\textbf{V} + \textbf{Adverbial}$:	*study in the United States*
$\textbf{Aux} + \textbf{V}$:	*can study*
$\textbf{Aux} + \textbf{V} + \textbf{Adverbial}$:	*can study in the United States*
$\textbf{V}$:	*study*

We may now further expand the formula representing the grammar underlying our sample sentence by specifying that the adverbial may be a prepositional phrase as well as a one-word adverb. To do this we use a convention of generative grammar which puts **alternates** between braces:

$$\textbf{Adverbial} \rightarrow \begin{Bmatrix} \textbf{ADV} \\ \textbf{prep} + \textbf{NP}_2 \end{Bmatrix}$$

The above formula indicates that instead of using a prepositional phrase like *in the United States,* we could have used an adverb like *here* or *there*.

The grammar which has generated the sentence

Many foreign students study English in the United States

may thus be expressed by the following formulas:

$$\textbf{S} \rightarrow \textbf{NP} + \textbf{VP}$$
$$\textbf{NP} \rightarrow (\textbf{det}) + (\textbf{ADJ}) + \textbf{N}$$
$$\textbf{VP} \rightarrow (\textbf{aux}) + \textbf{V} + (\textbf{N}_1) + \textbf{Adverbial}$$

$$\textbf{Adverbial} \rightarrow \begin{Bmatrix} \textbf{ADV} \\ \textbf{prep} + \textbf{NP}_2 \end{Bmatrix}$$

The above formula accounts not only for one sentence. It can be made to generate many more, if we specify additional words or lexicon to fit the formulas. Note that, in the example, N, N_1, N_2 refer to different types of nouns:

$$N \rightarrow \begin{Bmatrix} students \\ children \end{Bmatrix}$$

$$det \rightarrow \begin{Bmatrix} the \\ some \\ many \end{Bmatrix}$$

$$ADJ \rightarrow \begin{Bmatrix} good \\ young \\ foreign \end{Bmatrix}$$

$$aux \rightarrow \begin{Bmatrix} may \\ can \\ do \end{Bmatrix}$$

$$V \rightarrow \begin{Bmatrix} learn \\ study \end{Bmatrix}$$

$$ADV \rightarrow \begin{Bmatrix} here \\ there \end{Bmatrix}$$

$$N_1 \rightarrow \begin{Bmatrix} English \\ mathematics \end{Bmatrix}$$

$$prep \rightarrow in$$

$$N_2 \rightarrow \begin{Bmatrix} United\ States \\ Canada \end{Bmatrix}$$

The grammar (formulas + lexicon) specified so far can account for sentences such as:

Children learn.
Foreign children may study in Canada.
Some young students can study there.
The foreign students can learn mathematics in the United States.

The "rewrite formulas" used above simplify some of the problems involved in writing generative grammars, but they do convey the general concept on which generative grammars are based. In addition they illustrate that generative grammars must also be concerned with specifying precisely what classes of words, which types of verbs, nouns, adjectives, etc., can apply within those formulas. If we had not specified different types of nouns for the subject (**NP**), the direct object of the verb (**NP$_1$**), and the adverbial phrase (**NP$_2$**), our grammar could have generated sentences such as:

Young mathematics learn children in students.

To illustrate further, the sentence *the dog bites the boy* is generated by this grammar:

$$S \rightarrow NP + VP$$
$$NP \rightarrow (det) + N$$
$$VP \rightarrow V + (NP)$$

However, it is perfectly clear that not all English verbs fit into this system. Only verbs which can take a direct object can be used to fill the position of **V** in the above grammar. A sentence such as *the dog looks hungry* must be accounted for by a grammar in which the verb phrase takes the form of

$$VP \rightarrow V + ADJ.$$

Nevertheless, only a certain type of verb (*look, get, seem, be*) can take the place of **V** in the above formula. Formulas showing the various options according to which sentence elements may be rewritten must be supplemented with statements as to what classes of words, what types of verbs, nouns, adjectives, etc., are in fact available for each option.

Transformational grammars are concerned not only with showing how sentences are generated but also with indicating how sentences are related to each other. Most writers of transformational grammars assume that certain sentence types are basic while others are related to them through processes of transformations which follow clearly describable and fixed rules.

If we wanted to relate the sentence *many distinguished professors write important books* to sentences such as *many distinguished professors are writing important books* or *many distinguished professors do not write important books*, we could do this by specifying in the grammar evolved for the first sentence that there are options to use the progressive tense (**Prog**) or to make the sentence negative (**Neg**).

In the grammar the option for the progressive could be indicated by

$$(\textbf{Prog}): \textbf{V} \Rightarrow be + \textit{-ing } \textbf{V}.$$

The symbol $\Rightarrow$ is used to indicate a transformation. The formula indicates that the progressive is formed by replacing the verb by the corresponding form of *be* and the *-ing* form of the verb itself.

The negative option can be expressed by a rule which states that the negative is formed by placing *not* after the auxiliary verb:

$$V \rightarrow (\textbf{aux}) + V$$
$$(\textbf{Neg}): V \Rightarrow \textbf{aux} + not + V.$$

Note that in the latter of the two formulas the auxiliary is no longer optional. Even if the original positive sentence has no auxiliary, a mandatory auxiliary must appear in the negative transformation:

Foreign students study ...
Foreign students $\boxed{do}$ *not study ...*

In our approach to the problem of teaching English as a foreign language, we shall not attempt to produce a transformational grammar of English, nor shall we attempt to give an exhaustive description of English according to any one particular linguistic model; but we shall use the various models discussed so far as a general framework within which to approach the discussion of the problems faced by the non-native in his attempt to speak acceptable English. The main thrust of this work is not linguistic but pedagogical.

(B) THE MEANING OF "APPLIED LINGUISTICS"

During the past twenty years the views of linguists have had an ever-increasing influence on language instruction at all levels. The first major impact of linguistics upon language teaching took place during World War II when linguists were asked to create grammars of languages which had never or seldom been taught in the United States before, and to teach those languages to military personnel. The impact of linguists upon language teaching was also felt through the teaching of English as a foreign language. It was primarily during and after World War II that an ever-increasing number of foreigners (military personnel, students, etc.) came to the United States to study. These foreigners had to acquire as quickly as possible an audiolingual command of American English, and linguists had an essential part in preparing the teaching materials to be used in the teaching of American English. Through these two avenues, the linguistic view of language teaching spread first into the college curriculum and from there into the teaching of foreign languages in the high schools.

Before enumerating some of the relationships of linguistics to language teaching, we want to underline one fact: applied linguistics relates to linguistics in approximately the way in which any applied science field relates to the science itself. An engineer must know applied mathematics and applied physics in order to build bridges — but he cannot and should not expect the mathematician or physicist to tell him what bridges to build in a particular situation. In a similar way, the language teacher cannot expect the pure science (linguistics) to contain an automatic endorsement of any particular teaching procedure. It is a tool to be used by the practitioner; it can help the practitioner operate more effectively. The teacher who is familiar with linguistics will find certain teaching procedures more reasonable than others, but it is the teacher who must decide upon the method, and the best method is ultimately the one that is proved best by practical experience.

The following are some of the main areas in which linguistics has made an impact upon language teaching and in which language teachers have found that the use of linguistics was of particular help.

1. **Linguistics has generally discredited the grammar-translation approach**, probably for two reasons:

   a. The general semantic definitions on which this approach was based were found lacking in accuracy. The theory behind the grammar–translation approach was that **grammatical** analysis of **one** language was the prerequisite for translation into the other. Thus the analysis of the English sentence

The father sees the boy.

provided a grammatical framework:

Subject	Predicate	Direct Object
(noun, nominative)	(verb, present tense, third person)	(noun, accusative)

This grammatical framework enabled the student to "resurrect" the English sentence in any other language, provided he could identify the same grammatical frame. For example, in Latin:

Subject	Predicate	Direct Object
(noun, nominative)	(verb, present tense, third person)	(noun, accusative)
pater	*videt*	*puerum*

As we said before, there are theoretical objections to this

procedure of learning a foreign language. Some of the grammatical categories employed are not universals: they may fit some languages better than others. The categories of **nominative** and **accusative** can be easily identified in a language such as Latin where they correspond to very specific sets of case endings, but the same categories make little sense in a language such as English. While there may be, indeed, universal categories (that is, most or perhaps all languages have sentences which contain subjects, predicates, and objects), the emphasis on those universals may obscure the real difficulties of the learner — namely, the specific way in which these universals are expressed in specific languages. Thus, in the example quoted above, the subject/object relationship of English is expressed by word order, while in the Latin sentence the same relation is expressed by the endings alone. As a matter of fact, in transforming the English sentence into Latin while keeping the English word order, we illustrated how translation procedures may often — quite subtly — result in imposing the characteristics of one language upon another. While any permutation of the words *pater*, *videt*, and *puerum* will give a theoretically correct and understandable Latin sentence, in normal Latin style the word order *pater puerum videt* (verb in final position) would be preferred.

b. The other objection to the grammar–translation method stems from more practical considerations. It is a slow procedure since the student must always return to his native language and go through processes of grammatical analysis to arrive at foreign language utterances. Furthermore it almost forces the student to learn foreign language equivalents of words of his native language in isolation, or at least to apply such equivalents in contexts different from the ones in which they were learned in the first place. To give a simple example, the Spanish speaker who has learned that the English equivalent of the Spanish verb *hacer* is *make* may — as result of the translation process — produce English sentences like *he makes (instead of *does*) *his homework* or *it makes (instead of *is*) *cold*, simply because Spanish uses *hacer* in the Spanish equivalents of those English sentences. Perhaps the majority of the mistakes of the foreign language learner can be traced to his applying, or rather misapplying, native language = foreign language equations. No specific methodology can guarantee that misapplication of such pseudo-equivalents will never take place. But there is ample reason to avoid a teaching methodology which reinforces the danger of the occurrence of such errors.

2. **Linguists generally recommend that the starting point of any exercise be a construction in the foreign language**. This construction must be learned and can then be changed into other constructions by processes of transforming, expanding, etc.

3. **The "models" of languages developed by the linguist have had a profound influence on the teaching methods**. The descriptive linguists have generally assumed that the processes used in linguistic analysis are also useful teaching and learning procedures. Just as the linguist "finds out" that *boy* and *child* are nouns by substituting one for the other in the same sentence, so the student finds out about grammatical categories and sentence structure by substituting words of the same category within the same sentence. Just as the linguist finds out that /p/ and /b/ are phonemes of English by contrasting words such as *pit* and *bit*, so the non-English speaker (who may have difficulty distinguishing /p/ and /b/ and pronouncing them correctly) is taught to discriminate between the sounds by listening to and pronouncing series of words such as *Pete, beat*; *pat, bat*; *pin, bin*, etc.

So far the generative–transformational model has probably had somewhat less impact on foreign language teaching than the descriptive one. Of course language teachers, whether linguistically oriented or not, have always used **transformation** (that is, shifts from one tense to another, changes from active to passive, from positive to negative) as a device for the construction of exercises. However, the use of a transformational generative model for pedagogical purposes involves a great deal more than just the use of transformation drills. Some of the main features implied by it seem to be:

a. Basic sentence types from which all others can be derived either by expansion or by transformation processes are used as the starting point of instruction.
b. Careful attention is paid to the **sequence** in which expansion and transformation processes are learned.
c. Sentence patterns are grouped in the exercises in such a way that patterns related to each other are learned in their correct relationship.
d. Sentences which have only a surface relationship to each other

are not grouped together or produced in the same exercise (for example, the sentences *he is eager to please* and *he is easy to please* should not be produced as the result of a substitution procedure in the same drill or exercise).

e. Vocabulary is not learned indiscriminately, but preferably in terms of categories which fit specific types of sentences. For example, verbs such as *look, seem*, etc., which fit into the sentence pattern *he looks good, he is good*, must be distinguished from verbs which fit into a pattern **Noun + Verb + Noun** such as *the boy sees the man*.

4. **Linguists have always emphasized that one of the main stumbling blocks to learning a second language is the interference which comes from the first.** Through careful comparison of the language to be learned with the native language of the learner, we can pinpoint the reasons for the difficulties experienced by the student and help him to overcome them. For example, the reason that the native speaker of Spanish has difficulty pronouncing the sequence of *s* + **consonant** at the beginning of a word (as in *speak, stand*) is simply that in his native language such a sequence does not exist in word-initial position. *s* + **consonant** in Spanish is always preceded by a vowel. Awareness of the nature of this type of interference can help us give correct explanations and, even more important, it can help us conduct the most helpful exercises. Many linguists believe, therefore, that good teaching materials must be based on a careful **contrastive analysis** (comparison) of the native language and the language to be learned. Our analysis of the English sound system and its comparison with those of French, Spanish, and German — see Chapter IV, Section (C) — is an example of such a contrastive analysis.

5. **Most linguists have always insisted that language is primarily audiolingual activity and that writing is only a secondary reflection of speech.** This attitude has led has led to the writing of grammars which are based on speech rather than writing — on the analysis of certain parts of language which are usually overlooked or are only inadequately reflected in written materials (intonation, frequency of occurrence in speech rather than in written materials). The information furnished will obviously be useful to the language teacher.

6. **Descriptive linguistic analysis is based on examination of the observable facts of language.** Descriptive linguists have had a strong kinship to **behavioristic** schools of psychology — schools based on the

analysis of observable stimuli and reactions. In language teaching, descriptive linguists have emphasized that an important part of language learning consists of practice—having the student respond to stimuli so that the responses may be learned. Descriptive linguists are fairly unanimous in emphasizing that learning **about** the language is not necessarily the same activity as learning the language—acquiring the repertory of responses which characterize a native speaker of the language.

From the foregoing, it is clear that the relationships of linguistics to language teaching span a wide area in which the linguist must be looked upon as having various degrees of competence and authority. The linguist (as linguist) can ultimately give little advice as to whether the **direct method** (complete avoidance of the native language) is superior to any other. We can only point out that the avoidance of the native language is undoubtedly beneficial because it is likely to minimize interference. At the same time, the direct method depends largely on **realia**, classroom environment, and activities that can be carried out within the classroom. Therefore, the lesson or the course is likely to be structured according to principles other than those of structure or grammar. A simple direct method lesson may include sentences such as: *The teacher comes into the classroom. He says hello to the students. The students answer him. Now he sits down, opens his book and starts reading.*

These sentences include a great variety of constructions (for example, a two-part verb—*sit down*; direct objects; objects of prepositions; and so on)—a mixture which shows little linguistic control. This is perhaps not a **necessary** feature of the direct method. To the extent that it can be made compatible with attention to linguistic structure and linguistic sequencing, the direct method would certainly be endorsed by most linguists.

Some pedagogical practices which have often been associated with linguistics and the impact of linguistics on language teaching actually have little relation to linguistic science, and they reflect—at best—ideas used by particular linguists in particular teaching situations. One such practice is the utilization of audiolingual tactics before taking up reading and writing. While such a strategy reflects the linguist's concern for the importance of speech, its pedagogical efficacy must be determined by the language teacher in the specific learning situation. In a similar way the doctrine that **memorization of dialogues** is the most effective way of learning languages may have the endorsement of some linguists; but linguistic science has nothing to offer to prove the superiority of such purely pedagogical devices.

The suggestion that languages are learned best without any formal explanation of grammar may have been made by some linguists. Indeed, all experienced language teachers and linguists will agree that the learning of grammatical rules and grammatical explanations **by themselves** will not assure adequate **performance** in the foreign language. But linguistics will not furnish evidence for the withdrawal of grammatical rules. When or whether to offer grammatical explanations is ultimately a psychological problem which must be handled in the light of psychological insight and — above all — practical experience.

CHAPTER II

Some Psychological Aspects of Language Learning

From our description of language it can be gathered that learning a language system—native or foreign—is an extremely complex task. Modern learning theory is largely based on experimentation and theories derived from extremely simplified laboratory situations (often involving animals rather than humans). We must be careful when drawing conclusions from those theories and applying them to the complex task of language learning.

Perhaps one way of introducing the psychological problem of language learning is to take a description of language as a starting point and to ask precisely what is involved in the acquisition of this language. Obviously the person speaking any language (foreign or native) must have acquired control of the sound system. He must be able to produce the phonemes of the language and hear the contrasts between them. The morphemes and words (and their meanings) must be available to him as "responses" when they are suggested by the appropriate "stimuli." (In other words, if a speaker of English sees a cow, this sight must stimulate the word, and when the word is used it must evoke the appropriate concept.)

However, in addition to sounds, morphemes, and words, the learner of the language must also acquire the ability to manipulate the system. The native speaker learns somehow to put morphemes together according to "rules" and he learns to manipulate and use the patterns of his own language. Nobody memorizes (even in his native language) all the forms and sentences he is going to say in his lifetime. Somehow we know the patterns, we change them, we substitute in them, and we use

25

them for our purposes. The best proof that even native language learning involves some sort of awareness and manipulation of pattern comes from the mistakes of children. A three-year-old may say *I singed the song, not because he ever heard and learned the form *singed, but because he combined the stem sing with the -ed ending, attributing to sing the same **transformation pattern** as laugh/laughed; kill/killed, etc.

Language learning—native and foreign—involves two complex but very different tasks:

1. The acquisition of an amount of material immediately available to us for the purpose of understanding and self-expression. This material **must** include the sounds, the morphemes, the words, and it inevitably also includes a large number of phrases, clauses, etc., which follow the patterns of the language to be learned.

2. The acquisition of the ability to use the acquired **raw material** (a famous language teacher, Harold Palmer, called it **primary matter**) for the purpose of converting it — transforming it — into the large number of unpredictable utterances which we will speak or hear. Much of the pedagogical discussion, much misunderstanding is caused by language teachers stressing either the one or the other of these tasks. The fact is that both exist, that both are equally important: we must have a certain amount of raw material, primary matter, available — and we must also be able to convert these materials into **secondary matter** — the phrases and sentences required by the specific speaking situation.

An analysis of language aptitude and language aptitude tests (see Bibliography: Carroll-Sapon) seems to bear out the above statements. The most widely used language aptitude tests are composed of sections which first test the prospective students' ability to hear and analyze sound contrasts. Especially in an audiolingual course, this ability is prerequisite for easy mastery of all primary matter acquired through the ear. Another factor involved in language aptitude is memory. Without memory for sounds the acquisition of primary matter will become too difficult. A third factor of aptitude is the ability to recognize grammatical structure, to identify whether sentences belong to the same pattern. This ability to deal with grammatical structure is no doubt the component of aptitude involved in the manufacture of secondary matter out of the previously-learned raw material.

We have already stressed that a language cannot be memorized. The astonishing fact about both first and second language learning is that the learner must be able to expand a finite amount of learned materials by the conscious or subconscious application of a finite number of rules to a potentially infinite number of possible utterances.

It also seems obvious that the process of manufacturing new materials will be easier if the amount of raw material available is large. In the learning of the first language the amount of primary matter learned and available is extremely large, of course. Only years of exposure to the foreign language would increase the available primary matter to an amount equal to that available in the mother tongue.

The foreign language has an additional tremendous disadvantage in comparison with the native language: not only is there less primary matter available, but the manufacturing processes used in the native language will continue to interfere.

Whatever learning theory has to offer to language teaching must be interpreted with reference to the fundamental learning tasks involved in second language acquisition. In general, psychological theories can be divided into two major types: the **behavioristic** type and the **gestalt** type. The behaviorists — as the name indicates — insist that the scientific study of psychology cannot rely upon assumptions about unknown and unknowable interior processes, but must consist of the observation of overt, observable reactions (**R**) to observable stimuli (**S**).

Many psychologists who do not follow the strictly behaviorist approach believe that psychological phenomena — and with them learning — involve more than overt stimulus and response. They feel that the learner brings to the learning process his own creativity, his ability to detect patterns and configurations, to recognize analogies and contrasts. While he may indeed be influenced and shaped by outside stimuli, he also is an interacting organism, influencing the environment.

The behavioristic view of learning (the $S > R$ school of psychology) distinguishes basically between two types of learning. Both of them play a role in the acquisition of language.

The first type of learning, called **classical conditioning**, involves what is called an **associational shift**. This process may be described, in a very oversimplified form, somewhat as follows: a piece of candy placed in the mouth serves as a stimulus S which produces salivation and a sense of pleasure as a reaction **R**:

$$\text{candy} > \text{pleasure}$$
$$\text{(physical stimulus)} > \text{(reaction)}$$
$$\text{S} > \text{R}$$

The candy is now called by a name, *gumdrop*, which is repeated each time a piece of candy is presented. *Gumdrop*, a linguistic abstraction or symbol, is now associated with the physical object, candy, and becomes a participating or alternate factor with the original stimulus. We can denote this alternate factor as **A**, and summarize the new situation thus:

$$\text{candy} \qquad\qquad + gumdrop > \text{pleasure}$$
$$\text{(physical stimulus)} + \text{(name)} \quad > \text{(reaction)}$$
$$\mathbf{S} \qquad\qquad\qquad +\mathbf{A} \qquad > \mathbf{R}$$

As a result of this association, we soon find that the word *gumdrop* alone, in the absence of any actual candy, will produce salivation and what we might describe as an **echo** of sweetness and pleasure:

$$gumdrop > \text{pleasure}$$
$$\text{(name)} \quad > \text{(reaction)}$$
$$\mathbf{A} \qquad > \mathbf{R}$$

By the association of stimulus **S** with a substitute or alternate **A** we have conditioned the response mechanism or reaction **R**, so that it will function even when the associational shift from $\mathbf{S} > \mathbf{R}$ to $\mathbf{A} > \mathbf{R}$ has been completed: the organism has been conditioned to react to a symbol even when the physical stimulus is not present.

In the learning of the mother tongue, **S** corresponds to the complex of stimuli created by a situation, and **A** represents the linguistic symbols —words, forms, and structures—with which the stimuli are constantly associated. So persistent is this process of association that the linguistic symbol **A**, a substitute for reality **S**, comes to evoke whole complexes of responses or reactions **R**, and so to have meaning.

When the learning of a second language is undertaken, the process of associational shift cannot be repeated in this simple form. We do not refer here, however, to the simultaneous learning of two languages by a very young child in a bilingual environment, but to the acquisition of a new or foreign language by one who has already acquired the habits of his native tongue.

Much traditional methodology has focused the learner's attention on the association of elements of the new language, which we can designate as $\mathbf{A}^1$, with those of the native language, **A**. This gives us an additional substitution between **S**, the situation or external reality, and **R**, the response or meaning. Our formula would now be:

$$\mathbf{S} + \mathbf{A} + \mathbf{A}^1 > \mathbf{R}.$$

The meaning **R** of the foreign language **A¹** is not derived directly from the situational association. It is also identified with the meaning of the symbols of the native language.

Of course this interpolation of the native language is the reason for what we have called **interference**. It leads not only to a frustrating slow-down of the process of communication, but also to the intrusion of native sound and speech patterns into the second language as used by the learner.

The second basic type of learning is called **instrumental**: in addition to an association of stimulus and response, it also involves the idea of the **reward** or satisfaction which the individual receives as the result of his performance. As we watch an infant or a small puppy beginning to react to sounds and sights in his environment, it becomes apparent that, at first, responses may be almost completely random; but a chance few of the responses result in the satisfaction of some desire, or the lessening of an anxiety. This satisfaction or reward becomes associa-ted with the specific response after a number of chance occurrences and thus serves to **reinforce** the learning of a particular response to a particular stimulus.

In first-language learning, the child produces sounds at random, but certain configurations of sounds will win the approval of his parents or bring about certain results. The child is then communicating, and the reward will be his parents' attention. The response which brings reward will be learned.

In second-language learning, of course, **conscious imitation** of sounds produced by the teacher becomes an important and obvious basis for identifying bits of new behavior to be learned. Nevertheless the value of reward or reinforcement of correct responses in speeding real control seems beyond argument. Our problem will be to determine what teaching or learning devices are best calculated to provide for such reinforcement. We must observe carefully the way we use the term reward. A student may be anxious to get his homework done and may be worried about not finishing it in time so that he can get to the baseball game. The response he produces in the foreign language, no matter how wrong, will find an immediate reward in the lessening of his tension ("Thank God I'm done with the homework") and thus will be reinforced and learned. Our goal must be to guide the learning of the student in such a way that reward of any kind is reserved only for correct responses. We should keep in mind that it is more effective to reward correct responses than to punish (**extinguish**) incorrect ones and that the reward seems more effective if it comes immediately after the response. The effectiveness of the reward as a reinforcer diminishes with every increase in delay.

In general it may be stated that language pedagogy during the past years has been more under the influence of behavioristic approaches than gestalt assumptions. The reason for this is perhaps that the structural linguists were naturally more inclined toward behavioristic approaches. Another reason may simply be that the behavioristic view gives us very specific help in teaching responses to specific stimuli. The notion of shaping responses either by rewarding the correct ones or by rewarding successive approximations to correct responses is of course a very fruitful one in the classroom, as well as in the language laboratory.

At the same time, however, it seems that the behavioristic view of learning is more useful in the task of what we called acquisition of primary matter than in the other essential aspect of language learning, which involves control over a system of communication, not acquisition of specific responses to specific stimuli. The learning of the system evidently involves some sort of perception of the patterns used for communication – and the gestalt view of learning seems more pertinent to that particular task.

Whatever view of learning we adopt, the acquisition of specific responses to specific stimuli cannot completely account for language learning. Essential to any view of language learning, therefore, is the notion of **transfer**. The responses which are learned must also be available when stimuli different from the original ones are present – otherwise the student who has learned to respond *I am studying English* to the stimulus *what are you doing?* may be able to produce *I am studying English* **only** when he hears *what are you doing?*. Any previously unknown responses have to be created according to the learner's conscious or subconscious awareness of the foreign language pattern. In the behavioristic view the type of transfer we have been referring to is essentially accounted for by the external situation: a response is learned in situation A – but it can recur in situation B because situation B shares many elements with situation A. The nonbehaviorist is more likely to stress mental processes within the learner as being responsible for the transfer (or **transposition**) and is also more likely to insist that transfer is promoted through an understanding of the situation and its component elements.

Of course there is little doubt that understanding does promote transfer. A pupil who has memorized a sentence without understanding its grammatical structure (or perhaps even without understanding the sentence) is not likely to have this sentence or a similar sentence available in response to a changed stimulus. At the same time, the necessity for understanding, the intellectual comprehension of grammar, can — with many students at least — actually interfere with fluency in speaking and production. Here the language teacher is faced with a dilemma that appears to some extent in the teaching of any complex skill. The pupil who learns to drive or to dance must get detailed instruction in the various responses involved in the performance. The exact motions of manipulating the clutch, the accelerator, the gears (or in the case of dancing, the exact sequence of steps) must be analyzed. However, the **goal** of the instruction is not the analysis but, as a matter of fact, is a performance during which the pupil forgets about the analytical study. It is difficult to drive a car and at the same time think about the operation of the clutch, the gears, etc. It is difficult to speak a language — and at the same time think about the nominative, the accusative, the direct object, etc. — necessary, or at least helpful, as these concepts may be in the acquisition of the first faltering steps in the new medium.

There are probably two ways of attacking the problem of the dancer who falters because he has to keep his mind on the sequence of the steps:

1. a great deal of practice;
2. a partner who is so interesting that she keeps his mind off the analytical process.

The same remedies also apply in the language teaching situation. The analytical awareness of grammatical patterns doesn't substitute for practice; as a matter of fact, this awareness must in a sense be **counteracted** by practice. In addition, we can, and sometimes must, divert the student's attention away from the structure itself. In the initial stages of instruction this diversion may take the form of an exercise in which the student manipulates a structurally unimportant but obvious element of a grammatical construction. For example, perhaps with the help of flash cards, we can have the pupil change the subject of the sentence *my friend wishes he had more money*. The substitution of *professor, uncle, brother, etc.* in this construction will divert the student's attention from the complicated structure he is practicing. This will allow sufficient repetitions of the structure being taught for it to become automatic, while avoiding the boredom that would develop without the diverting element. On the higher levels of instruction the diversion process consists simply of giving the pupil something to talk about that is of real and genuine interest to him.

The main hindrance to language learning, however, is not the clinging to analytical understanding, but errors committed in the transfer process. Any language response — unless it is a response which has been **specifically** learned — is the result of a transfer process. The child who uses the form *he approximated*, without having heard or learned the past tense of *approximate*, is **transferring correctly** from his experience with forms like *wanted, waited*, etc. The child that forms the past tense **singed* or **thinked* is transferring out of the same experience — but **transferring incorrectly**. Such **incorrect transfers**, which are caused by exceptions and breaks in consistency in the pattern of a language, are committed quite often by the learner of a foreign language. Not only must the learner of a foreign language combat the inconsistencies of the foreign language system, he is also likely to be influenced by the transfer pattern of his native language. Now if these patterns of transfer — these manufacturing processes of the native language — correspond to those of the foreign language, they are likely to promote positive transfer in the foreign language; if they clash, they will lead to incorrect transfer. A speaker of Spanish who has learned to say *I have money* (Spanish: *tengo dinero*) will be helped by the pattern of his native language to transfer positively to *I have friends* (*tengo amigos*); *I have bread* (*tengo pan*). However, if on the basis of Spanish transfer possibilities he manufactures **I have thirst* (*tengo sed*), he has come up with an incorrect English sentence. It so happens that in English one "is thirsty" but does not "have thirst." In this particular case, the native Spanish has been the cause of **incorrect transfer** and **interference**.

The primary task of foreign language teaching is the maximization of positive transfer and the minimization of incorrect transfer (= interference coming from the native language). There are various ways or strategies we can employ to minimize incorrect transfer or interference.

We have already stated, for instance, that avoidance of the mother tongue, as in the **direct method**, is calculated to minimize incorrect transfer caused by interference from the native language. Another way to avoid incorrect transfer is simply to increase the amount of primary matter available to the individual and thus decrease the sector of expressions in which transfer plays a role. The more practice we have in the language, the more we memorize, the fewer mistakes we are likely to commit. However, just plain memorization — while always beneficial — may also be quite uneconomical if it includes memorization of many sentences and constructions which could most likely have been expressed by the pupil through correct transfer processes.

The **early start** in the foreign language is another possible way of minimizing incorrect transfer. In childhood the transfer processes utilized in the native language apparently have not yet been **overlearned** to the extent where they will necessarily interfere with foreign language acquisition. Children can learn several languages without accent and with only minimal interference, if any, of one grammatical system with the other. In addition, the early start also opens up the possibility of acquiring a larger amount of primary matter than is usually possible in a second language curriculum. The most important objection that could be made against the early start concerns the economy of the process. That is to say, the avoidance of **incorrect transfer** by the early start is most likely bought at the expense of a maximal utilization of **correct transfer**. To some extent, at least, the child makes an incorrect transfer less frequently because he cannot or does not utilize transfer to the same extent as the adult. The adult using the transfer processes of his native language is likely to learn the structure of the language faster than the child, but he will also probably make more mistakes as the result of incorrect transfer.

With the student who has reached the age when transfer (correct and incorrect) is likely to be a major factor — the student from junior high school age up — the best and most economical way of teaching is simply to concentrate explanation and practice at those points where incorrect transfer is likely to occur. The most likely points of incorrect transfer are those at which differences between the native language and the target language are revealed by a **contrastive analysis**. The availability of such a contrastive analysis or simply knowledge of the native language of the student are powerful tools in the construction of teaching materials as well as the daily teaching routine followed by the classroom teacher.

CHAPTER III

Teaching Procedures

The purpose of this textbook is not to discuss **methods** as distinct from the materials to which they are applied. There are, however, three aspects of a **linguistic approach** to teaching which apply to many different teaching problems and which are, therefore, discussed independently from the specific problems arising from the structure of English. They are: (A) the general concept of **pattern practice**; (B) the use of **visual aids**; and (C) the use of the **language laboratory**.

(A) PATTERN PRACTICE

The pupil who wants to say a sentence in the foreign language (English) has basically two avenues of approach to this sentence.

1) He can think of the sentence in his native language first, then fragment the sentence, unconsciously or consciously, through some sort of grammatical analysis. Then he can try to put together a sentence in English by thinking of the English equivalents of the fragments of his native language sentence and recombining them according to whatever rules of grammar he may remember. This process may take approximately the following form: A native speaker of Spanish wants to say: *I want my son to study English* (*quiero que mi hijo estudie el inglés*). Transposing the sentence word-by-word into English, he will come up with the English equivalent **want that my son study the English*. After producing these equivalents he will have to remember that: (1) the subject pronoun is obligatory in English: *I want*, not *want*; (2) that the definite article is **not** used with names of languages: *English*,

not *the English*; and, most important, (3) that the entire construction is wrong anyway because after *want*, English uses the pattern: **dependent object** + *to* + **verb** rather than a dependent clause (*I want her to study* rather than *I want that she studies*). The probability that the process will lead to the production of a correct English sentence is rather small. Nevertheless it is the type of operation which most poor language learners perform if they try to speak a foreign language. It is certainly not an operation which we should encourage by our teaching procedures.

2) The operation performed by a good language learner bypasses the fragmentation and analysis of sentences of his native language. He may not remember the sentence *I want my son to study English* as a unit. Most likely he has never either heard or said exactly this very same sentence; but perhaps he does remember a similar sentence used by someone in a similar situation or context. For example, he may have heard: *he wants everybody to follow his advice*. It is important that the learner remembers the pattern: ... *want* ... *to* ...; *he wants* is then changed quickly to *I want*; *everybody* is replaced by *my son* and *to study English* is quickly supplied, probably from a different sentence or context, such as *I came here to study English*. Thus the process of arriving from *he wants everybody to follow his advice* to *I want my son to study English* has involved a transformational type of change within the target language (*he wants* > *I want*) and two substitutions (replacement of *everybody* by *my son* and of *follow his advice* by *study English*).

In the process of pattern practice the student learns the various substitution and transformation procedures. The purpose of learning these procedures is:

1. To bypass the process of using the foreign equivalents of fragments of native utterances as a basis for utterances in the foreign language.

2. To teach the pupil through **practice** and **grammatical understanding** those processes which will enable him to create sentences in the foreign language.

The latter point needs special emphasis because it is not always clearly understood and brought out in pedagogical discussion. The substitution and transformation exercises which form the basis of pattern practice are not designed to bypass grammar. They rely on grammatical understanding and are in turn supposed to reinforce it. Furthermore, pattern practice is not **primarily** a device by which the student—through repetition and minimal manipulation of a sentence—is forced to utter sentences in the foreign language. **The ultimate goal of pattern practice is to teach the student those operations which will enable him to generate sentences in the foreign language—those grammatical procedures which allow him to convert primary matter into secondary matter with maximal speed and minimal interference from his native language.**

There are many ways of classifying types of pattern practice, and we shall discuss examples of pattern practice in connection with specific grammatical problems in Part Two of this book. However, broadly speaking, pattern practices may be classified into three types of operations:

1. Substitution
2. Expansion
3. Transformation

The essential characteristic of the **substitution** pattern practice exercise is that the pattern itself remains constant throughout the exercise. The sentence *many foreign students study engineering* represents the pattern:

$$det + ADJ + N + V + N.$$

This pattern could be practiced in an exercise in which substitution occurs for only **one element (single substitution)**, **two elements (double substitution)**, **three elements (triple substitution)** or perhaps—progressively—for all elements of the pattern (**progressive substitution**).

A **single substitution** exercise dealing with the **determiner** slot might take the following form:

TEACHER: *Many foreign students study engineering.*
CLASS: *Many foreign students study engineering.*
TEACHER: *Few.*
CLASS: *Few foreign students study engineering.*
TEACHER: *All.*
CLASS: *All foreign students study engineering.*
TEACHER: *Most.*
CLASS: *Most foreign students study engineering.* (Etc.)

The following is a **double substitution** exercise dealing with the two noun slots of the sentence:

TEACHER: *Many foreign students   study engineering.*
CLASS: *Many foreign students   study engineering.*
TEACHER: *Scientists.*
CLASS: *Many foreign scientists study engineering.*
TEACHER: *Mathematics.*
CLASS: *Many foreign scientists study mathematics.*
TEACHER: *Scholars.*
CLASS: *Many foreign scholars   study mathematics.*
TEACHER: *Economics.*
CLASS: *Many foreign scholars   study economics.*

A **progressive substitution** exercise utilizing the same pattern may take the following form:

TEACHER: *Many foreign   students study engineering.*
CLASS: *Many foreign   students study engineering.*
TEACHER: *American.*
CLASS: *Many American students study engineering.*
TEACHER: *Boys.*
CLASS: *Many American boys   study engineering.*
TEACHER: *Elect.*
CLASS: *Many American boys   elect engineering.*
TEACHER: *Mathematics.*
CLASS: *Many American boys   elect mathematics.*

In the **expansion type** of exercise the **basic pattern** which is practiced also remains the same. However, it is expanded—typically by adding elements either to the **noun** or **verb** section of the sentence. In terms of the linguistic principles discussed briefly in Chapter I, this expansion consists typically in an operation which amounts to a rewriting or restating of the **NP** or **VP** part of a formula.

A typical **noun expansion** exercise may take the form of adding an adjective or a prepositional expression.

TEACHER: *Many students study engineering.*
CLASS: *Many students study engineering.*
TEACHER: *Foreign.*
CLASS: *Many foreign students study engineering.*
TEACHER: *Intelligent.*
CLASS: *Many intelligent students study engineering.*
TEACHER: *From Latin America.*
CLASS: *Many intelligent foreign students from Latin America
           study engineering.*

A **verb expansion** exercise may involve the addition of adverbs or adverbial expressions:

TEACHER: *Many foreign students study engineering.*
CLASS: *Many foreign students study engineering.*
TEACHER: *Never.*
CLASS: *Many foreign students never study engineering.*
TEACHER: *In the United States.*
CLASS: *Many foreign students never study engineering in the United States.*

Expansion exercises may also take the form of the same expansion being performed on different sentences representing the same pattern. The following is a **verb expansion** exercise of this type:

TEACHER: *Let us add the adverb **never** to the following sentences:*
          Many students understand this rule.
CLASS: *Many students never understand this rule.*
TEACHER: *My friends study English.*
CLASS: *My friends never study English.*
TEACHER: *Our friends speak Spanish.*
CLASS: *Our friends never speak Spanish.*

In some ways the **transformation** exercise is quite similar to the expansion exercise just mentioned. It consists of applying the same linguistic operation to a series of sentences which all have the same or at least nearly the same structure. The linguistic operation, however, is one that brings about a radical change in the structure of the sentence.

The most typical kinds of transformation drills consist of making active sentences passive, changing them from one tense to another, making positive statements negative and/or interrogative. The following is an example of a **transformation** exercise:

TEACHER: *Make the following statements negative:*
          Many Americans study foreign languages.
CLASS: *Many Americans do not study foreign languages.*
TEACHER: *Many students take courses in science.*
CLASS: *Many students do not take courses in science.*

Question/answer type exercises are basically transformation exercises. In the following example the interrogative form is transformed into the negative:

TEACHER: *Answer the following question negatively:*
Does your brother study engineering?
CLASS: *No, my brother does not study engineering.*
TEACHER: *Do you receive a letter every day?*
CLASS: *No, I don't receive a letter every day.*

Perhaps the most essential aspect of pattern practice is the already-mentioned fact that its ultimate goal is to teach the student the tools and operations which will lead to self-expression. It is important that the transfer operation — the use of the pattern for expressing the student's **own** sentences — be made part of the individual pattern drill as much as possible. One way of accomplishing this goal consists of the gradual withdrawal (**fading**) of the cue until the use of the pattern for self-expression is introduced. To give an example:

Step 1: Repetition

TEACHER: *Repeat the following sentences:*
Charles wants his friends to help him.
CLASS: *Charles wants his friends to help him.*
TEACHER: *Charles wants his friends to explain this assignment.*
CLASS: *Charles wants his friends to explain this assignment.*
TEACHER: *Charles asks his neighbor to tell him the answer.*
CLASS: *Charles asks his neighbor to tell him the answer.*
TEACHER: *Charles expects his friends to help him.*
CLASS: *Charles expects his friends to help him.*

After the repetition exercise the teacher will want to make sure that the pattern involved (namely **NP + V + NP +** *to* **+ VP**) is understood by all the students. (As we will point out later, the pattern by which one action — **NP V(NP)**: *his friends help him* — is made dependent upon another action — **NP V**: *Charles wants* — by the use of *to* before the verb, is a fairly difficult one for many non-English speakers to grasp.)

Step 2: Noun Substitution: Single Substitution

TEACHER: *Repeat:*
Charles wants his friends to help him.
CLASS: *Charles wants his friends to help him.*
TEACHER: *Substitute the following for* **friends**:
Neighbor.
CLASS: *Charles wants his neighbor to help him.*
TEACHER: *Father.*

CLASS: *Charles wants his father to help him.*
TEACHER: *Teacher.*
CLASS: *Charles wants his teacher to help him.*

Step 3: Double Substitution

TEACHER: *In the sentence **Charles wants his friends to help him**,*
                    *substitute alternately for **wants** and **friends***
                    Repeat:
                    Charles wants his friends to help him.
CLASS: *Charles wants his   friends   to help him.*
TEACHER: *Expects.*
CLASS: *Charles expects his friends   to help him.*
TEACHER: *Father.*
CLASS: *Charles expects his father   to help him.*
TEACHER: *Asks.*
CLASS: *Charles asks his   father   to help him.*
TEACHER: *Neighbor.*
CLASS: *Charles asks his   neighbor to help him.* (Etc.)

Step 4: Progressive Substitution

TEACHER: *Let us take the sentence **Charles wants his friends to help***
                    ***him** and substitute progressively the following:*
                    My neighbor.
CLASS: *My neighbor wants his   friends   to help him.*
TEACHER: *Asks.*
CLASS: *My neighbor asks   his   friends   to help him.*
TEACHER: *Your.*
CLASS: *My neighbor asks   your friends   to help him.*
TEACHER: *Relatives.*
CLASS: *My neighbor asks   your relatives to help him.*
TEACHER: *Assist.*
CLASS: *My neighbor asks   your relatives to assist him.*

Step 5: Transformation

TEACHER: *Answer the following questions according to this model:*
                    Why do Charles's friends help him?
                    *Answer: **Charles wants his friends to help him.***
                    Now answer this:
                    Why does Charles's father help him?
CLASS: *Charles wants his father to help him.*

TEACHER: *Why does Charles's neighbor help him?*
CLASS: *Charles wants his neighbor to help him.*
TEACHER: *Why do Charles's friends explain the assignment to him?*
CLASS: *Charles wants his friends to explain the assignment to him.*
TEACHER: *Why does Charles's uncle write to him?*
CLASS: *Charles wants his uncle to write to him.*

Step 6: Nonverbal cue: Substitution

For this type of practice the teacher can use a series of pictures (or a chart containing a series of pictures) each of which has been associated with a specific noun (for example, *the teacher, the neighbor, the uncle, the aunt*). By simply pointing to a specific picture, the teacher can now cue a substitution:

TEACHER: *Charles wants his friends to help him.*
CLASS: *Charles wants his friends to help him.*
TEACHER: (points to the picture of *the teacher*)
CLASS: *Charles wants his teacher to help him.*

Step 7: Nonverbal cue: Transformation

The teacher can utilize a series of pictures (or a chart containing a series) each of which has been associated with a specific action (for example, *the teacher explains the lesson; the teacher answers the question; the director talks to the students*).

The teacher can now explain that whenever he points to a specific picture, the action represented by the picture is to replace the action of *his friends to help him* in the construction *Charles wants his friends to help him.*

TEACHER: (points to picture of *the teacher explains the lesson*).
CLASS: *Charles wants the teacher to explain the lesson.*
TEACHER: (points to picture of *the teacher answers the question*).
CLASS: *Charles wants the teacher to answer the question.* (Etc.)

Step 8: Situational Stimulus: Verbal Cue

In normal conversation, patterns are very rarely used in response to a stimulus which is identical or nearly identical with the pattern itself. In other words we rarely have occasion to repeat a language pattern because we want to substitute in, or transform it. The best way to teach the student the practical use of a pattern is to ask him to use it in response to a cue or description of a situation which does not contain the pattern at all. The student could be asked to use the pattern of our sample exercise (**NP** + **VP** + **NP** + **VP** + **NP**) in response to cues such as the following:

TEACHER: *Why is Charles talking to his friend?*
STUDENT: (possible answers:) *He wants his friend to explain the lesson. He wants his friend to help him.*
TEACHER: *Why are you in the United States?*
STUDENT: (possible answers:) *My parents want me to study English. My government wants me to study engineering.*
TEACHER: *Why are you afraid of the exam in mathematics?*
STUDENT: (possible answer:) *My teacher expects us to know everything.*

The importance of the practice just described is that it leads the student gradually from repetition to self-use and self-expression. It starts with repetition — an echo response in which the stimulus and response are identical. With each successive step the stimulus becomes increasingly **dissimilar** to the desired response. Transformation requires the student to change the stimulus structure. In pictorial cueing the stimulus has been faded into a nonverbal cue and requires the pupil to perform the substitution and the transformation on a sentence which he must recall. In the final step (situational stimulus) we have finally reached the normal speaking situation. The stimulus is completely dissimilar to the expected response: the original stimulus has been faded completely.

Another simple device, designed to make pattern manipulation into a creative activity for the student, consists of employing exercises of progressive substitution, telling the student to make sentences of his own choice by substituting for the different parts of speech in a specific sentence. The teacher assigns only the base sentence (for example, *if I had money, I would buy a car*). The students make up their own sentences by providing their own substitutions: *if I had enough time, ... if I had the opportunity ... I would take a trip ... I would not be here.*

It is also possible to designate a specific transformation or series of transformations as a special exercise. For example, one exercise consists of performing the negative, passive, and interrogative transformations on a sentence. These operations should be performed on the same base sentence, or they should be successive operations performed on the product of the preceding operation. For example, the teacher assigns the sentence: *Charles understands the explanation* and the student responds (orally or in written form) with *Charles does not understand the explanation. The explanation is understood by Charles. Does Charles understand the explanation?* In the **successive-chain** variation of this exercise the student's response would be: *Charles doesn't understand the explanation. The explanation isn't understood by Charles. Isn't the explanation understood by Charles?* Obviously this type of exercise can be used only after the student has had a great deal of practice in each of the steps involved as well as in the usage of reduced forms such as *isn't*. The purpose of the exercise is to make the student aware of the fact that the transformation procedures which he is learning are manufacturing devices available to him so that he may create sentences of his own from the sentences he has learned.

(B) VISUAL AIDS

There are various types of visual aids and many ways to use them in the language class. We shall comment on some of the most important categories from the linguistic viewpoint, beginning with those which are unrelated to teaching influenced by structural linguistics.

The most obvious way of using pictures is to employ them for teaching vocabulary items. The teacher may hold up a picture of a horse to the class, point to it, and utter the word *horse*. He may then ask a question such as *what is this?* in the hope of eliciting the response *this is a horse* from the class. Useful as this kind of pictorial aid may be, it has no immediate relation to the teaching of language structures.

Another possible use of the picture is the description of a scene or action. A picture is presented to the student; the words for all the persons or objects in the picture and the actions taking place are given. Then the student is asked questions about what is going on. This kind of pictorial aid has several useful applications. If typically American scenes and typically American settings are chosen, a great deal of cultural information can be conveyed.

Pictures can also be used to good advantage for the contextual presentation of vocabulary items and of structures previously drilled or to be drilled. Since the description of even a very simple picture is likely to elicit a variety of forms and patterns, it is an occasion for the use and testing of grammatical patterns rather than the learning of them.

Quite different use is made of the pictorial aid if it is of the type in which every sentence to be learned by the student is accompanied by one picture. With this kind of pictorial aid two quite distinct possibilities must be differentiated:

1. In the first method the picture is used to convey the exact semantic content of the sentence. The student hears the sentence *a man is entering the room*, and he sees the picture of a man entering a room. This kind of visual aid has been elaborated into a rather skillful teaching device in which stick figures are used, rather than pictures depicting real persons. These figures are systematically put through a series of actions which teach the student basic semantic concepts with the help of a basic vocabulary. This technique, an elaboration of the direct method, is quite useful but it is not organized according to the structure of English.

2. The other approach, which combines an individual structure with a single picture, conveys the visual reinforcement of the structure rather than the exact meaning of the structure. This visual reinforcement is supposed to be doubly effective if the picture is esthetically of high quality; we are at the opposite pole from the stick figures. The actual connection between the meaning of the sentence to be learned and the picture may be quite loose. For example, a picture of people skiing is accompanied by a sentence such as *many Americans like winter sports*. The value of this use of pictures, aside from the obvious possibilities in the representation of a cultural environment, lies in the supposed reinforcement of the structure to be learned. Whether such a reinforcement actually takes place (or could it be that the visual impact **diverts** the student's attention from the language structure?) remains to be confirmed by experiments. There is no obvious connection between teaching influenced by linguistics and the pictorial aid.

A more **linguistic** use of the pictorial aid is made when it serves to teach a difference in meaning or a construction which is difficult for the student to grasp or which is at least unusual from the point of view of his native language. To give an example: many languages have no grammatical gender. Others differentiate in pronoun replacement strictly according to grammatical gender and not to sex (for example, Spanish *mesa—table* is feminine and is referred to as *ella—she*. Spanish *reloj—watch* is masculine and is referred to as *él—he*). Speakers of such languages may have to be reminded of the English use of *he, she, it* by pictures which are used to tie the concept of *he* to a male, the concept of *she* to a female, and that of *it* to an object.

In a similar way pictorial aids may be used to illustrate the different meanings of expressions which may be confusing to the pupil because, as far as he is concerned, they lack clear differentiation in construction and sound very much alike. The so-called **two-part verbs** are a typical example for this situation. Pictorial help may be needed to illustrate and reinforce the differences between *get up, get off, get in*, etc. The fact that often many different meanings are associated with one word may also lead to a great deal of confusion. Frequently this confusion can be cleared up by pictures which illustrate these different meanings: *he is getting a letter; he doesn't get the solution of the problem; he is getting tired).*

A very different and direct application of the structural linguistic approach to the use of visual aids is the structural diagraming of sentence patterns. Various examples of the same pattern are presented to the student in such a way that the elements which fulfill identical functions in the pattern are lined up vertically and are put into the same slot in the structural frame.

Charles	will	get up	this morning
You	can	leave	today
We	must	take off	tomorrow

The same method can also be used in the usual presentation of substitution exercises.

Charles	will	get up	this morning
Robert	____	_____	_____
_____	may	_____	_____
_____	____	leave	_____
_____	____	_____	tomorrow

This type of presentation is an important aid in the teaching of structure. In many ways it is more effective than lengthy grammatical explanation in making the student aware of basic similarities and differences between patterns and in making him conscious of grammatical word classes.

A very direct and useful tie between language structure and pictorial aid exists when the picture chart is used to illustrate a grammatical category. For example, we may compose a series of pictures or a picture chart illustrating verbs which can be followed by adjectives (*the coffee smells good*; *the apple tastes sweet*; *the boy looks healthy*), or perhaps the verbs which do not normally occur in the *be* plus *-ing* form for the present progressive tense: *I speak* > *I am speaking*, but this same operation can not be performed with *I understand, I need, I know*, and so on. Such a chart may contain pictures associated with sentences such as *he understands English*; *he needs money*; *he knows my brother*; etc.

To give another example—we may combine on our chart a series of pictures illustrating **count nouns** (nouns which can be preceded by numerals and can be made plural) vs. **mass nouns** (nouns which normally cannot be made plural and which are not preceded by numerals; for example, *milk, bread, butter*).

The composite chart of the type mentioned above is probably the most immediate application of pictorial aids to linguistically oriented teaching, because it is this type of chart that can be used most effectively in the basic drill techniques of substitution, transformation, and expansion. A chart showing several objects or persons can provide the nouns to be substituted in a pattern. The teacher provides the pattern to be drilled—for example, *I want you to talk to the teacher*; and merely by pointing at different pictures, he elicits the responses *I want you to talk to the principal*; *I want you to talk to the director*.

Even more useful for pattern drills is the chart which is composed of a series of action pictures. The student learns the basic sentence which describes each action taking place on the chart: *the professor is looking for the book*; *the pupil is listening to the radio*. Once each sentence has been learned and associated with the appropriate picture, the chart becomes an efficient instrument for triggering students' responses in manipulative pattern drills. For example, the basic sentences may be transformed into different tenses. By pointing at a particular picture and using a key word (for example, *yesterday*), the teacher may drill his class to respond with a past tense: *the professor looked for the book*. The word *tomorrow* may be used to trigger a response in the future, the words *always* or *often* to elicit responses of habitual action, and so on. The teacher may ask the class or individual students to substitute different subjects in the actions of the chart—for example, he points to the chart and says *we* and the class responds with *we are looking for the book*. The basic sentences may be made negative or transformed into questions; the nouns may be replaced by pronouns; questions may be asked for the subjects or objects of the actions; and other words (for example, adverbs) may be inserted into the basic sentences.

(C) THE LANGUAGE LABORATORY

In many teaching situations, the pattern practice type of exercise discussed in the preceding sections has been primarily relegated to the **language laboratory**.

There are different types of laboratories. Some provide only listening facilities. Others provide facilities which enable the student to respond and hear his responses through the ear phones. The most advanced kind of laboratory enables the student to record his responses so that they may be available for his and/or the teacher's inspection.

But even more important than the facilities of the laboratory are the uses to which it is put. Here we must distinguish between two very different situations: (1) the laboratory provides flexibility according to individual student need; (2) the laboratory provides no such flexibility and is utilized instead of a block of time available for class instruction. There is little doubt that the **major** contribution of the laboratory is realized in the first situation, achievement of flexibility according to individual need and aptitude. This flexibility can be brought about in two quite distinct ways. One consists of giving the student flexible access to the laboratory. The good student (and the less motivated student) may use it for only a short time. The less capable student (as well as the more highly motivated student) has the opportunity to increase his contact with the language to whatever level he desires. This type of flexibility exists in many of the **library-type** laboratories, especially at the college level. The other type of flexibility is brought about by allowing the student to proceed at his own rate of speed. This necessitates a complete reorganization of the language course and the use of **programmed** materials, teaching materials which can be used for the purpose of **self-instruction**.

If the laboratory is used simply to replace classroom instruction, it can, of course, still provide certain advantages. It can provide welcome relief for a tired teacher who can relegate the more mechanical aspects of pattern practice (**repetition, substitution**) to the laboratory. It can give the pupil exposure to a variety of correct models. In the classroom the pupil can give only a limited number of individual responses per class-hour. In the laboratory the number of individual responses can be increased tremendously. The tape can provide immediate confirmation, and thus reinforcement, of every correct response. However, these latter advantages of the laboratory depend on the assumption that the pupil actually goes through the drills and exercises provided on the tape. If he sits in front of the microphone silently, with his mind wandering away from the business of language learning, the advantage of the laboratory will be only theoretical.

It is thus essential in any kind of laboratory work that the pupil's attention remain focused on his task. The good language teacher must learn to keep the pupil's attention on the lab work by providing **intrinsic** or at least **extrinsic** motivation for the lab performance. By intrinsic motivation we mean providing material that is of sufficient interest to the pupil to capture his attention. By extrinsic motivation we understand that the pupil's attention is somehow forced on the laboratory task: the tape provides material not otherwise available; the pupil knows that his performance is being monitored; the lab session ends with a very short quiz dealing with the material covered during the session.

In conclusion, we wish to emphasize again that the main potential of the lab consists of providing flexibility. Since education is moving toward the goal of flexibility of instruction, we can assume that increasing attention will be given to the development and the use of programmed materials for laboratory instruction. In programmed materials the course is divided into individual learning steps. These steps are typically small, so that a correct response by the pupil is likely. If the pupil responds correctly, the correct answer is confirmed (reinforced) and he is allowed to go on to the next step. An incorrect response may force the pupil to go through different versions of the same exercises or to take the same step over again. The control over the shaping of the pupils' behavior which programming affords gives a great deal of promise in increasing the success of the pupils and in reaching pupils which by other methods have not been able to become successful language learners. At the same time, however, at present many features of programming (for example, the optimal size of the learning step) remain problematical, and programs devised so far seem to have been more successful in insuring the pupils' learning of primary matter (in the programmer's language a **specific** or **formal** repertory of responses) than in bringing about the even more essential transfer skills.

PART TWO

CHAPTER IV

Teaching Pronunciation

(A) PHONEMICS

Before turning to a description of the English sound system, we wish to emphasize once more the difference between **phonetic** and **phonemic** approaches.

In the **phonetic** approach we attempt to describe the sounds of language as accurately as possible. In a **phonetic** transcription we try to match **every sound** to a **specific symbol**. In a **phonemic** approach we pay attention only to those differences in sound which can be utilized to express differences in meaning in a specific language. In a **phonemic** transcription we use different symbols for different sounds only if the difference can be used to express different meanings.

The criterion for an accurate phonetic transcription is therefore inherently vague, while that for an accurate phonemic transcription is rather precise. At what point can we say that there is enough variation within the pronunciation of a vowel sound so that we should say that it is really a **diphthong** (made up of two vowels rather than one)? How long must a vowel be so that we can say that it is long, not short, nor medium long? From the phonetic point of view these decisions must at times be made on an arbitrary basis. From the phonemic point of view we can make a clear-cut decision as to whether or not the feature under consideration (long vs. short, or diphthong vs. monophthong) can be utilized to convey differences in meaning within the linguistic system. If it can, then it must be considered phonemic and must be transcribed in a **phonemic transcription** (always put within / /). If it cannot be considered capable of conveying differences in meaning, then it is only

51

a phonetic feature and may be transcribed in a phonetic transcription (usually put within [   ]), but never in a phonemic one.

To illustrate: the vowel sound of English *play* [e] is normally longer than the vowel of *played*, which in turn is generally pronounced longer than the vowel of *plate*. These differences in vowel length are part of an English speech habit of pronouncing final stressed vowels longer than vowels that are followed by consonants — and of pronouncing vowels before voiced consonants (such as /d/) somewhat longer than vowels before unvoiced consonants (such as /t/). Most speakers of English are not particularly aware of this difference. The length of the vowel is predictable by its position: either final or before a voiced or unvoiced consonant. From the very predictability of this length distinction, it follows that it can never be used **by itself** to make a distinction in meaning: the difference in vowel length in *play*, *played*, *plate* is the allophonic variation of a phoneme. We can ignore it in a phonemic transcription and represent the three words just mentioned as /ple/ /pled/ /plet/. Only in a phonetic transcription could we attempt to account for the different vowel length in the three words and perhaps transcribe them as [ple:] [ple·d] [plet].

In our discussion of English pronunciation we shall refer primarily to phonemics and use phonemic transcriptions between /   /. In the discussion of purely phonetic facts and when referring to variants of a phoneme we will occasionally have to use phonetic transcription (between [   ]).

One additional characteristic of a phonemic transcription, which should be understood by the teacher, is that it constitutes a linguist's **interpretation** of the phonetic facts rather than the phonetic facts themselves. Just because two linguists may transcribe the same word differently does not mean that one of them must be wrong or that they are dealing with different facts. As we shall point out later in more detail, the vowel system of English is subject to different interpretations. The vowels of English *beat* and *bit* and the vowels of English *food* and *good* are obviously different. The vowel of *beat* is higher than the one of *bit*; the vowel of *food* is higher than the one of *good*. The vowels of *beat* and *food* are also more diphthongal than the vowels of *bit* and *good*. In the phonemic interpretation we can pin the title of **phonemic difference** on any one of these distinctions. If we emphasize the difference in height of the tongue as the significant one, we consider the difference of the vowels of *beat/bit*; *food/good*, as a difference between two phonemes: /bit/, /bɪt/; /fud/, /gʊd/. If we interpret the difference as being due to the distinction diphthong/monophthong, we can come to the conclusion that the vowel of *food* is really the one of *good* followed by an upglide and lip-rounding, while the vowel of *beat* is really the one of *bit*, followed by an upglide: /biyt/, /bit/; /fuwd/, /gud/.

The teacher then should never completely identify the phonemic transcription with the reality for which it stands. The advantage of phonemic interpretation and transcription, if properly understood, consists of giving a systematic understanding of the sounds — and differences between sounds — with which a particular language operates. We know that our student must be able to hear and produce the phonemic differences of English or he will never be able to understand or to communicate. The phonemic analysis of English will show us clearly just which sounds and which sound differences must be mastered by the student.

(B)   THE SOUND SYSTEM OF AMERICAN ENGLISH

1. Consonants

Consonant sounds are contrasted to vowel sounds on the basis of one characteristic: in the production of consonant sounds the airstream that moves through the speech organs meets an obstacle. In the production of vowel sounds no such obstacle is present.

Consonant sounds can be classified in several ways:

Manner of production

Consonants are classified according to the way in which the obstacle to the airstream is formed. If the airstream is actually interrupted during the production of the sound, we call the sound a **stop**. A stop is a sound which is produced by the act of closing and opening the path taken by the air during sound production. In this process of closing and opening, the air is allowed to build up pressure against the obstacle and is then permitted to escape suddenly when the obstacle is removed. Stop sounds are also frequently called **plosives**.

The following consonant sounds of English — corresponding to the letters in bold face italics in the words below — are all plosives or stops:

/p/	*pin*	/t/	*team*	/k/	*coal*
/b/	*bin*	/d/	*deem*	/g/	*goal*

There are some stops in which an obstacle to the airstream is formed, and then the obstacle is released so gradually that air goes through the speech organs slowly, producing a continuant sound at exactly the point at which the closure for the stop had been formed. A stop with such a slow release may be considered either as a combination of stop + continuant (see below) or as a single sound. If they are considered as a single sound, they are referred to as **affricates**. The English sounds transcribed below which correspond to the letters in bold face italics are affricates:

/č/   *chin*   /ǰ/   *gin*

All sounds that are **not** stops or affricates are referred to as **continuants**. In the production of continuants the airstream is allowed to pass through the speech organs without complete interruption.

If the consonant sound is produced by the friction of the air as it passes through the obstacle it is called a **fricative**. If the very narrow passage through which the air is allowed to escape during the production of the sound has the shape of a long slit (wide from side to side and narrow from top to bottom), the sound is called a **slit fricative**. The following English phonemes are slit fricatives:

/f/   *fit*   /θ/   *thin*   /h/   hole
/v/   *vine*   /ð/   *this*

If the fricative is produced with an opening that is narrow from side to side and deep from top to bottom and with the tongue simultaneously forming a small grove toward its tip, then the sound is called a **grooved fricative**. Since the grooved opening results in those sounds having a hissing quality, they are frequently called **sibilants**. The following English phonemes are grooved fricatives or sibilants:

/s/   *seal*   /ʃ/   *she*
/z/   *zeal*   /ʒ/   *treasure*

Consonants which are formed without any real narrow constriction of the speech organs are called **resonants**. Some resonants are formed by a complete closure of the oral air passage, but with a simultaneous opening of the nasal passage which allows the air to escape through the nose. These resonant sounds are referred to as **nasals**. The following English consonant phonemes are nasals:

/m/   *mine*   /n/   *neat*   /ŋ/   lo**ng**

In the production of some resonants the tongue may make contact with its tip either against the teeth or the grooves above the teeth, or it may be raised toward the back of the mouth; but the characteristic sound is produced by the sound escaping along the side or sides of the tongue. Resonants of this type are called **laterals**. The English phoneme /l/ is a lateral:

/l/   *leap*

Vowels may also be classified as resonants and the distinction between vowel and consonant—sharp and obvious if we compare vowels with stops or even fricatives—becomes blurred in the case of resonant sounds. From the strictly phonetic point of view, it is difficult to decide whether some sounds are vowels or consonants. Sounds in the border area between vowels and consonants can be classified as **semi-vowels**. The following English phonemes are semi-vowels:

/w/   *water*   /r/   *rather*   /y/   *yes*

There are other manners of articulation which can be used to produce consonants. None of these has any significance in the phonemic description of American English. We shall mention some of them briefly, because the teacher of English is likely to find these articulations in the sound production of non-native students.

Some sounds are produced by the vibration of one of the vocal organs. These sounds are called **vibrants** or **trills**. A common type of French or German *r* is produced by the vibration of the uvula. A Spanish *r* as in the word *perro* is a trill produced with the tip of the tongue.

A sound produced with only a single vibration is referred to as a **flap**. Some types of British *r* sounds are produced as flaps. The Spanish single *r* of *pero* is a flap sound produced with a single tap of the tongue against the alveolar ridge. The pronunciation often given in American English to an intervocalic *t*, as in *better* or *letter* (a quick flap of the tongue against the gums above the upper teeth), is also a flap sound.

The manner of production of a sound may vary according to the type of **release**, or in the **coarticulations**. We have already referred to the **aspiration** of sound. Aspiration occurs if a stop is released in such a way that a slight puff of air is heard immediately after the sound is produced. As mentioned earlier, initial /p/, /t/, /k/ of English (as in *pick, tick, kick*) are normally aspirated, while the same sounds after an *s* are not (as in *speak, stick, skate*). Aspiration is significant within the phonemic system of many languages but has no significant function in English.

The concept of coarticulation anticipates the next step in the classification of speech sounds — namely the place of production. Some consonants are produced in such a manner that more than one place of production is involved. For instance, if a stop is produced with a simultaneous rounding of the lips, as in the initial consonant group of English *quick* [kwik], it is referred to as **labialized**. If a sound is produced while the tongue is being raised to the back of the mouth it is called **velarized**. Many speakers of American English have the habit of velarizing their *l*-sounds, especially after vowels (*tall, spell, kill*). **Palatalization** occurs when a sound is pronounced with the tongue raised against the palate. Many languages (such as Russian) distinguish palatal consonants as opposed to nonpalatal ones. A **palatalized consonant** sounds somewhat like a combination of consonant + y. In the quick pronunciation of *how do you do?*, the first /d/ may become such a palatalized consonant.

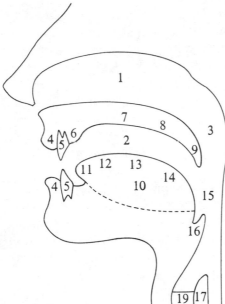

1. Nasal Cavity
2. Oral Cavity
3. Nasal Passage
4. Lips
5. Teeth
6. Alveolae (ridge behind upper teeth)
7. Hard Palate
8. Soft Palate (Velum)
9. Uvula
10. Tongue
11. Tip of Tongue
12. Front of Tongue
13. Middle of Tongue
14. Back of Tongue
15. Pharynx
16. Epiglottis
17. Glottis
18. Larynx
19. Vocal Cords

Lower Articulator	Upper Articulator	Type of Sound
lower lip (4)	upper lip (4)	bilabial
lower lip (4)	upper teeth (5)	labio-dental
tip of tongue (11)	upper teeth (5)	dental
tip of tongue (11)	alveolae (6)	alveolar

tip of tongue (11) (curled back toward the palate)	palate (7)	retroflex
front of tongue (12)	alveolae (6)	alveo-palatal
back of tongue (13/14)	back of palate (7)	palatal
back of tongue (14)	velum (8)	velar
back of tongue (14)	uvula (9)	uvular

Place of articulation

From this point of view consonants are classified according to the place in which they are produced — that is, according to where the obstacle impeding the airstream is formed. In following the classification of English consonants according to their place of production it is best to consult and study the accompanying chart of the speech organs and the summary of terminology. Note that the place of production is generally determined by an upper and by a lower articulator which combine to form the obstacle to the airstream. The conventional names used in the classification of sounds (third column) are derived sometimes from both (for example, **labio-dental, bilabial**) but usually from only one of the articulators (**dental, velar**). There is also a more general classification which groups sounds according to whether their articulation involves the lips (**labials**), the tip or **apex** of the tongue (**apicals**), the front of the tongue (**frontals**) or the back or **dorsum** of the tongue (**dorsals**).

The following list illustrates the English consonantal sounds classified according to their **place of articulation**. They are listed in a sequence from "front" to "back", starting with **bilabials** and ending with the **glottal** sound /h/. In studying and reading the list, it is best to say the words out loud while paying attention to the point of articulation of the consonant being illustrated and while consulting the chart describing the speech organs.

Bilabial

/p/	*pin*	*happy*	*hip*
/b/	*bin*	*rubber*	*rib*
/m/	*mine*	*hammer*	*ham*
/w/	*water*	*lower*	

Labio-dental

/f/	*fit*	*coffee*	*leaf*
/v/	*vine*	*never*	*love*

Dental

| /θ/ | thin | ether | breath |
| /ð/ | this | either | breathe |

Alveolar

/t/	team	latter	hat
/d/	deem	ladder	had
/s/	seal	basic	bus
/z/	zeal	razor	buzz
/n/	neat	sinner	man
/l/	leap	pillow	mail

Retroflex

| /r/ | rather | very | far |

Alveo-palatal

/č/	chin	catches	witch
/ǰ/	gin	badger	ridge
/ʃ/	she	pressure	rush
/ʒ/	____	treasure	rouge

Palatal

| /y/ | yes | beauty | ____ |

Velar

/k/	coal	hockey	back
/g/	goal	bigger	flag
/ŋ/	____	singer	long

Glottal

| /h/ | hole | cohort | ____ |

There is at least one point of articulation—the uvula—which is not illustrated by the English consonant system. As stated previously, an example of a uvular sound is the German or French trilled r-sound. Sounds other than those listed do exist in English but must definitely be considered as variants of phonemes. Thus some speakers of American English replace the t sound in a word like bottle by a glottal stop /ʔ/: a stop produced by the closure and sudden opening of the vocal cords themselves.

Voicing

Voicing refers to the vibration of the vocal cords during the production of a sound. The actual mechanism which correlates the vibration of the vocal cords and the production of a consonant is quite complicated. But, in a somewhat simplified fashion, we may call a sound **voiced** if the vocal cords vibrate throughout the production of the sound, while we consider a consonant **voiceless** if vibration of the vocal cords is absent throughout most or all of the production of the sound. Most of the English consonants can be grouped in pairs which are phonemically distinguished only by the presence or absence of **voice**. In the list of English consonant sounds above the voiceless member of the pair is always listed before the voiced.

Voiceless: /p/   /f/   /θ/   /t/   /s/   /č/   /ʃ/   /k/
Voiced: /b/   /v/   /ð/   /d/   /z/   /j/   /ʒ/   /g/

The list of consonant sounds does not give us complete information concerning the consonant system of English. To indicate that a specific sound exists is not enough. We must also realize in which positions and in what combinations it occurs. Thus the sounds /ŋ/ (*strong*) and /ʒ/ (*garage, treasure*) do not occur in word initial position in English. In fact, a native speaker of English may experience considerable difficulty in producing these sounds at the beginning of a word. Another feature of American English pronunciation which is often confusing to the foreigner is the variation in pronunciation of the voiceless stop sounds (/p/, /t/, /k/) in initial, intervocalic, and final position. These sounds are aspirated in initial position (pronounced with a slight puff of air), unreleased in final position, and in intervocalic position they have a soft unaspirated pronunciation which – particularly in the case of intervocalic /t/ – often sounds like their voiced counterparts (/b/, /d/, /g/) to the ear of the non-native.

It is especially important for the teacher of English as a foreign language to realize that English is comparatively rich in consonant clusters. A student may have no difficulty in producing a consonant in isolation or in conjunction with a preceding or following vowel, but that student may find the same consonant "unpronounceable" in conjunction with other consonants. Certain sequences of consonants may present considerable difficulty even if the individual consonants of the sequence do not by themselves represent pronunciation problems. In many languages the typical pattern of the syllable is **CV** (**consonant +
vowel**) and/or **VC**. Double consonants in initial or final position – **CCV**

or **VCC** — may be rare or nonexistent. English has the possibility of almost 40 (the exact number depends on the dialect) different **CC** combinations before vowels (such as *pray, skin, glow, thwart*, etc.) and at least 5 combinations of the **CCC** type in the same position, namely /skr/ (*scribe*), /spr/ (*spring*), /spl/ (*splash*), /skw/ (*squeak*), /str/ (*stream*).

In word final position English admits an even larger number of consonant clusters. Considering only the composition of individual of consonant clusters. Considering only the composition of individual morphemes and without taking into consideration the grammatical endings, English has in this position approximately fifty combinations of two consonants (*tend, desk, card*, etc.) and fifteen combinations of three consonants (for example, /mpt/ (*attempt*), /ndθ/ (*thousandth*). /rmθ/ (*warmth*)).

However, the actual number of word final consonant clusters is further increased by the inflectional endings -*s* (plural of nouns, third person singular of verbs) and -*ed* (past participle and past tense), which create additional clusters of two, three, and even four consonants — for example, /bz/ (*cabs*), /bd/ (*robbed*), /nθs/ (*months*), /rbz/ (*curbs*), /lmd/ (*filmed*), /mpts/ (*attempts*), /rsts/ (*bursts*), /lfθs/ (*twelfths*), /ltst/ (*waltzed*). etc.

Just which consonant clusters of English turn out to be serious pronunciation problems depends on the native language of the learner. The possibility of combining many consonants in large clusters in pre- and post-vocalic position is a feature of English which is likely to create considerable difficulties for the learner. The post-vocalic clusters which are created by the grammatical endings -*s*, -*ed* are especially likely to present problems, since failure to pronounce the final consonant is not only a pronunciation mistake but also a grammatical mistake which is likely to interfere with the intelligibility of the intent of the communication (for example, *I learned* pronounced like *I learn*; *my friends* pronounced like *my friend*; etc.)

2. Vowels

Since vowels are produced without any obstacle to the airstream, we must classify them according to a method different from the one used for consonants. Again we can use different points of reference to establish categories. A most important point of reference for vowel classification is the **position of the tongue** during the production of the vowel.

We can divide the oral cavity into a **front**, **central**, and **back** area. We can then classify vowels as **front**, **central**, or **back vowels** according to whether the main hump or bulk of the tongue is in any one of these areas during the production of the sound. The following vowel sounds correspond in pronunciation to the letters of the sample words:

Front vowels

/i/	beat	bead	bee
/ɪ/	bit	bid	
/e/	bait	laid	bay
/ɛ/	bet	bed	
/æ/	bat	bad	

Central vowels

/ɑ/	pot	cod	pa
/ə/	but	mud	

Back vowels

/u/	food	goose	do
/ʊ/	foot	good	
/o/	goat	robe	go
/ɔ/	bought	lawn	straw

In addition to the **front**, **central**, **back** classifications we can also consider the position of the tongue relative to the vertical axis. Again we can divide the oral cavity into three general areas: **high**, **mid**, and **low**, and classify vowels accordingly.

According to this classification the English vowels enumerated above distribute themselves as follows:

High vowels

/i/	beat	/u/	food	
/ɪ/	bit	/ʊ/	good	

Mid vowels

/e/	bait	/ə/	but	/o/	goat
/ɛ/	bet				

Low vowels

/æ/	bat	/ɑ/	pot	/ɔ/	bought.

By utilizing the classification according to tongue position in the horizontal (front, central, back) and vertical (high, mid, low) dimension it is possible to describe any vowel system according to a scheme in

which the vowels are placed in either a square or a trapezoid representing the oral cavity. For the English vowel system this scheme appears
as follows:

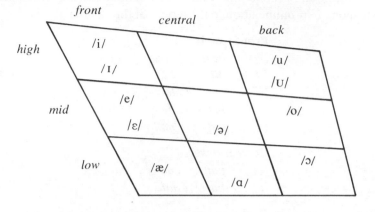

In addition to these tongue positions other criteria may be utilized
to classify and describe vowels. One of the most important of these is
the shape of the lips during the production of the sound. The lips may
be **spread** (as in the /i/ of *eat*) or may be rounded (as in the /u/ of *do*).
There is also the possibility of the lips being in neither definitely rounded nor spread but in a relaxed in-between position. In English the lips
are usually spread with the front vowels, generally quite rounded with
the back vowels and usually neither spread nor rounded with central
vowels. In other words lip-rounding by itself turns out **not** to make a
phonemic difference in English, though it does in many other languages (such as French or German in which some front vowels may be
pronounced with spread lips and others with rounded lips).

We consider a vowel as a **monophthong** if the same quality (tongue
position) is maintained throughout its production. If the tongue changes its position, we may feel that the vowel is really composed of two
vowels fused into one. If this is the case we call the vowel **diphthongal**
(or a **diphthong**). The English vowel sounds /i/ *be*, /e/ *bait*, /u/ *food*,
/o/ *go* are very definitely of diphthongal nature since the tongue glides
up during their production. However, according to the interpretation
of the English vowel system used in this textbook, English has only
three diphthongs: /aɪ/ *eye*, *ice*; /aʊ/ *cow*, *about*; /ɔɪ/ *soil*, *boy*.

There are several other ways of characterizing vowels, most of
which are usually not considered as phonemically distinctive in the
description of English.

Vowels may be distinguished on the basis of **nasality**. During the production of a vowel, if the sound is allowed to escape through the nasal cavity, the vowel becomes nasalized. Speakers of English nasalize their vowels to varying degrees when the vowels stand after and especially before nasal consonants, as in words such as *man, down, ample*. Nasality by itself is not a distinguishing phonemic characteristic of English, as it is in some other languages, such as French.

Two other important features in the description of vowels are the **length** of the vowel and the degree of **tenseness** of the lips and the tongue muscles during the production of the vowel. We have mentioned that English vowels tend to be of different length depending on whether they are syllable final or followed by voiced or unvoiced consonants in the same syllable: *be* [bi:], *bead* [bi·d], *beat* [bit]. But by itself length is not a phonemic distinction in English. The same is also true about the degree of tenseness. The higher vowels /i/ *seal*, /e/ *bait*, /u/ *food*, /o/ *goat* are more **tense** than the corresponding lower vowels /ɪ/ *bit*, /ɛ/ *bet*, /ʊ/ *good*, /ɔ/ *bought*. It is easy to check on this difference in tension by saying words like *beat/bit*, or *bait/bet* in rapid succession and noting the relaxation of the lip and tongue tension which characterizes the second vowel of each pair. But, the **tense** vs. **lax** contrast is not considered a phonemic distinction according to the analysis presented here.

So far we have not discussed allophonic variations of the English vowels. One of the most important and obvious of these concerns the central vowel /ə/ (*but*). This vowel occurs in several variants which are phonetically quite distinct. All the variants are central vowels produced without lip-rounding. But the stressed variant (as in *but* or *enough*) is produced with the tongue quite a bit lower and farther back than its unstressed counterpart (as in the unstressed pronunciation of *the* or the initial vowel of *enough*). Phonetically the stressed variant is usually transcribed as [ʌ], the unstressed as [ə]. However, since their distribution is mutually exclusive, they can be interpreted as the same phoneme. Thus, while **phonetically** *enough* can be transcribed as [ənʌf], the **phonemic** transcription is /ənəf/. In addition, the /ə/ phoneme has also a variant which appears only before *r* (as in *sir* or *furry*). This variant (phonetically [ɝ]) is quite a bit higher and more central than the sound used before other consonants (such as [ʌ] in *enough*). Again, since the occurrence of [ɝ] seems restricted to the position before /r/, the [ɝ] sound can be interpreted as the phoneme /ə/. Thus *sir* is **phonetically** [sɝr], but **phonemically** /sər/ (Note: in some

American dialects there is a contrast of [ə][ʌ] vs. [ɝ] even before /r/. But for our discussion it does not seem warranted to set up /ɝ/ as a separate phoneme on the basis of such regional contrasts as *hurry* /həri/ vs. *furry* /fɝri/.)

Just as in the case of the consonants, the information concerning the production of the vowels must be supplemented by some indication as to their possible distribution. Basically all the vowels can occur in the accented syllable. The vowels /ɪ/ (*bit*), /ɛ/ (*bet*), /æ/ (*bat*), /ʊ/ (*foot*) can occur only if they are followed by a consonant in the same syllable. Depending on dialectal variation, there is also an additional minor restriction which applies to the occurrence of these vowels in stressed accented position. The difference between the sounds /i/ : /ɪ/, /e/ : /ɛ/ : /æ/, /u/ : /ʊ/, /o/ : /ɔ/ may be lost before the sound /r/. Thus in some eastern dialects of the United States the words *Mary, merry, marry* are pronounced differently, while in some other eastern dialects *Mary* and *merry* are pronounced alike, but distinguished from *marry*. In much of the United States, however, *Mary, merry, marry* are all pronounced with the same /e/ sound. Of course the phonemes /e/, /ɛ/, /æ/ (*bait, bet, bat*) are kept distinct before other consonants. It is only before /r/ that this distinction is lost or—to use the technical term—**neutralized**. This neutralization is of no particular concern to the foreign student (except that he may at times be bothered by not hearing an expected differentiation in pronunciation). However, the concept and the fact of neutralization are important for the teacher of any foreign language to remember: a distinction between phonemes, easily made and maintained in one position, may be completely lost in another.

The most important neutralization occurring in American English is the reduction of unstressed vowels to /ə/. This happens particularly in unstressed final position, as well as in other unstressed positions within the word. In initial unstressed position vowel sounds which are followed by a consonant tend to be replaced by the unstressed variant of the /ə/ phoneme: *divide* /də ' vaɪd/ *, believe* /bə ' liv/, *polite* /pə ' laɪt/, *maternal*, /mə ' tɝnəl/. However, if the vowel in initial unstressed position is followed by another vowel sound, the contrast is maintained: *react* /ri' ækt/, *biology* /aɪ' aləji/, *chaotic* /ke' atɪk/, *poetic* /po'ɛtɪk/.

The result of the tendency to neutralize all vowel distinctions into /ə/ in preconsonantal unstressed position is that in many instances the

---

*Note that stress marks precede the stressed syllable.

meaningful units (morphemes) will appear in initial unstressed position in a form which is different from the one which they have if they are under the stress: Thus the morpheme /stebəl/ of *stable* changes to /stə'bɪl/ in *stability*, the morpheme /æ'təm/ of *atom* becomes /ə'tɑm/ in *atomic*. By a switch of stress, the noun /ˈrɛkərd/ (*record*, stress on the first syllable) becomes the verb /rə'kɔrd/. The noun /ˈkɑntɛst/ (*contest*, stress on first syllable) corresponds to the verb (kən'tɛst/. The difference in pronunciation according to stressed or unstressed position also applies to many one-syllable words which change their vowel to an unstressed /ə/ if they are used in unstressed position. Thus the word *do* /du/ will normally become /də/ if in unstressed position — as can be seen by the sentence *how do you do?* which is normally pronounced /haʊ də yə du/. These changes or neutralizations of vowel contrasts to /ə/ form one of the major problems of English for the foreign student and will be discussed at greater length in the chapter on morphology.

Before leaving the summary description of the English vowel system, we must refer to an alternate description and method of analysis which assumes that English has only nine simple vowels and interprets some of the vowels which we called single unit phonemes as phonemic diphthongs. Since this latter analysis is used fairly widely in the pedagogical literature as well as in some student textbooks, we shall describe it here very briefly. Obviously the description may be omitted at the option of the teacher and/or student in case it is felt that the presentation of an alternate system will lead to confusion.

The alternate analysis assumes that the English vowel system has three front, three central and three back vowels:

Front vowels

/i/	(/ɪ/)	*bit*
/e/	(/ɛ/)	*bet*
/æ/		*bat*

Since the system recognizes only one /i/ phoneme and one /e/ phoneme, any symbol for /i/ or /e/ can be used. There is no need to make sure that there are two distinct symbols for /i/ and /e/ as in the system which contrasts /bɪt/ and /bit/, /bɛt/ and /bet/.

Central vowels

/ɨ/	*just*
/ə/	*but*
/ɑ/	*pot*

The central vowels /ə/ and /ɑ/ are the same as in the other system. However, the nine-vowel system introduces an additional central vowel, which—as a monophthong—can be exemplified by the rapid pronunciation of the adverb *just* (as in *I just did it* [ɑɪ jɨst 'dɪd ɪt]) which contrasts with the pronunciation of *just* as an adjective (as in *a just man* [ə jəst mæn]).

Back vowels
/u/ (/ʊ/)	*foot, good*
/o/	*I'm "gonna" do this*
/ɔ/	*watch, cot* (New England pronunciation)

Since the system recognizes only one /u/ phoneme, any kind of symbol can be used. One of the problems of the nine-vowel system is that in most varieties of American speech its two *o*-phonemes are quite difficult to find as single vowels. Thus the New England pronunciation of *road*, or the pronunciation of *o* in the shortened form of *going to* ("*gonna*") are the usual examples quoted for the /o/ phoneme of the system while *watch* or the New England pronunciation of *cot* (/kɔt/, not /kɑt/) furnish examples of /ɔ/.

The rest of the English vowels can then be interpreted as diphthongs composed of the above mentioned nine vowels plus semivocalic glides. The diphthongs /ai/, /au/, /ɔi/ (*eye, cow, boy*) of the first system are thus interpreted as being composed of **vowels + semivowels:**

/ay/	*buy*
/aw/	*cow*
/ɔy/	*boy*

Similar diphthongs are used to account for the other glided vowels:

/iy/	*beat*
/ey/	*bait*
/uw/	*food*
/ow/	*goat*

In other words the analysis assumes that the last element of the diphthongs in *buy, beat, bait* is really a variant of /y/ (as in *yes*), which appears only after the vowel. In the same way the last element of the vowel sounds (diphthongs) in *cow, food, goat* is assumed to be a variant of the phoneme /w/ as in *water, with,* etc. Phonetically there is probably not too much similarity between the /w/ in /wɔtər/ and the /w/ of /gowt/. However, since the sounds are in exclusive (**comple-**

mentary) distribution, they may be interpreted as variants of the same phoneme. In addition to the post-vocalic glides [y] and [w] which are assumed to be variants of the phonemes /y/ and /w/, the second system also recognizes a **vocalic glide** or lengthening which is usually interpreted as a variant of the phoneme /h/. This lengthening is always present if the /ɔ/ vowel is syllable final and thus lengthened: *law*, *paw* = /lɔh/, /pɔh/. It can be used to distinguish pairs like *cot* (if pronounced with /ɔ/), *caught*: /kɔt/, /kɔht/. It can also be used to transcribe the glides which exist in most varieties of American speech before /r/: *poor* = /puhr/, *war* = /wɔhr/, *far* = /fɑhr/, *dear* = /dihr/, etc.

There are certain advantages to the second system: it can be used much more efficiently than the first system to describe differences between varieties of English. It also makes clear in transcription that vowels such as those in *bait*, *beat*, *food*, *bone* are diphthongal: /beyt/, /biyt/, /fuwd/, /bown/. But there are also disadvantages: the pure, monophthongal phonemes (/o/, /ɔ/) are difficult to illustrate. From the purely theoretical point of view, a phonemic system should be based on the description of a specific language or dialect and should not be created for the convenience of comparing dialectal differences. From the purely practical pedagogical point of view, the dialectal differences which can be spelled out by the use of the second system are usually of little importance to the foreigner learning American English. If they are to be dealt with, then they must be simplified and explained briefly, preferably without recourse to different phonemic transcriptions.

3. Non-segmental phonemes

So far we have discussed only those elements of the sound system which can be isolated by cutting the stream of speech into successive segments: for example, *father* = /f/ + /ɑ/ + /ð/ + /ə/ + /r/). Actually there is more to the stream of speech than the successive units of sound. We could construct (and some scientists have already done so!) a machine that could pronounce successive sound segments. But such speech would sound unreal, monotonous. Some of the very essential signals might be completely missing, because the intonation patterns, the different stresses and pitches with which various parts of the sound stream are pronounced, are an essential part of the phonemic inventory of every language. The following must be considered part of the phonemic system of English:

1. **Stress** – the relative prominence given to any one syllable.
2. **Pitch** – the relative tone level with which a syllable is pronounced.
3. **Juncture** – the manner in which sounds are connected with each other.

English can give prominence to almost any word of a sentence by simply applying a heavy stress (**emphatic stress**) to it: $\overline{I}$ ⌐ *saw John yesterday* (stress on *I*), does not mean exactly the same as *I* ⌐ *saw* ⌐ *John yesterday*, or *I saw* ⌐ *John* ⌐ *yesterday*, or *I saw John* ⌐ *yesterday* ⌐. To the native speaker of English this way of stressing the importance of any one part of an utterance seems a most natural way of conveying emphasis. There are many languages in the world, however, (for example, French) where this possibility of giving emphasis by simple syntactical stress does not exist.

In addition to emphatic stress, English also uses **word stress** on a phonemic basis – to differentiate word meanings. We can easily demonstrate that word stress is phonemic in English by comparing words like *discus* (/'dɪskəs/) and *discuss* /dɪs'kəs/ or pairs like *'accent/ ac'cent, 'pervert/per'vert*, in which the switch from one word class to the other (noun/verb) is indicated by a switch in the stress.

The comparison of *discuss* and *discus* allows us to isolate two degrees of stress: primary (′) and weak (˘): *discus* = /'dis˘kəs/, *discuss* = /˘dis'kəs/. If we compare pairs such as *animate* (verb) and *animate* (adjective) or *refugee* and *effigy*, we can isolate a degree of stress which is intermediate between the primary and the weak: the last syllable of the verb *animate* and of *refugee* is not stressed as heavily as the first, but at the same time it is stressed more heavily than the last syllable of the adjective *animate* or of *effigy*: it carries a **secondary stress** (transcribed as ˋ): *animate* (verb) = /'æ˘nɪˋmet/, *animate* (adjective) = /'æ˘nɪ˘mət/; *effigy* = /'ɛ˘fɪ˘ji/; *refugee* = /'rɛ˘fyʊˋji/.

English possesses a rather intricate stress system. In a fairly subtle way (still subject to further research), this system is linked with a system of using pitch. There are many languages in the world which can use pitch to differentiate words from each other in somewhat the same way English can use stress (as in *discuss* vs. *discus*). For example, in Chinese a word *ma* pronounced with a high pitch is different from a word *ma* pronounced with lower pitch, or with a rising or falling pitch. There are languages which distinguish as many as five different levels of pitch to contrast words. This use of pitch is not known to English. English does utilize pitch, however, to form the overall **sentence melody**. This sentence melody can be described best by assuming that the voice of a speaker of English operates on four mutually contrasting levels of pitch, which can be compared to four registers or levels on a musical staff numbered from 1 to 4:

4		extra high	eh
3	or referred to as	high	h
2		medium	m
1		low	l

Normally a declarative statement in English starts at the medium level, rises to the high level, and then descends to the low level.

2   3   1
I am leaving.

A typical question intonation may be described as 2   3   3:

2   3   3
Are you leaving?

The use of level 4 (extra high) is comparatively rare in normal speech and will usually indicate emotional involvement of the speaker. In a question like *What are you doing?* a note of disgust or surprise may be expressed if *do* receives emphatic stress and with it level 4 pitch:

2   4 1
What are you doing?

In addition to describing the overall intonation pattern, it may also be useful to show specifically how an utterance is terminated. English distinguishes three types of **terminals**: fade ($\downarrow$), rise ($\uparrow$), and sustained ($\rightarrow$).

A fading terminal is used quite typically at the end of a declarative statement and indicates finality, the fact that the communication has come to a close. Thus the simple word *no* (with the meaning: *no, I mean no, that's definite*) will normally be pronounced with a fading terminal *no*($\downarrow$). However, when pronounced with a rising terminal, it will indicate surprise on the part of the speaker, perhaps surprise caused by the *no* answer of the previous interlocutor:

SPEAKER A: (with definiteness and conviction) *No.* ($\downarrow$)
SPEAKER B: (with surprise) *No?* ($\uparrow$)

The sustained terminal (→) indicates normally that the communication is not really finished:

SPEAKER A: *Do you want to help him?*
SPEAKER B: *No (→) . . . but (→) . . .*

A very important feature of English nonsegmental phonemic structure is the way in which sound segments can be connected with each other. It is important to realize that English possesses two alternate ways: **closed juncture** (usually no special symbol) and **open juncture** (+). In closed juncture the sounds are closely linked or run together, while open juncture signals some sort of boundary: *nitrate* /nɑitret/, but *night rate* /nɑit + ret/. It is also easy to demonstrate that the place at which open juncture occurs can make a significant difference: *a name* /ə + nem/, but *an aim* /ən + em/.

Open juncture is normally not expressed by an actual pause, but rather by the way the consonants before and after the juncture are produced. Thus the first *t* of *nitrate*, in syllable initial position, is fully pronounced with aspiration, while the first *t* of *night rate*, in syllable final position, is unreleased. Open juncture occurs in English quite typically at what one might call **grammatical boundaries** (that is, between words or the constituents of words). In any event, it is an important signal contributing to the intelligibility of English utterances. Obviously its omission on the part of speakers whose native language does not employ this signal will interfere quite seriously with the comprehensibility of their English utterances.

(C) THE MAIN PRONUNCIATION PROBLEM: INTERFERENCE

The main and perhaps ultimately the only reason why a non-native has any trouble pronouncing the sounds of a foreign language is that he has already acquired the sound system of his native language which interferes with the acquisition of new speech sounds and new sound patterns. The best way of illustrating the problem of pronunciation is a comparison of sound systems. We will contrast very briefly the main features of English with those of Spanish, French, and German.

The comparison of sound systems can be approached through an inspection of phonemic charts. In the following comparison we shall rely largely on the phonemic charts of the textbooks *Teaching French*, *Teaching Spanish*, and *Teaching German*. In those books the charts are used to illustrate and discuss the problems of the native speaker of American English in learning those foreign languages. In this text we shall utilize the same material for what we might call the **reverse** purpose, the discussion of the problems of native speakers of Spanish, French, or German in learning English. In the discussion we shall also attempt to establish the main types or categories of pronunciation mistakes.

We shall start our comparison by contrasting the consonant systems of the four languages with the help of phonemic charts:

	Bilabial	Labio-Dental	Dental	Alveolar	Retroflex	Alveo-Palatal	Velar	Uvular	Glottal
ENGLISH									
stop	p, b			t, d			k, g		
affricate						č, ǰ			
fricative slit		f, v	θ, ð						h
fricative groove				s, z		ʃ, ʒ			
lateral				l					
nasal	m			n			ŋ		
semivowel	w				r	y (palatal)			
SPANISH									
stop	p, b		t, d				k, g		
affricate						č			
fricative slit		f	(θ)				χ		
fricative groove				s					
lateral				l		λ (palatal)			
nasal	m			n		ɲ			
trill			ʀ						
flap			r						
semivowel	w					y			
FRENCH									
stop	p, b		t, d				k, g		
fricative slit		f, v							

	Bilabial	Labio-Dental	Dental	Alveolar	Retroflex	Alveo-Palatal	Velar	Uvular	Glottal
fricative groove			s, z			ʃ, ʒ			
lateral			l						
vibrant								r	
nasal	m		n			ɲ			
semivowel	w					y, ɥ			
GERMAN									
stop	p, b			t, d			k, g		
affricate	(pf)			(ts)		(tʃ)			
fricative slit		f, v				ç	χ		h
fricative groove				s, z		ʃ, ʒ			
lateral				l					
vibrant								R	
nasal	m			n		ŋ			
semivowel						y			

For the reader familiar with Spanish, French, or German, the following words will illustrate the sound values of the symbols used in the phonemic charts, and will also indicate the most important allophonic variants of some of the phonemes. (Remember that phonemes are always surrounded by slants / /, while variants are given in brackets [ ].)

Spanish

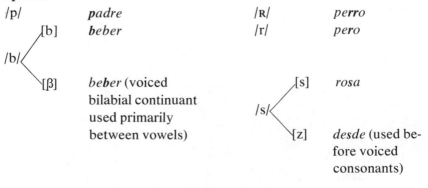

/p/   padre   /ʀ/   perro
    [b]   beber   /r/   pero
/b/
    [β]   beber (voiced   [s]   rosa
               bilabial continuant   /s/
               used primarily
               between vowels)   [z]   desde (used be-
                                                      fore voiced
                                                      consonants)

/m/	*madre*	/l/	*el*
/w/	*cuento, hueso*	/ʎ/	*ella* (Castilian)
/f/	*fuente*	/č/	*mucho*
/t/	*tengo*	/k/	*carne*

/d/⟨[d] *dedo*
[ð] *dedo* (voiced dental continuant used primarily between vowels)

/g/⟨[g] *gallo*
[ɣ] *lago* (voiced velar continuant used primarily between vowels)

| /θ/ | *hacer* (Castilian) | /ɲ/ | *año* |

/n/⟨[n] *niño*
[ŋ] *ángulo*

| /y/ | *yo* |
| /χ/ | *deja* |

French

/p/	*père*	/l/	*belle*
/b/	*boire*	/n/	*non*
/m/	*main*	/ʃ/	*cheval*
/w/	*oui*	/ʒ/	*général*
/f/	*fin*	/ɲ/	*agneau*
/v/	*vin*	/y/	*bien, fille*
/t/	*ton*	/ɥ/	*lui*
/d/	*don*	/k/	*car*
/s/	*brosse*	/g/	*gant*
/z/	*rose*	/r/	*rue* (also pronounced as a uvular trill: [ʀ] *rue*)

German

/p/	*Pein*	/l/	*lachen*
/b/	*Bein*	/n/	*nein*
/pf/	†*Pfeife*	/tʃ/	†*Tscheche*
/m/	*mein*	/ç/	‡*ich*

†Note that the German affricates are interpreted as a combination of two phonemes.
‡Since χ appears almost without exception only after back vowels, where /ç/ does not appear, /χ/ and /ç/ are considered by some linguists as variants of one phoneme.

/f/	*fein*	/χ/		‡*ach*
/v/	*Wein*	/ʃ/		*Schuh*
/t/	*Tante*	/ʒ/		*Genie*
/d/	*danke*	/y/		*ja*
/ts/	†*zu*	/ŋ/		*Ding*
/s/	*Wasser*		[R]	*Ruhe* (syllable initial)
/z/	*Rose*			*irr* (after stressed
/h/	*haben*	/r/		short vowels,
				syllable final)
			[ʌ]	*ihr* (vocalized
				after long stressed
				vowels, syllable
				final)
				aber (vocalized
				after unstressed
				vowels)

Pronunciation problems may be classified according to several categories, which can be illustrated by the difficulties which native speakers of Spanish, French or German will experience in learning English:

1. **The most important and most obvious problem occurs if the language to be learned — English in this case — utilizes a phoneme which has no counterpart in the learner's language.** If we inspect our phonemic charts only for the absence or presence of sounds, we find that the following English sounds simply do not occur in the other three languages:

Bilabials

Speakers of German do not have the phoneme /w/. As a result, they are likely to substitute /v/ for /w/: *water* pronounced like [vɔtər].

Labio-Dental

Speakers of Spanish do not have the sound /v/. Therefore they will substitute [b] or its allophone [ß] (a continuant pronounced with both *lips): vest* is pronounced as [bɛst] or [ßɛst].

Dental

English /θ/ is absent in German, French, and most varieties of Spanish. Only Castilian Spanish has a /θ/ sound; most other varieties use /s/ where Castilian uses /θ/. German and French have no /ð/ sound. (Spanish does possess the sound as a variant of /d/.) Speakers of French, German or Spanish will therefore have difficulties pronouncing *thin* and may substitute either [t] or [s] giving [tɪn] or [sɪn]). A similar substitution will occur for /ð/: *the* pronounced [də̇] or [zə].

Retroflex

The English retroflex semivowel /r/ has no counterpart in any of the three languages. Speakers are likely to substitute their own *r* sounds: dental, velar or uvular trills or fricatives which have little resemblance to the English /r/.

Alveo-Palatal

English /č/ is absent in French. The most obvious and likely substitute is [ʃ]: *chin* pronounced like [ʃɪn]. /ǰ/ is absent in all three languages (though, as we shall point out, some speakers of Spanish actually do use a [ǰ] sound). The most likely substitutes are the voiceless [č] (for Germans): *German* pronounced like [čərmən] or /ʒ/ (for Frenchmen): *General* pronounced like [ʒenərəl].

Both /ʃ/ and /ʒ/ are absent in most dialects of Spanish. The most likely substitution is [č]: *shine* pronounced as [čɑin]. Since there is no contrast [č]:[ʃ] for the speaker of Spanish, he may also confuse [č] and [ʃ] once he has learned to pronounce the latter: *shine* may become [čɑin] but *chicken* may be pronounced [ʃɪkən]. This happens especially with speakers of Spanish in whose native dialect the stop element of /č/ is very weak (/č/ almost like [ʃ]).

Velar

The /ŋ/ sound has no phonemic counterpart in French (and, as we shall point out, exists only as an allophone in Spanish). The most likely substitute is [n]: *sing* pronounced like *sin*.

Glottal

The phoneme /h/ does not exist in either French or Spanish. The most likely mispronunciation for speakers of French is simply omission of the sound: *have* pronounced [æv]. Speakers of Spanish may either omit the sound or substitute the farther front, more fricative velar [χ]: *have* pronounced [χæv].

2. **Another set of problems arises if the sound of English does exist in the native language of the learner but is utilized in a different way.** From the theoretical point of view this kind of pronunciation problem should be easier to cope with than the one caused by complete absence of the sound. In practice this is evidently not necessarily the case. This category may be illustrated by the following examples:

The speaker of Spanish possesses a sound very similar to English /ð/ (*the*)—but only as the intervocalic allophone of /d/ (the Spanish word for finger—*dedo*—is pronounced [deðo]). Even though the [ð] sound does exist in Spanish, most native speakers of Spanish have great difficulty transposing this intervocalic variant to the beginning of the word. They are likely to mispronounce *the* as [də]. The existence of a variant of *n* pronounced [ŋ] before a velar (for example, *ángulo* pronounced [áŋgulo]) does make it easier for the Spanish speaker to produce the /ŋ/ of English (*sing, bring*) in isolation, but when /ŋ/ is followed by a labial or dental, he has great difficulty pronouncing it.

Another problem of the same type is illustrated by the Spanish speaker's difficulty with the /z/ phoneme. In Spanish the sound [z] occurs only as a variant of /s/ pronounced before voiced consonants. But in all other positions Spanish speakers will have difficulty producing or hearing a /z/: *zeal* nay become [sil], *roses* may be pronounced [rosəs].

Even /w/ and /y/—which, according to the phonemic chart, should represent no problem for the speaker of Spanish—may turn out to be stumbling blocks. All speakers of Spanish pronounce sounds like [w] and [y] after consonants: Spanish *bien* [byen] or *fuego* [fweɣo]. However, in many varieties of Spanish in word initial position the /y/ phoneme becomes [ʒ] or [j] and /w/ becomes [gw]. As a result, *yes* may be pronounced as [ʒes] or [jes] and *water* as [gwɔtər].

If certain sound combinations are absent in the language of the learner, the many problems which arise belong in the category of **different utilization**. We have already mentioned the many **CC(C)V** and **VCC(C)(C)** patterns possible in English. Without going into an exact comparison of these patterns with those of German, French, or Spanish, we can state that this particular feature of English will cause comparatively little trouble to the speaker of German, some trouble to the speaker of French, and a great deal of trouble to the speaker of Spanish. German rivals English in richness of consonant clusters before or

after the vowels: *nichts* /nıçts/ (*nothing*), *spricht* /ʃprıçt/ (*speaks*),
etc. The latter, incidentally, illustrates a possible problem for the
speaker of German: especially in standard or Southern German, initial /s/ cannot occur before another consonant. Orthographic *s* in
fact stands for [ʃ]. As a result, the speaker of German may have a
tendency to say [ʃpiks] instead of [spiks] (*speaks*); [ʃton] instead of
[ston] (*stone*), etc.

French also admits a number of **CC** and **CCC** patterns in initial
position (*splendide, scrupule, prendre, bien*). However, as far as intervocalic or final position is concerned, the occurrence of consonant
clusters is limited in French by the so-called **law of three consonants**
which states that a combination of three or more consonants is possible only if the group of consonants remaining after omitting the first
can also occur in word initial position. Thus a group like *rdr* (*perdre*
/perdr/) is possible because *dr* can occur in word initial position
(*drogue*); but a French speaker may show some uneasiness in pronouncing groups like [rvd] (*curved*), [skt] (*asked*), etc., since word
initial groups like *vd, kt* do not exist in French. To make such groups
pronounceable he will most likely interpolate an /ə/ sound: *asked*
pronounced [æskəd] instead of /æskt/.

The speaker of Spanish uses in his own language only a very limited
number of initial combination **CC** before vowels, some combinations
of C + /r/ (such as *traer*), C + /l/ (*placer*), C + /y/ (*bien* /byen/),
C + /w/ (*bueno* /bweno/). Word initial /s/ before a consonant does not
exist. Whenever the Spanish speaker encounters any of the English
initial consonant clusters beginning with /s/ (*Spanish, small, snow*)
he will tend to make them pronounceable by adding an initial vowel —
a tendency reinforced by the fact that, for many of the words having
initial /s/ + C in English, the corresponding Spanish word begins with
/e/ (*Spanish = español*): *Spanish* becomes [ɛspæniʃ], *small* may
become [ɛsmɔl], etc. The existence of the C + /y/ and C + /w/ clusters
in Spanish does little to facilitate the Spanish speaker's accuracy in
English pronunciation. In many cases in which English uses the
combination C + /y/, Spanish does not use it in corresponding **cognate**
words — for example, English *mule* /myul/, Spanish *mulo* /mulo/;
English *Cuba* /kyubə/, Spanish *Cuba* /kuba/; English *fume* /fyum/,
Spanish *fuma* /fuma/. The Spanish speaker will be tempted to say
[mul] instead of /myul/, [fum] instead of /fyum/. On the other hand, in
the majority of words in which Spanish does use a C + /y/ combination,
English does not use it in the corresponding cognate: Spanish *cuestión*

/kwestyon/, English *question* /kwɛsčən/. The result will be that Spanish speakers will tend to introduce pronunciations like [misyon], [kwɛstyon] into their English. A somewhat similar problem also exists with respect to the Spanish C + /w/ cluster = English C + /u/ + V. In many cases the consonant preceding the /u/ of the English cluster does not correspond to the consonant of the similar Spanish word: Spanish *visual* /bis'wal/, but English *visual* /'vɪʒuəl/; Spanish *gradual* /gra'dwal/, English *gradual* /'græjuəl/; Spanish *puntual* /pun'twal/, English *punctual* /'pəŋkčuəl/.

Spanish does have several syllable initial **CCC** combinations (of which the last two consonants are /ry/, /rw/; /ly/, /lw/: *prieto, prueba, pliego, fluir*). Since none of the Spanish combinations can include initial /s/, the Spanish speaker will have a major problem dealing with English **CCC** combinations in which /s/ is the first element: *scroll, script, spring, squeal*. Again, the addition of an initial vowel ([əskript] for /skrɪpt/) will be the usual way out.

When it comes to producing the various **VCC(C)** combinations of English, the specific problems of Spanish speakers are almost unpredictable. For all practical purposes, syllable or word final clusters do not exist in Spanish. Any English cluster is likely to present a problem that will probably be solved either by the interpolation of a vowel (*friends* becomes [frɛndɛs]), or by the omission of one or even several consonants (*friends* becomes [frɛn], [frɛns]). Even the number of possible single word final consonants of Spanish is limited — and many Spanish dialects are losing the few that exist in the standard Castilian language: for example, *verdad* (*truth*) is pronounced [berða], *amigos* (*friends*) is pronounced [amiɣo], with only a very faint indication of a final consonant, or none at all. The result is that many speakers of Spanish tend to speak English without word final consonants or with final consonants which are not identifiable to English ears: [maɪ ne i χose χimene] (*my name is José Jiménez*).

3. **Closely related to the set of problems just mentioned are those which are best analyzed as the result of a neutralization process in the native language**: a contrast between phonemes maintained in some positions is completely lost in others.

Spanish and German furnish good examples of this situation. Speakers of Spanish distinguish /m/, /n/, and /ɲ/ in most positions (at the beginning of a word or between vowels: for example, [mama], [niɲo], [vano], [aɲo]. However, before a consonant the distinction between

/m/, /n/, /ɲ/ is lost: only [m] appears before a labial, only [n] before a dental, and [ŋ] before a velar. As a result, when speaking English, the Spanish speaker may pronounce *sometime* as [səntaɪm], *some coffee* as [səŋ kɔfi], *in bed* as [ɪmbɛd]. Speakers of German have no difficulty distinguishing voiced and voiceless sounds in all positions — except word or syllable finally. In the latter positions sounds are voiceless and the contrast voiced/voiceless is neutralized: *time* vs. *dime* does not represent any problem, but *hat* and *had* may **both** be pronounced [hæt].

4. **Another important type of pronunciation mistake is the close substitute sound.** In most instances the mistake caused by substituting a native sound very similar or almost identical to the English phoneme will cause little trouble or misunderstanding. In the long run, it is likely to be a most persistent but perhaps less serious aspect of a foreign accent. A good example for this category is the substitution of the unaspirated French or Spanish /p/, /t/, /k/ for the aspirated English /p/, /t/, /k/ phonemes in word initial position, or the substitution of the clearly dental Spanish or French /t/, /d/, /n/, /l/ for their English counterparts.

We can furnish further examples of the various categories of pronunciation problems by comparing the vowel systems of the languages we are discussing.

Note that the descriptions of the Spanish, French and German systems are slightly schematized. Also, the international phonetic alphabet symbols /y/, /æ/, /ø/ have been utilized to transcribe the rounded front vowels of French, while the "Umlaut symbols" /ü/, /ö/, etc. are used

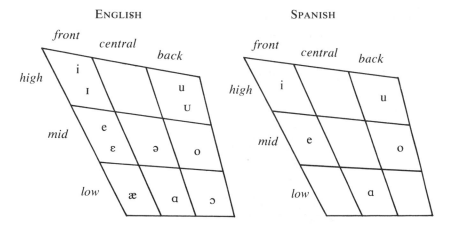

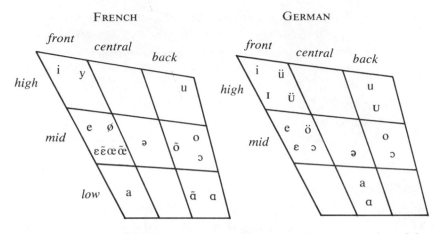

FRENCH   GERMAN

to describe the rounded front vowels of German. Some examples of the vowels of the Spanish, French and German systems follow:

Spanish:

/i/	*vivir*		/u/	*uva*

/e/ ⟨ [e] *pero*
    [ε] *tengo* (variant usually occurs in syllable ending in a consonant)

/o/ ⟨ [o] *cosa*
    [ɔ] *donde* (variant usually occurs in syllable ending in a consonant)

/a/   *casa*

French:

/i/	*lit*	/y/	*du*	/u/	*doux*	/ɛ̃/	*vin*
/e/	*les*	/ø/	*peu*	/o/	*beau*	/œ̃/	*un*
/ɛ/	*dette*	/œ/	*peur*	/ɔ/	*botte*	/õ/	*mon*
/a/	*patte*	/ə/	*le*	/ɑ/	*bas*	/ã/	*tante*

German:

/i/	*Lied*	/ü/	*Güte*		/u/	*gut*
/ɪ/	*bitte*	/Ü/	*Mütter*		/ʊ/	*Mutter*
/e/	*beten*	/ö/	*Goethe*		/o/	*Sohn*
/ɛ/	*Bett*	/ɔ̈/	*Götter*		/ɔ/	*Gott*
		/ə/	unstressed, *Rosen*			
		/a/	*Stadt*	/ɑ/ *Staat*		

From the comparison of the vowel systems it becomes immediately clear that the speaker of Spanish (with only five vowel phonemes) is likely to have the most trouble with the English vowel system. Both he and the speaker of French share one pronunciation problem belong-

and /ʊ/ phonemes of English (*bit*, *good*). In other words, in the general articulatory area of English /i/ and /ɪ/, speakers of Spanish or French have only one phoneme /i/; and in the general area of English /u/ and /ʊ/ they have only one phoneme /u/. As a result they may have difficulty hearing the difference /i:ɪ/ (*beat*/*bit*) and /u:ʊ/ (*fool*/*full*), and may pronounce *bit* like *beat* /bit/ or *full* like *fool* /ful/. The comparison of the vowel systems also makes it quite clear that in fact none of the other three languages possesses a counterpart to the English phoneme /æ/ (*bat*). Thus, native speakers of all the three languages may have trouble with this particular sound.

They may also have trouble discriminating /æ/ from either /ɛ/ or /ɑ/ (/pɛt:pæt/; /pæt:pɑt/) and may substitute /ɛ/ or /ɑ/ for /æ/ (*pat* pronounced like *pot* or *pet*). The kind of difficulty caused by the absence of a sound in the native language is also illustrated by the /ə/ phoneme of English. Here we must keep in mind that at least the stressed variant [ʌ] (*but*) has no counterpart in the other three languages. Thus [ʌ] is likely to be confused with the much lower /ɑ/ or the further back /ʊ/. Speakers of French, German or Spanish may have difficulty in discriminating *luck* /lək/ from *lock* /lɑk/ or *look* /lʊk/.

A pronunciation problem belonging to Category 2 is illustrated by the Spanish speaker's difficulty in pronouncing and discriminating English /e/, /ɛ/. The Spanish [e] [ɛ] sounds are variants of the same phoneme. In most Spanish dialects the open sound [ɛ] is pronounced only if followed by a consonant in the same syllable; the closed sound [e] is produced if the vowel is syllable final. The result is that the speaker of Spanish has difficulty distinguishing /e/ and /ɛ/ (*bait*, *bet* and may confuse pairs like *bait*/*bet*, *gate*/*get*, etc., in pronunciation.

Category 3 (neutralization of a phonemic contrast in the native language) does not present any special problems to speakers of French, German, or Spanish. The real problems are created by the neutralizations taking place in *English*. The substitution of /ə/ for other vowels in unstressed position will especially confuse and confound the learners: for example, the words that have been learned and identified as /ði/ (*the*), /ænd/ (*and*), /yu/ (*you*) must also be identified and learned as /ðə/, /ən/ or /n/, /yə/, etc. The morpheme /ætəm/ (*atom*) must be Reidentified and pronounced at /ətám/ (in *atomic*).

The problem of the close substitute sound (Category 4) is best illustrated by the German, French, Spanish pronunciations of the English vowels /i/ (*beat*), /e/ (*bait*), /o/ (*bone*), /u/ (*food*). As we have pointed out already, the English vowels are diphthongal (therefore the interpretation [iy], [ey], [ow], [uw] in the second system), and they start with a lower tongue position than their French, German, or Spanish counterparts. As a result English *do* may be pronounced like French *doux* or German *du*; English *gay* like German *geh* or French *gai*; etc. The mispronunciation is not likely to cause misunderstandings but it can be a most persistent feature of the foreign accent.

To complete our brief survey of possible pronunciation problems, we will consider the **nonsegmental phonemes** of the languages involved in our comparison. Briefly the inventory of the nonsegmental phonemes may be summarized as follows:

Stress

English: Stress is phonemic. There are three degrees of word stress.

German: Stress is phonemic. There are three degrees of word stress.

Spanish: Stress is phonemic. There are two degrees of word stress.

French: Stress is nonphonemic. Stress (and lengthening) are used to indicate the end of a word (group).

Pitch

English: Pitch is phonemic on the utterance level. It can be analyzed as having four levels.

German: Pitch is phonemic on the utterance level. It can be analyzed as having four levels.

Spanish: Pitch is phonemic on the utterance level. It can be analyzed as having three levels.

French: Pitch is phonemic on the utterance level. Analysis by levels is difficult.

Juncture

English: Internal open juncture is used to mark boundaries within the utterance.

German: Internal open juncture is used to mark boundaries within the utterance.

Spanish: Internal open juncture is rare. (Its existence is questioned by some scholars.)

French: Internal open juncture is rare or absent. (Its existence is questioned by some scholars.)

From the above comparisons it is evident that speakers of German will have minimal – and speakers of French maximal – trouble with the interpretation and imitation of the English sentence melody and stress. The German and English inventory correspond exactly. This does not necessarily mean that German and English intonation will always correspond (the inventory can be used differently in sentences with identical meaning), but by and large the intonation problems of speakers of German will be minor. Like **any** foreigner learning English, they may still have trouble putting the stress on the right syllable – a problem inherent in the very fact that English stress is phonemic. If we could always predict on which syllable the stress must be put, it would, by definition, be no longer phonemic and would become useless for expressing meaning differences like *'discus, dis'cuss; 'pervert, per'vert,* etc.). In quite a few cases the placement of stress does not correspond in German and English; especially in words which are quite similar in both languages the speaker of German may misplace the stress: for example, English *'atom,* German *A'tom,* English *'president,* German *Präsi'dent.* As a result, a German may stress English *atom* on the second syllable, *president* on the third, and so on.

The speaker of Spanish lacks the device of secondary stress. He is therefore accustomed to producing rather long sequences of syllables with weak stress. English is more likely to require the alternation of strong (or secondary) stress with weak stress: for example, English *pròclamátion* but Spanish *proclamación* (with only one heavy stress, on the last syllable). The example also illustrates the fact that, like the speaker of German, the Spanish speaker also may be misled into putting the stress on the wrong syllable in English – especially in words which are cognate. Thus English *animal* /'ænəməl/ corresponds to Spanish *animal* /ani'mal/ with stress on the last syllable; English *telephone* /'tɛləfon/, corresponds to Spanish *teléfono* /te'lefono/ with stress on the second syllable. The speaker of Spanish will also have difficulty in hearing and producing the open juncture signal of English. The result will be that, in his speech, word boundaries will not be marked clearly (*beautiful eggs* pronounced exactly like *beautiful legs*) and thus the general intelligibility of his English is likely to suffer.

An examination of Spanish and English pitch contrasts goes beyond the scope of this discussion. Briefly, the pitch patterns of the languages will not always correspond: the three Spanish pitch levels are much more closely spaced than the English ones. As a result the Spanish intonation will often sound monotonous if imposed on English utterances.

The speaker of French does not have any kind of phonemic stress in his language. There is a lengthening which marks the last syllable of a word or word group but, except for this, all syllables of his language are produced with the same amount of stress and with equal length. If we pronounce the word *liberty* with the same stresses that we would use in counting *'one, 'two, 'three ('li-'ber-'ty)*, we can give a pretty good imitation of a French stress pattern imposed upon English. The English stress will almost never be on the last syllable: English *'liberty, phi' losophy, a' cademy*. Pronounced with a French accent, they become ['li'bɛr'tɪ], ['fi'lo'zo'fi], ['ɑ'ka'de'mi] under the influence of French *liberté* [libɛr'te], *philosophie* [filɔzo'fi], *academie* [ɑkade-'mi].

The possibility of signaling word boundaries through internal open juncture is also lacking in French. As a matter of fact, to an even greater degree than Spanish, French is spoken by syllables which end, whenever possible, in vowels and which do not necessarily coincide with word boundaries. In other words, *I cannot understand you* becomes ['ɑi'kæ'nɑ'tə'ndɛr' stæn' dyu].

As far as intonation is concerned, French cannot easily be reduced to definite pitch levels. It has very characteristic pitch contours: up and down (↗ ↘) for simple statements, up for *yes* and/or questions (↗), down for commands (↘). In contrast to Spanish, the total range of pitch in French is considerably broader than the normal range of the pitch contours of English. As a result the sentence melody of French may sound excited, exaggerated or emotional to English ears.

The absence of familiar intonation patterns and juncture signals will always result in the learners of any language believing that the native speakers of the language to be learned speak rapidly and not as distinctly as they should. Most likely, Frenchmen or speakers of English learning each other's language would give each other the advice that in **their** language sounds must be pronounced clearly and distinctly. The fact is that the absence of juncture signals and the pronunciation by syllables rather than words will give the native speaker of English considerable difficulty in his effort to learn French. The junctures and stresses of English — not a part of the French equipment — will be of little help to the Frenchman; he (and to some extent also the speaker of Spanish and even German) will be considerably confused by the English habit of lengthening stressed syllables at the expense of unstressed ones. Syllables of French or Spanish all take approximately the same amount of time (except for the already mentioned lengthening of word or phrase final syllables in French). The speaker of English swallows the unstressed syllables at the expense of the stressed ones. Unlike French or Spanish, English is not a syllable-timed but a stress-timed language. In French or Spanish, an utterance of six syllables will take approximately twice the time of an utterance of three syllables. In English, the duration of the utterance is not primarily determined by the number of syllables but by the number of stresses it contains: the English word *about* (two syllables) does not take considerably less time to be pronounced than the word *approximately* (five syllables); the time difference is nearly equalized by the more rapid pronunciation of the unstressed syllables. The result of this speech habit is that, to the ears of many non-natives, it seems that the speaker of English hurries from stress to stress, swallowing the intervening syllables rapidly. To the non-native ear, English is spoken rapidly and indistinctly. And to the native speaker of English, the foreigner who pronounces all syllables, stressed or unstressed, with equal length sounds strange and quite "un-English" and may even be difficult to understand.

The comparison between English and the Spanish, French, and German systems is not meant to be exhaustive. It has been undertaken primarily to illustrate the **types** of pronunciation problems foreigners encounter in English. Obviously speakers of other languages may encounter many **specific** problems not mentioned so far: for example, speakers of languages in which [p] and [f] or [r] and [l] are variants of the same phoneme (as in several Oriental languages) may have difficulty learning the distinctions /p:f/ or /l:r/. They may mispronounce English by using /p:f/ or /l:r/ according to the distribution patterns of their language; for example, if [p] is used initially and [f] intervocalically, then *father* may become [paðər] and *apple* may become [æfəl]. If [l] is used initially and [r] intervocalically, then *right* will be pronounced as [lɑɪt] and *melon* as [mɛrən]. In Japanese [t] and [tˢ] are variants of the same phoneme, with [tˢ] used before [u] and [t] used elsewhere; English *suit* might then be pronounced [tˢut], and so on.

(D) SPECIAL TEACHING PROCEDURES

1. Auditory discrimination training

One of the main strategies behind pronunciation training is dictated by the assumption that the pronunciation problem is basically connected with a hearing or discrimination problem. Any speaker has been trained to hear the various sounds which are phonemic (significant) in his native language and to neglect others which are not linguistically significant. Therefore, learning a new language requires training the ear to become aware of the sound differences which are phonemic in the language to be learned. The learner must be able (1) to identify the sounds of the new language; (2) to hear the distinctions among the sounds of the new language; and also (3) to hear the differences between the sounds of the new language and those of his native language which he may want to use as substitutes. However, the acquisition of auditory discrimination is not a **guarantee** that accurate pronunciation will be developed; rather, it seems to be a prerequisite for the latter. If a person does not **hear** that he is mispronouncing, he is likely to continue to mispronounce. He has no way of checking up on the accuracy of what he is saying and he has no incentive or guide for improvement. However, it is quite possible that a person may **hear** his own mispronunciation without being able to make the necessary corrections. Training in auditory discrimination is a first step in the teaching of pronunciation, but not necessarily the only one.

The chief method of auditory discrimination training consists of making the learner listen to and identify so-called minimal pairs which are based on sound differences not utilized in his native language, either because the sound differences are not phonemic or because they are neutralized in specific positions. A minimal pair consists of two utterances (typically simple words) which are differentiated only by the specific sound contrast to be learned; for example, *pit* and *bit* are a minimal pair. A learner whose native language does not have both a phoneme /b/ as well as a phoneme /p/ would listen to pairs like *pit/bit*, *pat/bat*, *pin/bin*, *pack/back*. He could be asked to identify the difference between /p/ and /b/ in various ways:

1. Indicate which of the following words begins with /p/, which with /b/, by writing 1 on your answer sheet whenever you hear a word beginning with /p/ and by writing 2 whenever you hear a word beginning with /b/: *pin, bin, bat, pat*. (Answer: 1   2   2   1.)

2. Which of the following words is different from the others in the same series? 1. *pit* 2. *pit* 3. *bit* 4. *pit*. (Answer: 3.)
1. *bin* 2. *pin* 3. *bin* 4. *bin*. (Answer: 2.)

3. You will hear first one word, then three others. Indicate which of the three words is the same as the first word: *pin* – 1. *bin* 2. *pin* 3. *bin*. (Answer: 2.)

4. You will hear a series of pairs of words. Indicate whether the pairs are made up of identical words or different ones:

pin, pin.	(Answer: same.)
bat, pat.	(Answer: different.)
Pete, beat.	(Answer: different.)

If the difficulty of the learner is caused by a neutralization process rather than by the absence of a phoneme, the minimal pairs would need to contrast the phonemes only in the environment in which the neutralization occurs. For a native speaker of German, for example, the /p:b/ contrast would have to be practiced only in final position (since the voiced/voiceless contrast is lost in German in this position). To discriminate *pit/bit* would cause no difficulty for a speaker of standard German, but he might need extensive practice in establishing differences like *nap/nab*; *tripe/tribe*; *rope/robe*.

Auditory discrimination exercises of the type discussed above can be used both as a training device and as a diagnostic device for determining the auditory discrimination and pronunciation problems of the student. Since teachers may want to use minimal pair contrast tests for diagnosis and teaching, we shall list some examples of minimal pairs illustrating the most common auditory discrimination problems encountered by non-native speakers of English. As a general rule, depending on the native language of the student, any two or more English phonemes which are phonetically close to one another can be trouble spots in auditory discrimination: sounds which are distinguished by only **one** phonetic feature (such as stop vs. continuant; voiced vs. voiceless; velar vs. glottal) are much more likely to cause trouble than sounds which are distinguished by several features: /b:v/, /t:d/, /h:χ/ are likely candidates for discrimination trouble, while /m:g/, or /n:k/ will present no difficulty. Vowels produced with similar or neighboring tongue and/or lip position are more likely to be on the trouble list than vowels which are markedly distinguished by lip and tongue position. Many learners are likely to have problems discriminating /ɪ:i/ (*bit/beat*) or /ə:a/ (*hut/hot*). However, contrasts like /i:a/

(*heat*/*hot*) or /iːu/ (*feed*/*food*) are most unlikely to cause discrimination problems.

The most frequently missed phonemic contrasts of English:

Vowel contrasts

/iːɪ/	*beat*/*bit*	*sheep*/*ship*	*seat*/*sit*
/eːɛ/	*bait*/*bet*	*late*/*let*	*taste*/*test*
/ɛːæ/	*bet*/*bat*	*set*/*sat*	*better*/*batter*
/æːɑ/	*hat*/*hot*	*cat*/*cot*	*stack*/*stock*
/ɑːə/	*shot*/*shut*	*hot*/*hut*	*lock*/*luck*
/əːɔ/	*but*/*bought*	*cut*/*caught*	*sung*/*song*
/ɔːo/	*bought*/*boat*	*caught*/*coat*	*call*/*coal*
/uːʊ/	*Luke*/*look*	*suit*/*soot*	*fool*/*full*
/ʊːə/	*look*/*luck*	*put*/*putt*	*could*/*cud*

Consonant contrasts

Labial, labio-dental:

/pːb/	*pit*/*bit*	*pat*/*bat*	*pole*/*bowl*
	rope/*robe*	*tripe*/*tribe*	*mop*/*mob*
/bːv/	*boat*/*vote*	*ban*/*van*	*best*/*vest*
/fːv/	*fan*/*van*	*fast*/*vast*	*fail*/*veil*
	leaf/*leave*	*safe*/*save*	*grief*/*grieve*
/pːf/	*pine*/*fine*	*pun*/*fun*	*pan*/*fan*
/vːw/	*vine*/*wine*	*vest*/*west*	*veal*/*wheel*

Dental, alveolar:

/tːd/	*time*/*dime*	*to*/*do*	*tale*/*dale*
	hat/*had*	*can't*/*canned*	*wrote*/*rode*
/tːθ/	*tin*/*thin*	*tanks*/*thanks*	*wit*/*with*
/dːð/	*day*/*they*	*dare*/*there*	*ladder*/*lather*
/sːθ/	*sin*/*thin*	*sing*/*thing*	*sigh*/*thigh*
/zːð/	*rise*/*writhe*	*bays*/*bathe*	*tease*/*teeth*
/zːs/	*zinc*/*sink*	*razor*/*racer*	*prize*/*price*
	buzz/*bus*	*lazy*/*lacy*	*maze*/*mace*

Note that /θ/ can also at times be confused with the **labio-dental slit fricative** /f/:

/fːθ/	*fin*/*thin*	*fought*/*thought*	*miff*/*myth*

Alveolar, alveo-palatal:

/sːʃ/	*Sue*/*shoe*	*sin*/*shin*	*same*/*shame*
/čːʃ/	*chin*/*shin*	*chew*/*shoe*	*watch*/*wash*

/č:ǰ/	chin/gin	chew/jew	etch/edge
	rich/ridge		
/ʃ:ʒ/	(few if any pure minimal pairs exist:		
	fission/vision	pressure/treasure	
	Aleutian (islands)/allusion		
/ǰ:y/	jail/Yale	jeer/year	joke/yoke

Velar:

/k:g/	come/gum	coat/goat	cold/gold
	pick/pig	back/bag	tuck/tug

Glottal:

/h : ∅/	hand/and	hold/old	hit/it

Nasals:

/m:n/	dime/dine	some/sun	ram/ran
/n:ŋ/	win/wing	sun/sung	ran/rang
/m:n:ŋ/	ram/ran/rang	rum/run/rung	
	(Note that /ŋk:ŋ/ can also be confused:		
	think/thing	sink/sing	bank/bang)

Semivowels and l

/r:l/	right/light	rode/load	read/lead
	green/glean	pray/play	fry/fly
/r:w/	ripe/wipe	run/won	raid/wade.

Training in auditory discrimination is by no means identical with pronunciation training. It is only part of it. It aims to assure that a prerequisite of pronunciation is present, but the presence of the prerequisite does not imply that accurate pronunciation will follow. It is likely that the person who can discriminate between two English phonemes will also distinguish them in his speech. However, he might make the distinction between the two phonemes by substituting two more or less similar sounds for them. For instance, a speaker of German will have no difficulty discriminating between /ɪ:i/ (bit/beat) but in actual pronunciation he will substitute his short [ɪ] (bitte) for English /ɪ/ (bit) and his long nondiphthongal [i] (bieten) for English /i/ (beat). This is certainly preferable to the confusion of beat/bit which may be committed by a French or a Spanish speaker—but the nondiphthongal [i] of German will still impress the native American as a distinctive "foreign accent."

To counteract the substitution of phonetically similar sounds of the foreign language, we can try to develop in the student the ability to discriminate aurally between English sounds and the likely substitute sounds of his native language. For example, we can train a speaker of German, French, or Spanish to perceive the difference between his native nondiphthongal [i], [e], [o], [u] and the English diphthongal counterparts: German *du*, French *doux* vs. English *do*; German *See* vs. English *say*; Spanish, French *si* vs. English *sea*; etc. This kind of auditory discrimination training presupposes, of course, that the teacher has a good knowledge and accurate pronunciation of the pupil's native language. In actual practice this is not always the case.

Interlingual auditory discrimination training is a device to be kept in mind by those who have the background and opportunity to use it. In most situations the teacher will have to do without it and will try to achieve accuracy of pronunciation of the English sounds by insisting on accurate (or at least increasingly accurate) imitation and repetition, and by using some of the other teaching devices to be discussed later in this chapter.

2. Articulatory description

To help the pupil in the pronunciation of speech sounds, it is important to understand precisely the articulation of those sounds, and it is essential to be familiar with the general description and names of the speech organs.

The following information reviews and to some extent repeats points made in connection with the description of the English sound system; however, the emphasis is put on the most characteristic features of the sounds, those that help the student when called to his attention. Also, in certain instances, some descriptions exaggerate particular features of a sound. But it has been found that this exaggeration is helpful in the initial learning process.

Vowels

/i/ (*beat*):   Tongue in a high position toward the front of the mouth; lips spread and tense. During the pronunciation of the sound, the tongue shifts to an even higher position and the lips spread even more.

/ɪ/ (*bit*):   Tongue in a high front position, but less so than for /i/. Lips are slightly spread but relaxed.

/e/ (*bait*):   This is a diphthongal sound, and can best be described as a combination of /ɛ/ and /i/. The /e/ sound begins in the more relaxed position of /ɛ/, then shifts to the higher, tenser, and more forward position of /i/.

/ɛ/ (*bet*):   Lips are relaxed and neither spread nor rounded. The jaws are open a little wider than for /i/ with the tongue in a median position slightly toward the front of the mouth.

/æ/ (*bat*):   This is the most open of the front vowels, produced with nearly maximum aperture, low front tongue position, and slightly spread lips.

/ə/ (*cut*):   The tongue is in a central position with a medium degree of aperture; lips and jaws relaxed.

/ɑ/ (*cot*);   Maximum aperture, lips relaxed, tongue low.

/u/ (*food*):   Tongue in a high position toward the back of the mouth; lips firmly rounded and tense.

/ʊ/ (*foot*):   Tongue slightly lower than for /u/; lips still rounded, but relaxed.

/o/ (*boat*):   Another diphthongal sound, beginning from a position somewhere like that for /ə/ and shifting back and higher with gradual rounding of the lips as for /ʊ/.

/ɔ/ (*bought*):   Nearly maximum aperture, tongue drawn slightly back, lips rounded.

Diphthongs

/ɑɪ/ (*buy*):   Begins at the position for /ɑ/ and shifts quickly to the high front position of /ɪ/, with slightly spread lips.

/ɑʊ/ (*bough*):   Begins at the position for /ɑ/ and shifts quickly to the back position for /ʊ/, with slightly rounded lips.

/ɔɪ/ (*boy*):   Begins at the low position for /ɔ/, with rounded lips, and shifts quickly to the high front position for /ɪ/, with slightly spread lips.

The degree of difficulty students may have in producing the English vowel sounds will vary considerably according to how complex or simple the vowel system of their native languages may be. People whose native language has a simple five-vowel system (such as Spanish) will usually have more difficulty in perceiving and producing sounds like /ɪ/, /ə/, /ʊ/ than those whose language contains a greater variety of vowels (such as German). The sound /æ/ seems to be difficult for speakers of all languages, while the glide sounds /e/ and /o/ seem especially difficult for some Southeast Asians (Thai, Vietnamese).

In any case, undue emphasis on the actual mechanics of producing a sound is to be avoided. For children and most young people, simple imitation is usually the easiest way to learn a sound, and complicated articulatory descriptions may only prove confusing, since most people haven't even a vague notion of what positions their tongues may assume during speech.

For some of the more common problems specific tactics have evolved which are quite helpful in teaching the student sounds which he finds difficult. The /i/ sound does not seem to create problems for anyone, however /ɪ/ presents a different picture. The Spanish speaker, for instance, finds /ɪ/ an extremely difficult sound both to hear and reproduce. (After some months of study, a Spanish speaker may still tell you of his plans to go to Europe *by sheep*.) For most people emphasis on **relaxing** the muscles of the tongue, lips, and jaw while saying /i/, without actually changing their position, will produce the desired effect.

Another sound which is usually easy is /ɛ/, but /e/ is a different story. The sound many speakers use for English /e/ is not diphthongal, but it is sufficiently different from /ɛ/ to be a comprehensible substitute; and if being understood is the only goal of the student, this may be acceptable. However, for those who wish to work toward a native pronunciation, the sound /e/ may be practiced as a combination of /ɛ/ and /i/, first spoken slowly to make the student aware of the shift of position, and then more and more rapidly until a normal diphthongal sound is achieved.

Whenever a pronunciation problem is initially attacked, it is most effective to exaggerate its vocal quality, and the student should be encouraged to continue this exaggerated pronunciation during practice drills. Experience shows that even a student who can produce a sound quite correctly in the classroom under the teacher's observation will probably continue to mispronounce it in uncontrolled conversation. The more he practices the exaggerated pronunciation, the better his chances of acquiring a normal correct pronunciation in ordinary speech, because there seems to be less than 50 percent carryover from the pronunciation class to free conversation. So, to develop the habit of pronouncing the diphthongal sound /e/ correctly, the student might practice words such as *paid*, *bake*, *save*, as [pɛ-id]. [bɛ-ik].]sɛ-iv], gradually increasing speed until the two vowel sounds merge into the diphthongal /e/.

Many students have great difficulty in producing the /æ/ sound—some seem almost embarrassed at making the effort. By making a joke of the situation, and getting the students to laugh while trying to produce the sound, success is usually achieved, since the more widely open mouth with drawn-back lips, which is automatic when laughing, is very appropriate for the pronunciation of /æ/.

Another difficult sound for many students is /ə/, and this is also particularly difficult for many to hear. Discrimination between /ə/ and /ɑ/ or /ə/ and /ʊ/ is nearly impossible for some students, and a great deal of patient drill is often necessary to enable them to distinguish these three vowel sounds. And of course the student must be able to distinguish between sounds before he can be expected to produce them. Students who cannot produce /ə/ by imitation can be told to "relax everything" (lips, tongue, jaw, even let the head roll back and forth), and make a sound. What comes out is usually a pretty good approximation of /ə/. In this manner the student can be made to realize that in order to say /ə/ he should avoid doing anything, and merely relax the speech organs as much as possible.

The /ʊ/ sound can be taught as a relaxation from the /u/ position in much the same way as the /ɪ/ is taught from the /i/ position. The diphthongal /o/ can be broken down into /ə/ + /ʊ/, and pronunciations such as [bə-ʊt] (*boat*), [kə-ʊd] (*code*) can be practiced with gradually increasing rapidity until a normal diphthongal /o/ is produced.

Finally, /ɑ/ and /ɔ/ do not usually present any difficulty once discrimination is achieved, and the amount of practice required to establish the difference between them may vary considerably according to the native language of the student. How difficult it sometimes is to establish this ability to discriminate may be illustrated by the question of a dignified Chinese gentleman, who interrupted an explanation of the expression *wear down* to ask: "Excuse me, but isn't [wɛ-ʊ dɑn] what I say when I order steak?"

Consonants and Semivowels

If you put your hands over your ears and say /b/, /d/, /g/ (as in *bin, den, got*), then /p/, /t/, /k/ (as in *pin, ten, cot*), you will notice a buzzing sound in yours ears while saying /b/, /d/, /g/ which is absent during the pronunciation of /p/, /t/, /k/. The buzzing noise is produced by the vibration of the vocal cords, which makes the sounds /b/, /d/, /g/ voiced sounds.

You can also notice the vibration of the vocal cords by placing your fingers lightly against your throat. Say /s/ (as in *sink*) and then /z/ (as in *zinc*), and note how the vocal cords vibrate if /z/ is produced with the correct voicing.

Labial

/p/, /b/:   The mouth is closed with the lips pressed together. The airstream comes up against the obstacle created by the closed lips and the sound is produced by releasing the obstacle suddenly; /p/ is voiceless. /b/ is voiced.

/m/:   Produced at the same point of articulation as /p/ and /b/. The lips are kept closed and the sound is allowed to escape through the nasal passage.

/w/:   Lips are firmly rounded and tense. and the tongue is in the high back position as for the /u/ sound. Lips are then suddenly relaxed and the tongue glides into the position required by the vowel which follows the /w/. (Note that /w/ is a glide and that the tongue does not make contact with the roof of the mouth during the pronunciation of the sound.)

Labio-Dental

/f/, /v/:   The upper teeth are placed against the lower lip. The sound is produced by the friction of the air passing between the lip and the teeth; /f/ is voiceless. /v/ is voiced.

Dental

/θ/, /ð/:   The front of the tongue is against the upper teeth, with the tip slightly between the teeth. The air is forced through the opening between the tongue and the upper teeth; /θ/ is voiceless, /ð/ is voiced.

Alveolar

/t/, /d/:   The tip of the tongue is against the alveolar ridge (the ridge behind the upper teeth), creating a firm closure.   The sound is produced when air coming up against the obstacle is allowed to escape by the sudden release of the obstacle; /t/ is voiceless; /d/ is voiced.

/n/:   The tip of the tongue is against the alveolar ridge (same position as for /t/ and /d/), and the sound escapes through the nasal passage.

/s/, /z/:   The front of the tongue forms a groove. The airstream is directed along the groove against the upper teeth; /s/ is voiceless; /z/ is voiced.

/l/:   The middle of the tongue is raised and the front (not the very tip) touches the alveolar ridge. The sound escapes at the sides of the tongue, which do not make contact with any part of the mouth. The /l/ after vowels is often pronounced with the tip or front of the tongue making no contact in the front of the mouth, and the middle of the tongue drawn back toward the soft palate (velum).

Retroflex

/r/:   **Before vowels:**   The tongue is raised and slightly curled back toward the roof of the mouth, lips slightly rounded. The tongue makes no contact with either the roof of the mouth or the teeth. The tip of the tongue points toward the alveolar ridge, but does not touch it. Post-consonantal *r* before vowels (as in *pray, try, broom*) presents a special problem for many learners. In general it is best to teach first the pre-vocalic /r/ not preceded by a consonant (*ray, rye, room*) and to introduce words with the consonant + *r* combination (*pray, try, broom*) only after the pronunciation of word initial /r/ has been mastered.

After vowels: Note that English /r/ is much more like a vowel sound than a consonant. The /r/ after vowels consists of a light lip-rounding and a gliding of the tongue into the /r/ position (tongue slightly curled back, tip pointing to alveolar ridge, but without contact). Post-vocalic final /r/ in some varieties of American speech is practically not pronounced (New England, the South, etc. — the so-called *r*-less speech). The position for post-vocalic /r/ is somewhat similar to that for /ə/, except that the lips are slightly rounded and the tip of the tongue is slightly curled back. When the sounds /ə/ and /r/ are pronounced together as a syllable /ər/, the position for the /r/ is anticipated during the pronunciation of /ər/ so that the result is a blend of the two into a single sound, as in *bird, learn*, etc.

Alveo-Palatal

/ʃ/, /ʒ/:   The lips are slightly rounded with the tip of the tongue near the alveolar ridge, but not touching it. The middle of the tongue is raised toward the palate without touching it. The front of the tongue is grooved, and the sound is created by the friction of the airstream passing through this groove against the alveolar ridge; /ʃ/ is voiceless; /ʒ/ is voiced.

/č/, /ǰ/:   These sounds correspond to /ʃ/, /ʒ/, except that the tip of the tongue touches the alveolar ridge very quickly at the beginning of the production of the sound. In other words, /č/ can be described as a very quickly produced /t/ followed by /ʃ/; /ǰ/ can be described as /d/ followed by /ʒ/.

Palatal

/y/: The tongue is in high front position (as for the vowel /i/) and glides from there quickly to the position required by the following vowel. Note that /y/ is a glide and that the tongue does not make contact with the alveolar ridge or the roof of the mouth during its production.

Velar

/k/, /g/: The back of the tongue touches the soft palate (velum), creating a closure. The airstream pushes against the obstacle created by the tongue and velum, and the sudden release of the obstacle produces the sound; /k/ is voiceless; /g/ is voiced.

/ŋ/: The back of the tongue is raised against the velum as for /k/, /g/. The closure is maintained, and the sound escapes through the nasal passage.

Glottal

/h/: This sound is produced by friction in the glottis (vocal cords) preceding a vowel sound. Since the sound is produced in the glottis alone, the lip and tongue position assumed during the production of the /h/ sound is simply the one required by the following vowel.

Students can usually be taught to produce nearly all of the consonant sounds in supervised classroom practice, but it is not quite as easy to transfer this correct production to ordinary speech. This can be accomplished only with the student's determination to practice the problem sounds until they become automatic. The sounds /θ/ and /ð/, for example, are initially difficult, but with patient encouragement most students can be taught to say them correctly in the classroom. Incorporating them into speech, however, is quite another matter. Depending on the native languages of the students, a variety of exercises may be needed, depending on whether the student substitutes /t/, /d/ or /s/, /z/ or /f/, /v/ for the /θ/, /ð/ sounds. (The /f/, /v/ substitution appears with fair regularity in the speech of some Polish and French students, for example.)

A method which has produced good results for students who are willing to make the effort is to provide the student with a small card or paper containing a list of minimal pairs of words contrasting the problem sound and the one the student substitutes, plus two or three sentences utilizing these sounds. For example:

/θ/	/s/	/ð/	/z/
thing	*sing*	*then*	*Zen*
thaw	*saw*	*clothe*	*close*
theme	*seem*	*breathe*	*breeze*
thumb	*some*	*teething*	*teasing*
path	*pass*	*withered*	*wizard*
I want to thaw this.		*The baby is teething.*	
I want to saw this.		*The baby is teasing.*	

The student should post this exercise someplace where he will see it several times a day (the bathroom mirror is usually an ideal spot), and each time he sees it he must repeat the exercise with the utmost concentration on producing the problem sound correctly. This takes only one or two minutes each time. Students who have conscientiously followed this method have noticed results, in the form of correct production of the sound in casual conversation, in about three weeks time, with two or more repetitions of the exercise daily. Naturally the teacher must be very sure that the student really can and does produce the sound correctly when he is paying attention to it. The method works equally well with both consonants and vowels.

The English /r/ sound is particularly difficult for a great many people, regardless of their native language. Some never master it, but since the sounds substituted for it—such as the uvular [R] of French or German, the trilled [r] of Italian or Spanish—are usually heard as [r] sounds (with a foreign accent), this inability to produce a correct English /r/ sound does not interfere with communication.

The glides /y/ and /w/ are difficult for some students. Typically a Spanish speaker will tend to substitute /ǰ/ for /y/, a German or Slavic speaker /v/ for /w/. To help overcome such difficulties, the vocalic quality of the sounds must be emphasized. For example, words like *yes, you,* may be practiced by having the student begin with an exaggerated /i/ sound, then shift to the following vowel: /i-ɛs/, /i-u/, gradually accelerating until he reaches /iɛs/, /iu/, then /yɛs/, /yu/. For the /w/ sound, the same technique can be used starting with an exaggerated

/u/ with very tightly rounded lips: *win* /u-ɪn/, *wet* /u-ɛt/, proceeding through many repetitions to /uɪn/, /uɛt/, and then /wɪn/, /wɛt/.

Another potential problem is the /h/ sound. It is important that speakers of languages which do not contain this sound understand that they must **not** try to assume a specific tongue or lip position, but simply breathe audibly. If any part of the tongue is raised, the air friction will be created at a point within the oral cavity and not in the glottis alone, and will lead to pronunciations like /χæv/ for *have* /hæv/.

An important overall strategy of pronunciation training consists of leading the student from a known sound which he can produce, to a new sound. In most cases it will be neither necessary nor advisable to give the student a complete articulatory description. It is far better to have him produce a familiar sound and then introduce the modifications which lead to the new, difficult sound. Obviously a knowledge of the sound system of the pupil's native language can be very helpful in following this procedure. But even if the native language is not known to the teacher, the latter can plan his strategy based on his observation of the student's performance in English. For example, even a teacher who is not familiar with Spanish would note very quickly that the student who is a native speaker of Spanish has no difficulty with the pronunciation of /f/, but experiences trouble with the sound /v/. Thus, the logical strategy for teaching the Spanish speaker the sound /v/ would be to tell him to pronounce /f/, keep his lips in exactly the same position and try to voice the sound. If the student has difficulty in producing /ŋ/, he can be told to pronounce /g/ and then to allow the resonance to escape through the nasal passage without changing the tongue position. If there is trouble with /θ/, the suggestion can be made to say /s/ with the tip of the tongue between the teeth.

3. Visual aids in pronunciation training

The most frequently used visual aids in pronunciation training are of three types: (1) description or diagrams of the speech organs — especially the tongue position — during sound production; (2) graphic presentation of intonation patterns; and (3) phonetic or phonemic transcription.

The description of the speech organs can be a very important aid in explaining pronunciation to the pupil. Whether or not it is employed will depend primarily on the textbook rather than on the teacher. Few teachers are good enough artists to draw their own picture of sound production on the blackboard on the spur of the moment. We shall show only a few typical sound production graphs.

For vowels a diagram indicating the oral cavity and dividing it into the low–mid–high and front–central–back compartments may be sufficient. Within the diagram the tongue position required by a specific sound can then be indicated. For example:

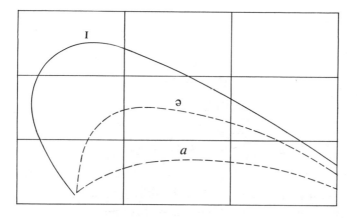

For consonants—for which the point of articulation is usually the crucial factor—a more complete diagram of the speech organs is necessary.

For example, here is the dental tongue position for /θ/, /ð/:

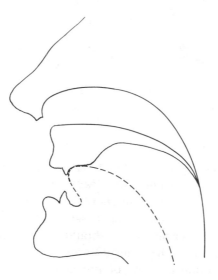

And this is the velar position for /ŋ/:

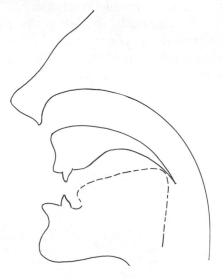

The drawing of intonation lines to illustrate sentence melody is a device used by several textbooks, and it is one that can be employed quite easily by the teacher. For example, the typical 2   3   1 (mid–high–low) intonation of a declarative sentence can be drawn in the following way:

and, if desired, it may be superimposed upon a sentence:

He is my | friend   or   *He came | yesterday.*

A much debated and critical issue in the teaching of foreign languages is the use of phonetic or phonemic transcription. Two problems are discussed here: (1) whether a phonetic **or** a phonemic transcription should be used; and—a more crucial issue—(2) whether **any** kind of transcription, phonetic **or** phonemic, should be employed.

As we pointed out earlier, the difference between a phonetic or phonemic transcription consists of the simple fact that a phonemic transcription employs the same symbol for the different variants of the same phoneme while the phonetic transcription attempts to distinguish between the different variants of the same phoneme. The less the effort to make these distinctions, the broader the transcription; the greater the effort, the narrower the transcription becomes. From the pedagogical point of view the decision of phonetic versus phonemic depends strictly on how important it may be to differentiate variants of the same phoneme. For example, in spite of a phonemic interpretation which assigns all the vowels of the words *sir* and *enough* to the same phoneme, we may decide to use different symbols for these vowels, simply because they are phonetically dissimilar: [sɜr] [ənʌf] rather than /sər/ /ənəf/. For students who insist on pronouncing final /p/, /t/, /k/ with the same strong release as initial /p/, /t/, /k/, it may be helpful to be reminded of the special pronunciation of the final consonants by some of special symbol: [pɪn], [kæn], [taɪm], but [lɪp°], [gɛt°], [sɪk°].

The reason for employing phonetic or phonemic transcriptions is to make clear to the student various facets of English pronunciation and to avoid or counteract as much as possible the interference coming from orthographic representation. Of course the interference coming from orthography could be counteracted by not letting the student see the normal spelling or by not using any kind of writing or reading at the beginning of the course—until good pronunciation habits are established. However, this complete withdrawal of any kind of visual symbol corresponding to the sounds to be learned is a negative measure, not a positive one. It simply eliminates the visual aid. For many students—especially older and/or "visual-minded" ones, it may create serious learning problems. In any case, it is only a temporary measure, because reading and writing must be introduced eventually in any case. In a language in which the "fit" of orthography and pronunciation is as irregular or, at any rate, as complicated as in English, it may be highly desirable to utilize phonemic (or phonetic) transcription, at least in the initial stages of a course. This does not necessarily mean that the student should be required to learn to write a phonemic (phonetic) transcription—but he could learn to read it and follow it in pronunciation exercises. If the student is already familiar with English orthography or if English orthography is introduced later in the course, the teacher could still have recourse to transcription to make clear some of the facts of English pronunciation which are disguised by the conventions of English spelling.

(E) A SPECIAL PROBLEM: ORTHOGRAPHIC
INTERFERENCE

So far we have concentrated on the discussion of what might be called genuine pronunciation problems: difficulties created by the differences between the sound system of English and that of the pupil's native language. But there are pronunciation problems of still another kind: those created by the orthographic presentation of the sounds. The pupil learns to associate a particular sound or sounds with a particular symbol or sequence of symbols. Then, when he sees the symbol or symbols again, he uses the sound associated with them — even though the association may no longer hold true in the new situation. This wrong transfer of sound/symbol relations may occur from the pupil's native language to English — or it may occur **within** English as a result of the complicated spelling patterns of English.

Of course, wrong transfer of sound/symbol relations from the foreign language to English is possible in all cases in which the pupil's native language uses the same alphabet as English. In many instances this wrong transfer will combine with and aggravate genuine pronunciation problems. For example, the English phoneme /r/ is a new and difficult sound for the native speaker of French, Spanish, or German. But the already-established association of the letter *r* with the sound [r] of his native language will make it doubly difficult to associate the new English /r/ phoneme with the letter *r*.

Examples of possible wrong sound/symbol relation transfers from the foreign language to English are numerous. To indicate some of the most typical problems, we shall cite some of the most frequent ones that might be made by native speakers of Spanish, French, or German.

The speaker of Spanish will normally pronounce the following orthographic symbols in the way indicated below (and thus will mispronounce English words using these symbols, as shown by the examples in the right-hand column):

Sample mispronunciations

$i = ([i])$	*bite* [bit] instead of /baɪt/
$e = ([\varepsilon])$	*pretty*, [prɛti] instead of /prɪti/
	England, [ɛŋlænd] instead of /ɪŋlənd/
$a = ([ɑ])$	*cat*, [kɑt] instead of /kæt/
	chamber, [čɑmbər] instead of /čembər/

	ball, [bɑl] instead of /bɔl/
	face, [fɑs] instead of /fes/
$o = ([o])$	*golf*. [golf] instead of /gɑlf/
	come, [kom] instead of /kəm/
	women, [womən] instead of /wɪmən/
$u = ([u])$	*mule*, [mul] instead of /myul/
	study, [studi] instead of /stədi/
v(initial) $= ([b])$	*van*, [bæn] instead of /væn/
$qu = ([k])$	*quick*, [kɪk] instead of /kwɪk/
$g + e$ or $i = ([χ])$	*general*, [χenerəl] instead of /jɛnərəl/
$j = ([χ])$	*jam*, [χɑm] instead of /jæm/
$h = \emptyset$	*have*, [æv] instead of /hæv/
$s + i +$ vowel $= ([sy])$	*mission*, [misyon] instead of /mɪʃən/
$ch = ([č])$	*chef*, [čef] instead of /ʃef/
	chemistry, [čemɪstri] instead of /kemɪstri/

In addition we must keep in mind that English uses a fairly large number of so-called **digraphs**, **trigraphs**, and even **tetragraphs** (2, 3, and even 4 symbols to indicate a single phoneme). Any one of those, especially the vowel digraphs, is a possible source of mispronunciation, since the learner may try to interpret the spelling symbols as individual sounds. In other words, *asked* may become [ɑskɛd] instead of /æskt/, *people* may be pronounced [peoplɛ] instead of /pipəl/, and so on.

The speaker of French is likely to encounter the same vowel spelling pronunciation problems as the speaker of Spanish. In addition, because of native language sound/symbol patterns, he may mispronounce the following:

ei	as	[e]	*receive*, [rɪsev] instead of /risiv/
oi	as	[wa]	*boil*, [bwɑl] instead of /bɔɪl/
ou	as	[u]	*couch*, [kuʃ] instead of /kɑuč/
u	as	[y]	(front vowel with rounded lips):
			full, [fyl] instead of /fʊl/
			put, [pyt] instead of /pʊt/
			but, [byt] instead of /bət/

He might also nasalize vowels followed by nasal consonants: *chamber* may become [ʃãbr] instead of /čembər/. Among the consonants the French speaker is likely to mispronounce are:

il	as	[y]	*travail*, [travɑy] instead of /trævel/
j	as	[ʒ]	*joke*, [ʒok] instead of /jok/

$g+e, i$	as	[ʒ]	*general*, [ʒeneral] instead of /jɛnərəl/
ch	as	[ʃ]	*church*, [ʃərʃ] instead of /čərč/
qu	as	[k]	*quite*, [kit] instead of /kwaɪt/
t + vowel	as	[sy]	*attention*, [atɛnsyən] instead of /ətɛnʃən/
h	as	∅	*have*, [æv] instead of /hæv/

The German speaker will again have basically the same vowel/ symbol association as the Spanish speaker. In addition, he might also mispronounce the following:

ei	as	[ɑi]	*receive*, [rəsɑiv] instead of /rəsiv/
ai	as	[ɑi]	*bait*, [bɑit] instead of /bet/
au	as	[ɑu]	*gauge*, [gɑuǰ] instead of /geǰ/
			laundry, [lɑundrɪ] instead of /lɔndri/
			caught, [kɑut] instead of /kɔt/
eu	as	[ɔɪ]	*Europe*, [ɔɪrəp] instead of /yʊrəp/
ie	as	[i]	*friend*, [frind] instead of /frɛnd/
			lie, [li] instead of /lai/

Consonant spelling mispronunciations are likely to be the following:

k or *g* pronounced before /n/:	*knight*, [knɑɪt] instead of /naɪt/
	foreign, [fɑrəgn] instead of /farən/
z pronounced [ts]	*zinc*, [tsɪŋk] instead of /zɪŋk/
w pronounced [v]	*when*, [vɛn] instead of /wɛn/
v pronounced [f]	*vast*, [fæst], instead of /væst/
ti before vowel pronounced [tsy]	*nation*, [nætsyon] instead of /neʃən/
si before vowel pronounced [sy]	*mission*, [mɪsyon] instead of /mɪʃən/
j pronounced [y]	*jelly*, [yɛli], instead of /ǰɛli/
g before *e* pronounced [g]	*germ*, [gərm] instead of /ǰərm/

As can be seen from the preceding examples, the student who approaches English from a native language which uses a writing system radically different from our English one may well have an advantage; he will not be subject to spelling pronunciations transferred from his native language. Of course, he will still be subject to the mispronunciations caused by the complications and inconsistencies of English orthography itself. The problem of sound/symbol relations in English is a complex one and much discussed, usually in connection with the teaching of reading or writing to native speakers of English. Since there are many books devoted to the problem, we shall only summarize very briefly the main sound/symbol correspondences and patterns of English from the symbol → sound as well as the sound → symbol point of view.

Main Symbol/Sound Correspondences of English

1. Vowel Symbols

Symbol	Sound	Examples
a	1. /æ/	*fat, captain, candy*
	2. /e/	*take, make, able*
	3. /ɑ/	*car, tar, star, calm*
	/ɔ/	*war, warm*
	4. /ə/	*parade, about, cottage, sofa*
e	1. /ɛ/	*get, desk, check, berry*
	2. /i/	*be, these, even, cede, here*
	3. /ə/ [ɝ]	*her, prefer*
	4. /ə/	*misery, deserve, market, benefit*
i	1. /ɪ/	*sick, miss, fill*
	2. /ɑɪ/	*fine, dine, polite, fire*
	3. /ə/ [ɝ]	*fir, firm, bird*
	4. /ə/	*aspirin, director, university*
	5. /i/	*machine, sardine*
o	1. /ɑ/	*hot, rob, respond*
	2. /o/	*hope, alone, cold*
	3. /ɔ/	*cord, for, store*
	4. /ə/	*pronounce, philosophy, alcohol, custody, contain*
	5. /ə/ [ʌ] [ɝ]	*come, love, word, world*
	6. /u/	*move, lose, whose*
u	1. /ə/ [ʌ]	*but, hundred, custody*
	2. /yu/	*mule, amuse, bugle, cure*
	/u/	*rude, June*
	3. /ə/[ɝ]	*fur, purr, murder*
	4. /ə/	*superior, difficult, album*
	5. /w/ (*u* + V)	*persuade, suite*

The details of the patterning which governs the correspondences of single-vowel symbols and sounds are too complicated to be discussed here. (See Bibliography: Axel Wijk). At any rate, they could only confuse the beginning student.

Some general patterns, however, are easily discussed. The single-vowel symbols correspond mainly to a so-called "short" pronunciation (1. above) or to a "long" pronunciation (2. above). The "long" pronunciation is very often marked by an unpronounced *e* after the following consonant. The alternation of the "short" vs. "long" pronunciations of the single-vowel letters can be illustrated by pairs such as *fat*:*fate* (/æ:e/); *pet*:*Pete* (/ɛ:i/); *bit*:*bite* (/ɪ:aɪ/); *hop*:*hope* (/a:o/); *cut*:*cute* (/ə:yu/). In addition — as illustrated under 3. above — there is a typical pronunciation for each symbol before *r*: *a* usually becomes /a/ or /ɔ/; the other symbols usually correspond to /ə/[ɝ], especially if the *r* is syllable final or followed by another consonant.

Finally, from the examples under 4. above, it can be seen that all vowel symbols can correspond to /ə/ in unstressed position. This indeterminacy of symbol corresponding to the unstressed /ə/ is, of course, a major source of misspelling of English and the source of exasperation for the elementary school teacher. The listings under 5. above illustrate some of the major — though by no means all — exceptions to the just-mentioned patterns of sound/symbol correspondence.

2. Vowel Digraphs, Trigraphs

The following is a listing of the most frequent combinations of two or more vowel letter symbols and their most frequent pronunciation. In this list the first entry represents the most frequent sound/symbol correspondences, the second lists the various alternate possibilities. Under 3., some of the sound/symbol correspondences in unstressed position are listed. It will be noted that some of the digraphs tend to keep their stressed pronunciations in unstressed syllables, while others take part in the general reduction to the /ə/ sound.

Symbol	Sound	Examples
ai (ay)	1. /e/	plain, day, stay
	2. /aɪ/	aisle
	3. /ə/	certain, bargain
	/i/	Monday, yesterday (in some pronunciations)

Symbol	Sound	Examples
au, aw	1. /ɔ/	*cause, law, fault*
	2. /ɑ/ or /æ/	*aunt*
	/o/	*gauche, chauffeur*
	3. /ə/	*restaurant*
awe	1. /ɔ/	*awe*
au(gh)	1. /ɔ/	*caught, daughter*
	2. /æ/	*laugh, draught*
ea	1. /i/	*each, teach, feast, ear, dream*
	2. /ɛ/	*bread, spread, feather, treasure*
	/e/	*great, steak, break*
	/ə/	*earn, earth*
	/ɑ/	*heart, hearth*
ee	1. /i/	*feel, feet, tree, breed*
	2. /ɪ/	*breeches* (pants)
	3. /i/	*committee, coffee*
ei (ey) + (gh)	1. /e/	*vein, reign, they, sleigh, eight, their*
	2. /ɑi/	*eye, neither* (in some pronunciations), *height*
	/i/	*ceiling, deceive, seize*
	/ɛ/	*leisure* (note also pronunciation /liʒər/)
	3. /ə/	*foreign*
	/i/	*honey, money*
eo	1. /ɛ/	*jeopardy, leopard*
	2. /i/	*people*
eou	3. /ə/	*gorgeous, courageous*
eu, ew	1. /yu/	*feud, Europe*
	/u/	*Jew, blew, chew*
	2. /o/	*sew*
	3. /u/	*neutrality, rheumatic*
eau	1. /yu/	*beauty*
	2. /o/	*beau*
ie (ye)	1. /i/	*brief, chief, niece, fierce*
	2. /ɑi/	*die, lie, rye, drier*

Symbol	Sound	Examples
	/ɛ/	*friend*
	/ɪ/	*sieve*
	3. /ɪ/	*mischief*
	/i/	*movie*
oa	1. /o/	*oak, boat, road*
	2. /ɔ/	*broad*
	3. /ə/	*cupboard*
	/o/	*cocoa*
oe	1. /o/	*foe, toe, goes*
	2. /u/	*shoe*
	/ə/ [ʌ]	*does*
	3. /o/	*oboe*
oi, oy	1. /oɪ/	*boy, oil, toilet*
	2. /wɑ/	*soiree, reservoir*
	/wɑɪ/	*choir*
	3. /ɔɪ/	*typhoid*
	/ə/	*porpoise*
oo	1. /u/	*food, doom, moon, poor, boor*
	2. /ʊ/	*book, cook, soot*
	/ə/ [ʌ]	*blood, flood*
	/o/	*brooch*
	3. /u/	*cuckoo*
ou (ow)	1. /ɑu/	*couch, cloud, spouse, devour, growl*
	2. /o/	*soul, own, below, know*
	/ɔ/	*four, pour, court*
	/ə/ [ʌ]	*couple, double, journal, courage*
	/ʊ/	*could, should, would*
	/u/	*group, soup, you, youth*
	3. /o/	*borrow, narrow, shadow* (but note also reduction to /ə/ in some dialects: *borrow* = /bɑrə/)
	/ə/	*famous*
ough	1. /ɔ/	*bought, ought, thought, fought*
	2. /ɑu/	*bough, slough*
	/o/	*dough, though, although*

Symbol	Sound	Examples
	/ɔf/	**cough, trough**
	/əf/ [ʌf]	**enough, rough, tough**
	/u/	**through**
	3. /o/	**borough**
	/əp/ [ʌp]	**hiccough**
owe	1. /o/	**owe**
ue	1. /yu/	**cue,** hue
	2. /u/	**blue,** true
	3. /yu/	**argue, value, virtue**
ui	1. /(y)u/	**suit, nuisance**
	/u/	**fruit, bruise**
	2. /ɪ/	**build**

3. Consonant Symbols

A number of the consonant letters represent only one sound value each; they are *b, h, k, l, m, p, r, v, w*. The only sound/symbol correspondence problem they offer within the English system is that several of them are also used in certain words or spelling patterns as **silent letters** with no corresponding sound value. Students may pronounce such silent letters, giving them their normal sound value (*doubt* mispronounced [dɑʊbt] instead of /dɑʊt/, for example.) These letters are included in the following list for that reason.

Symbol	Sound	Examples
b	1. /b/	**bad, rob**
	2. ∅ (before *t*)	**subtle, debt, doubt**
	(after *m*)	**lamb, bomb,**
		plumber
c	1. /k/	
	(before *a, o, u*)	**cat, could, cut**
	(before other consonants)	**clip, creep**
	(in final position)	**sac**
	2. /s/	
	(before *e, i, y*)	**city, ceiling, cycle**
	3. ∅	**indict, Connecticut**

Symbol	Sound	Examples
ch	1. /č/	*Charles*, **church**, *watch*, *each*
	2. /ʃ/	*Charlotte*, *chaise*, **chic** (and other loans from French)
	3. /k/	*Christ*, **chronology**, *technique* (and other loan words from Greek)
d	1. /d/	*dime*, *rod*, *dry*
	2. /t/	This pronunciation occurs in the verbal ending after voiceless consonants other than *t* (see Chapter V); for example, **packed** /pækt/. *laughed* /læft/, *helped* /hɛlpt/
	3. ∅ (after *n*, before another consonant)	*handkerchief*, *handsome*
f	1. /f/	*father*, *half*
	2. /v/	*of*
g	1. /g/ (before *a, o, u*)	*game, goal, gun, again, forgot*
	(sometimes before *e, i*)	*get, give, begin*
	(before consonants)	*glad, great, regret*
	(final or syllable final)	*bag, big, rug, magnet, sigma, suggest*
	(in the combination *gg*)	*piggy, rugged*
	2. /j/ (before *e, i, y*)	*gem, gin, gyp, angel, region,*

Symbol	*Sound*	*Examples*
	3. /ʒ/	engine, suggest mirage, rouge, beige (and other French loan words)
	4. ∅ (before *m* and *n* in final position)	paradigm, sign, resign
ge	1. /ǰ/ (in final position)	courage, savage, allege
gh	1. /g/	ghost, ghetto
	2. /f/	laugh, tough
	3. ∅	night, bought
gn	1. /n/	gnat, campaign
	2. /ny/	vignette, cognac
gu	1. /gw/	language, distinguish
	2. /g/	guard, guess, guest
h	1. /h/	have, half
	2. ∅	heir, honest, hour (loans from French), see also *wh* below
j	1. /ǰ/	jar, job, judge
k (ck)	1. /k/	kick, kind, sick
	2. ∅ (before *n*)	know, knight, knock
l	1. /l/	love, shelve
	2. ∅ (in a few words after *a*)	calf, half, alms, balm
n	1. /n/	neat, run
	2. /ŋ/ (before *k*)	think, uncle
	3. ∅ (after *m*)	damn, autumn

Symbol	Sound	Examples
ng	1. /ŋ/ (usually in final position and words derived from others in which ng is final)	sing, hang, long singer, hanging
	2. /ŋg/ (usually in intervocalic position, or before l, r)	singular, finger, single, hunger, hungry
nge	1. /nj/ (in word final position)	change, hinge, lunge, orange
ph	1. /f/	phrase, orphan, nephew
qu (que)	1. /kw/	quantity, equip, acquit
	2. /k/	conquer, liquor, torque
p	1. /p/	pit, lip
	2. ∅	pneumonia, psalm, psychology
s	1. /s/	
	(in initial position)	sick, sack, smoke
	(in final position -s)	gas, yes, chaos
	(vowel + se)	vase, cease, lease
	(consonant + se)	false, verse, horse
	(vowel + s + vowel)	basin, thesis
	(consonant + s)	ransom, handsome
	(vowel + s + consonant)	ask, grasp, must
	-s as grammatical ending after voiceless consonants:	
	(plural of nouns)	books, cups, cats
	(possessive of nouns)	Robert's, Jack's
	(third person singular verb form)	helps, laughs
	2. /z/	
	(in final position)	has, was, his
	(vowel + se)	praise, raise, tease

Symbol	Sound	Examples
	(consonant + *se*)	*cleanse*
	(vowel + *s* + vowel)	*busy, music, rosy*
	(consonant + *s*)	*clumsy, Wednesday*
	(vowel + *s* + consonant)	*raspberry, measles*
	-s as grammatical ending after vowels and voiced consonants:	
	(plural of nouns)	*boys, cows, eyes*
		dogs, hands, ribs
	(possessive of nouns)	*boy's, Mary's,*
		baby's, father's,
		Bob's, woman's
	(third person singular verb form)	*studies, borrows,*
		pays, learns,
		sings, dreams
3. ∅	(in French loans)	*aisle, chassis, isle*

In the above list the pronunciation /s/ is predictable for *s* in initial position and for the grammatical endings after voiceless consonants, while /z/ is predictable for the grammatical ending after voiced sounds. Beyond this, however, there is really no absolute way of predicting the pronunciation /s/ vs. /z/ for the *s* symbol.

Symbol	Sound	Examples
ss	1. /s/	*assist, class*
	2. /z/(rarely)	*dessert, dissolve*
sch	1. /sk/	*scholar, school, schedule*
sh	1. /ʃ/	*she, ship, wash*
si (*ti, ci*)	1. /ʃ/	*mission, action, social*

In a large number of words the original /sy/, /zy/ pronunciation of *si* (*ti, ci*) before a vowel changed to /ʃ/ during the late middle ages. The substitution of the /sy/ for the /ʃ/ pronunciation is a common mistake of speakers of other European languages in which the /sy/ pronunciation was kept in cognate words: for example, English *mission* /mɪʃən/ but French *mission* /misyō/, Spanish *misión* /misyon/, German *Mission* /misyon/, etc.

Symbol	Sound	Examples
s (+ u)	1. /ʃ/	*censure, insure, sugar*
	2. /ʒ/	*measure, usual, exposure*
t	1. /t/	*time, get*
	2. /č/ (before *u*)	*nature, torture, century*
	3. ∅ (in the combinations *-sten, -stle, -ften*)	*hasten, castle, often, soften*
th	1. /θ/	
	(initially)	*thief, thick, thin*
	(medially)	*ethics, method*
	(finally)	*bath, oath, breath*
	2. /ð/	
	(initially)	*the, they, them, this, that, those, though*
	(medially)	*father, rather, together, neither*
	(finally)	*smooth*
	(before silent final -*e*)	*bathe, breathe, teethe*
	3. /t/	*thyme, Thomas, Theresa,* (and other proper names)

Initial *th* is usually /θ/, but is pronounced as /ð/ in the function words: the article, the demonstrative, the words *than, then, though, thus*. Final *th* is usually /θ/; the /θ/ pronunciation is usually also preserved when morphological endings are added to words in which *th* is final: *length* /lɛŋθ/, *lengthy* /lɛŋθi/. Since final *th* is usually /θ/ and *th* + final *e* is /ð/, the final -*e* is used to mark the alternation between nouns (-/θ/) and verbs (-/ð/): for example, *breath—breathe* (/brɛθ/—/brið/), *bath—bathe* (/bæθ/—/beð/), *teeth—teethe* (/tiθ/—/tið/). Beyond the rules given above, the alternations of the /θ/—/ð/ pronunciations are difficult to predict. Note that in some words final /θ/ changes to /ð/ before the plural ending -*s*: *bath—baths* (/bæθ/—/bæðz/), *oath—oaths* (/oθ/—/oðz/); but *smith—smiths* (/smɪθ/—/smɪθs/).

Symbol	Sound	Examples
w	1. /w/	*water, win*
	2. ∅ (see *wh* below)	*who, whose*
wh	1. /w/	*when, wheel, whistle*

While, in some of the words above, *wh* is pronounced /hw/ by some speakers of English, it seems simplest to teach only the pronunciation /w/, used by the majority of American speakers.

Symbol	Sound	Examples
	2. /h/	*who, whose, whom, whole, whooping cough*
x	1. /ks/	*axe, sex, execute*
	2. /gz/	*examine, exaggerate*
y	1. /y/	*yard, yellow*
z	1. /z/	*zinc, zeal, seize, size*
	2. /ʒ/	*brazier, azure*
	3. /ts/	*Nazi, schizophrenia*

Main Sound → Symbol Correspondences of English

For the convenience of the teacher we shall also list the correspondences just given from the sound/symbol point of view.

1. *Vowel Phonemes and Diphthongs*

Phoneme	Symbol	Examples
/i/	*e*	*be, these, cede*
	i	*machine, sardine*
	ea	*each, teach*
	ee	*feel, feet, keep*
	ei	*ceiling, deceive*
	eo	*people*
	ie	*brief, belief*
/ɪ/	*i*	*sick, miss, fill*
	ee	*breeches*
	ui	*build*
/e/	*a*	*take, make*
	ai (ay)	*plain, day, vain*
	ea	*great, steak, break*
	ei (ey)	*vein, reign, they*
/ɛ/	*e*	*get, check, desk*
	ea	*bread, spread, dread*
	ie	*friend*

Phoneme	Symbol	Examples
/æ/	a	*fat, cat, candy*
	au	***aunt*** (in some pronunciations), *laugh*
/ɑ/	a (r)	*car, tar, father*
	o	*hot, rob, response*
	ea(r)	*heart, hearth*
/ɔ/	a(r)	*war, warm*
	o(r)	*for*
	augh	*caught, daughter*
	au(aw)	*cause, law*
	oa	*broad*
	ou(gh)	*cough*
/o/	o	*dope, alone, stone*
	oe	*foe, toe, goes*
	au	*gauche, chauffeur*
	oa	*oak, boat, toad*
	ew	*sew*
	oo	*brooch*
	ou (ow)	*soul, own, throw*
	ough	*dough, though, although*
	eau	*beau*
/ʊ/	oo	*book, cook*
	ou	*could, should*
/u/	u	/yu/ *mule, amuse*
		/u/ *rude, June*
	eu (ew)	/yu/ *feud, few* (sometimes *neuter, dew*) *Europe*
		/u/ *Jew, blew, chew*
	oe	*shoe*
	oo	*food, doom, moon*
	ou	*group, soup, you*
	ue	/yu/ *cue, hue*
		/u/ *blue, true*
	ui	/(y)u/ *suit, nuisance*
		/u/ *fruit, bruise*
/ə/	eau	/yu/ *beauty*

Phoneme	Symbol	Examples

stressed position:

	u	*but, hundred, custody*
	o	*come, love, won*
	oe	*does*
	oo	*blood, flood*
	ou	*couple, double, trouble*
	ou(gh)	*enough, rough*

**stressed position
before *r*:**

	e(r)	*her, prefer*
	i(r)	*fir, firm*
	u(r)	*fur, purr, furnace*
	ea(r)	*earn, earth*
	ou(r)	*journal*

unstressed position:

	a	*about, sofa*
	e	*misery, pretend*
	i	*director, aspirin*
	o	*pronounce, nobody*
	u	*superior, difficult*
	ai	*certain, bargain*
	au	*authority, restaurant*
	ei	*foreign*
	oa	*cupboard*
	ou	*famous, momentous*

| /ɔɪ/ | *oi, oy* | *boy, oil* |

/aɪ/	i	*fine, dine, fire*
	ais	*aisle*
	ei, ey	*eye, neither* (in some pronunciations)
	ie (ye)	*lie, die, rye*

| /aʊ/ | *ou* | *couch, cloud, spouse* |
| | *ough* | *bough, slough* |

2. *Semivowels and Consonants*

Phoneme	*Symbol*	*Examples*
/p/	p	*lip*, *hip*
	gh	*hiccough*
/b/	b	*bat*, *rob*
/m/	m	*man*, *some*, *ram*
/w/	w	*water*, *with*
	o(i)	*soirée*
	u	*persuade*, *suite*
	(g)u	*language*
	(q)u	*quick*, *equip*
	wh	*when*, *what*
/f/	f	*fan*, *puff*
	gh	*laugh*, *tough*
	ph	*phase*, *nephew*
/v/	v	*van*, *love*
	f	*of*
/θ/	th	*thin*, *method*, *bath*
/ð/	th	*the*, *father*, *smooth*
/t/	t	*time*, *hit*
	d	*helped*, *laughed*
	th	*Thomas*, *Theresa*, *thyme*
	z /ts/	*Nazi*
/d/	d	*dime*, *load*
/s/	s (ss)	*sit*, *assist*, *helps*
	c (+ e, i)	*city*, *ceiling*
	x /ks/	*axe*, *sex*
	z /ts/	*Nazi*
/z/	s	*has*, *was*
		praise, *raise*
		cleanse
		busy, *music*
		Wednesday, *raspberry*
		dogs, *hogs*, *robs*

Phoneme	Symbol	Examples
	ss	*dissolve, dessert*
	z	*zinc, zeal, size*
	x (/gz/)	*examine, exaggerate*
/l/	*l* (*ll*)	*light, well, call*
/n/	*n* (*nn*)	*not, can, runner*
/r/	*r* (*rr*)	*right, berry, far*
/č/	*ch*	*church, chin*
	tch	*watch*
	t(*u*)	*nature, century*
/ǰ/	*g* (+*e, i*)	*gem, gin, engine, angel*
	j	*jar, job, judge*
	dg(*e*)	*judge*
/ʃ/	*sh*	*shine, rash*
	ch	*Charlotte, chic*
	si (*ti, ci*) + vowel	*mission, social, action*
	s(*u*)	*sugar, censure, insure*
	sch	-*schist*, (some words and names of German derivation)
/ʒ/	*g* (*e*)	*garage, rouge*
	si (+ vowel)	*invasion, conclusion*
	s (+ *u*)	*measure, usual*
/y/	*y*	*yard, yes, yellow*
	gn(/ny/)	*vignette, cognac*

Before the phoneme /u/:

	ue	*cue, due, value*
	ui	*suit, nuisance* (in some dialects)
	eu, ew	*few, Europe*
	u	*mule, amuse*
	eau	*beauty*
/k/	*k*	*kick, kind*
	ck	*lick, stack*

Phoneme	Symbol	Example
	c (before a, o, u)	can, could
	(before consonant)	clerk, creep
	(final)	sac
	ch	Christ, technique
	qu (/kw/)	quick, acquit
	qu (/k/)	conquer, liquor
	x (/ks/)	sex, axe
/g/	g	good, get, got
	gg	piggy
	gh	ghost, ghetto
	gu	guard, guest
	x (/gz/)	examine, exaggerate
/ŋ/	ng	hang, sing, singer
	n (before k, g)	think, uncle, hunger
/h/	h	have, hit
	wh	who, whose

From the preceding summary of sound/symbol and symbol/sound correspondences it can be concluded that English orthography is by no means **irregular**, if by irregular we mean that the sound/symbol relation makes no sense whatsoever. Yet the sound/symbol relations are complicated enough to present a rather formidable obstacle to the learner of English as a second language — and even to the native speaker learning to read and write his own language. Of course the complications of the orthographic system will cause comparatively few pronunciation problems for the native speaker. Pronunciation problems and errors will be restricted to a relatively few rare words — cases in which extensive audiolingual use did not fortify the native speaker against orthographic interference.

Ultimately the best hope for foreigners in overcoming the complications of orthography and in helping them to avoid orthographic interference lies in giving them a large amount of audiolingual practice. This practice may very well be combined with the use of a phonemic spelling that can give temporary visual reinforcement to the auditory memory of the student.

In most cases it is necessary for the student to learn the sound/symbol patterns, but it does not seem advisable to introduce the student to these patterns until after a good basic vocabulary has been learned audiolingually.

However, there may be situations in which a speaking knowledge alone, rather than literacy, may be the goal of instruction. In such cases the sound/symbol patterning should be introduced in special types of exercises in which patterns (for example, the function of the final mute -*e*, the pronunciation of *c* before *e* and *i*) are pointed out to the student. Symbols which stand for the same sound, or different sounds expressed by the same symbol, can be drawn together in special reading or dictation exercises.

The student could receive dictations like *be, these, each, teach, meat, feel, feet, meet,* to show him the different spellings of the /i/ phoneme; or *fat/fate, mat/mate, rap/rape* could be contrasted in an exercise to show how the symbol *a* can stand for /æ/ or /e/, according to the absence or presence of the final mute -*e*. After practicing a reading selection, the student can be asked to underline all the symbols that stand for the sound /u/ — or he can make a list of the different pronunciations given to the same symbol within the selection.

The question of spelling reform is often raised because of the complications of English orthography. Would not a system in which each sound corresponds to only one symbol (in other words a **phonemic transcription**) be an ideal writing system? Obviously the much-debated problem of English spelling reforms goes beyond the scope of this discussion. But we must point out one complication which the use of a phonemic writing system would face, because it affects the use of the phonemic system by the foreign learners as well as the sound/symbol problems faced by him. Some of the irregularities of the English sound/symbol fit are created by the fact that English preserves morphological regularity or consistency at the expense of phonemic fit. In other words, variants of the same morpheme (which are pronounced differently) are spelled the same. A phonemic system of spelling would force us to spell /kæts/, /dɔgz/ (the plural morpheme spelled /s/, /z/) or /læft/, /rɑbd/, /fɪtəd/ (the past tense morpheme spelled /t/, /d/, /əd/); regular English orthography retains the same spelling for variants of the same morpheme: *cats, dogs; laughed, robbed, fitted.*

As far as quick readability of the language is concerned, there may be a strong advantage to giving the same spellings to the different versions of the same meaningful unit. In addition, words are not always pronounced the same by different speakers of English. Many phonetic or even phonemic spellings would be foreign to speakers from dialect areas different from that of the writer of the text or dictionary. For the foreign student, the regularity of spelling from the morphemic point of view increases the possibility of spelling mispronunciation and points up another serious learning problem—namely, the fact that the same morpheme, though spelled the same, will assume different forms in speech. A more detailed discussion of the problems created by the variations of pronunciation of morphemes is reserved for the next chapter.

CHAPTER V

Teaching Morphology

(A) MORPHOPHONEMICS: ORTHOGRAPHIC INTERFERENCE CONTINUED

We have stated that the morpheme may be defined as the smallest unit that has an identifiable meaning. Just as a phoneme can appear in several forms (allophones), the same morpheme can also appear in various forms (allomorphs). If the appearance of specific allomorphs depends on phonetic conditions, then we can say that the choice of the allomorph is a matter of **morphophonemic alternation**: the choice of the plural allomorphs /z/ in *dogs* /dɔgz/, *seas* /siz/; /s/ in *cats* /kæts/; and /əz/ in *dishes* /dɪʃəz/ is a result of the morphophonemic patterning of English. The choice is determined by the final sound of the stem of the noun: the voiceless /t/ of *cats* demands the allomorph /s/; the voiced /g/ of *dogs* and the vowel /i/ of *seas* require /z/; and the grooved fricative /ʃ/ of *dish* is one of the six sounds of English (/z/, /s/, /ʒ/, /ʃ/, /ǰ/, /č/) which must be followed by /əz/. The choice of the third person singular allomorphs /s/, /z/, /əz/, is similarly determined by the preceding sounds: *he laughs* /læfs/, *he robs* /rabs/, *he wishes* /wɪʃəz/, etc. The allomorphs of the regular past tense and past participle endings are also examples of a morphophonemic alternation: /t/ after voiceless consonants (*laughed* /læft/), /d/ after vowels and voiced consonants (*studied* /stədid/, *robbed* /rabd/), /əd/ after *t, d* (*fitted* /fɪtəd/).

At the end of the preceding chapter we pointed out that one of the characteristic features of English consists of not taking cognizance of such morphophonemic alternations in the spelling system. For the learner of English as a foreign language, the fact that morphophonemic

123

alternations are not represented orthographically causes two major problems. It increases the possibility of **spelling pronunciation** (mispronunciation due to spelling; for example, *robbed* pronounced /rɑbəd/ because of its spelling and by analogy the actual pronunciation of /fitəd/ for *fitted*); and they also render comprehension much more difficult. A morpheme that has been heard as /əd/ and visually identified as *-ed* must also be recognized aurally as /t/ or /d/.

Another major morphophonemic alternation of English, referred to earlier, is the tendency of English to reduce unstressed vowels to the vowel /ə/. This tendency may exist in varying degrees within the same geographical region or even with the same speaker. An individual may sometimes use the /ə/ sound (in less careful speech), sometimes the full unreduced vowels. In general, many elementary school teachers discourage their students from reducing vowels to /ə/ because it makes the problem of learning to spell unaccented vowels even more confusing than it already is. Nevertheless, the tendency is progressing rapidly, and the foreigner learning English must be prepared to identify and understand the "reduced" pronunciations.

In many cases the reduction is accompanied by changes in the pronunciation of consonants, especially the fusion to an affricate of alveolar stops followed by /y/: *did you*, /dɪjə/; *don't you*, /dončə/; *would you*, /wʊjə/; *can't you* > /kænčə/. While such forms are usually not used or practiced in the classroom, they do occur in colloquial usage and may puzzle and bewilder the student. Some attention and practice should be devoted to the phenomenon.

One of the authors of this book recalls the bewilderment of a foreign student who reported to her that he had heard an American student, meeting a friend outside the cafeteria, ask: "/jit/?" and get a reply: "/načɛt/." The two utterances were the reduced forms of the question "*Did you eat?*" and the reply "*Not yet.*" Comprehension practice of this reduced type of pronunciation may be given with patterns like *What did you do?* /wɑdɪjədu/, or *Aren't you coming?* /arənčəkəmɪŋ/.

The morphophonemic alternation of full vowel: /ə/ operates in conjunction with another peculiarity of English: the shift of stress from one syllable to another in the process of certain types of word formation. Again the result is that the student (who has learned to identify the pronunciation of a morpheme in certain words and to associate it with a specific spelling) is likely either to mispronounce under the influence of that spelling, if he finds the same morpheme in another word, or to fail to recognize and reidentify the morpheme when he hears it with a different pronunciation in a different context.

The following are some examples of the reduction of stressed vowels to /ə/:

/i/ → /ə/	*details* /'ditelz/(noun)	*details*	/də'telz/(verb)
	legal /'ligəl/	*legality*	/lə'gæləti/
/e/ → /ə/	*stable* /'stebəl/	*stability*	/stə'bɪləti/
	fate /'fet/	*fatality*	/fə'tæləti/
/ɛ/ → /ə/	*necessary* /'nɛsəsɛri/	*necessity*	/nə'sɛsəti/
/æ/ → /ə/	*aristocrat* /ər'ɪstəkræt/	*aristocracy* /ærə'stɑkrəsi/	
	atom /'ætəm/	*atomic*	/ət'amɪk/
/ɑ/ → /ə/	*politics* /'pɑlətɪks/	*political*	/pə'lɪtəkəl/
	catastrophic /kætəs'trafɪk/	*catastrophe* /kət'æstrəfi/	
/ɔ/ → /ə/	*author* /'ɔθər/	*authority*	/əθ'arəti/
/o/ → /ə/	*phoneme* /'fonim/	*phonemic*	/fə'nimɪk/
/u/ → /ə/	*accuse* /ə'kyuz/	*accusation* /ækyə'zeʃən/	

Note that, in the change from stressed to unstressed position, the shift of pronunciation occurs primarily in words of Latin or Greek origin — words which are likely to be familiar to the speaker of Spanish or French through cognate words in his own language. He will have a tendency to import a wrong pronunciation from his native language. The fact that there is a dual pronunciation in English is likely to compound his difficulties. Therefore, especially in the more advanced stages of the course, the multiple pronunciations of the same roots should be contrasted and the student should be made aware of the differences: for example, *he is a stable person*; *he is a man of great stability.*

Perhaps even more important, especially in the initial stage of instruction, is that the dual pronunciation problem affects also a small number of extremely frequent function words. With them the variation in pronunciation depends on whether or not the words appear under syntactical stress. Since in the majority of cases these words are not stressed, the reduced unstressed pronunciation is typically the more frequent one. Again the orthographic representation does not distinguish between the stressed and unstressed forms. The learner must be made aware of both pronunciations and must learn to recognize and use them. The alternation of full vowels with unstressed /ə/ in function words is illustrated by the following examples.

/i/ → /ə/   the   /ði/   the bird   /ðə bərd/
                                    (before consonants; but note: the eagle
                                    /ði igəl/)

/e/ → /ə/   a   /e/   a bird   /ə bərd/

/æ/ → /ə/   an   /æn/   an eagle   /ən igəl/
                 and   /ænd/   he and she   /hi (ə)n ʃi/
                 can   /kæn/   he can leave   /hi kən liv/
                 have   /hæv/   we should have left   /wi ʃud əv lɛft/
                 as   /æz/   as early as possible   /əz ərli əz
                                        pasəbəl/

/ɛ/ → /ə/   them   /ðɛm/   see them leave   /si ðəm liv/

/u/ → /ə/   do   /du/   how do you do   /haʊ də yə du/
                 to   /tu/   he began to sing   /hi begæn tə sɪŋ/
                 you   /yu/   what do you want?   /wɑt də yə wɑnt/

In addition to the alternation /full vowel/–/ə/, some of the extremely
frequent function words are subject to even further and different reductions. These reductions — some of which usually do not appear in spelling — must be taught quite specifically so that the student learns to use
and recognize the reduced forms. The most important of these instances of reduced forms are the following:

The possessives:

Full Form   Reduced Form

our   /aʊr/   He's our friend   /ar frɛnd/
your   /yʊr/   He's your friend   /yər frɛnd/
her   /hər/   He's her friend   /ər frɛnd/
his   /hɪz/   He's his friend   /ɪz frɛnd/

The pronouns:

him   /hɪm/   I know him   /no ɪm/
her   /hər/   I know her   /no ər/
them   /ðɛm/   I know them   /no əm/

The present tense of be (note that these are often written as
contractions):

I am   /aɪ æm/   I am here   /aɪm hir/   (I'm here)
you are   /yu ɑr/   You are here   /yur hir/   (You're here)
they are   /ðe ɑr/   They are here   /ðer hir/   (They're here)

he is	/hi ɪz/	*He is here* /hiz hɪr/ (*He's here*)
it is	/ɪt ɪz/	*It is here* /ɪts hɪr/ (*It's here*)
there is	/ðɛr ɪz/	*There is enough* /ðɛrz ənəf/ (*there's enough*)

The negation *not* (these forms are often written as contractions):

is not	/ɪz nɑt/	*He is not* (*isn't*) *here*	/ɪzənt/
was not	/wəz nɑt/	*He was not* (*wasn't*) *here*	/wəzənt/
does not	/dəz nɑt/	*He does not* (*doesn't*) *go*	/dəzənt/
do not	/du nɑt/	*I do not* (*don't*) *go*	/dont/
did not	/dɪd nɑt/	*I did not* (*didn't*) *go*	/dɪdənt/
could not	/kʊd nɑt/	*I could not* (*couldn't*) *go*	/kʊdənt/
would not	/wʊd nɑt/	*I would not* (*wouldn't*) *go*	/wʊdənt/
should not	/ʃʊd nɑt/	*I should not* (*shouldn't*) *go* /ʃʊdənt/	
cannot	/kæn nɑt/	*I cannot* (*can't*) *go*	/kænt/

Note the reduction in the affirmative form *can* /kæn/ > /kən/ when the main verb is stressed: *I can gó* /aɪ kən go/. Native speakers depend heavily on this to distinguish between affirmative and negative in rapid speech: *I can talk now* /aɪ kən tɔk nɑʊ/, as opposed to *I can't talk now* /aɪ kænt tɔk nɑʊ/.

The auxiliary verb *will* (and its negative form):

I will	/aɪ wɪl/	*I will* (*I'll*) *go*	/aɪl/
you will	/yu wɪl/	*You will* (*you'll*) *go*	/yul/
he will	/hi wɪl/	*He will* (*he'll*) *go*	/hil/
she will	/ʃi wɪl/	*She will* (*she'll*) *go*	/ʃil/
it will	/ɪt wɪl/	*It will go*	/ɪtəl/
we will	/wi wɪl/	*We will* (*we'll*) *go*	/wil/
they will	/ðe wɪl/	*They will* (*they'll*) *go*	/ðel/
Bob will	/bɑb wɪl/	*Bob will go*	/bɑbəl/
I will not	/wɪl nɑt/	*I will not* (*won't*) *go*	/wont/ or /wunt/

Other frequently reduced forms:

I have to go	/aɪ hæv tu go/	/aɪ hæftə go/
She has to go	/ʃi hæz tu go/	/ʃi hæstə go/
I used to go	/aɪ yuzd tu go/	/aɪ yustə go/
I am going to go	/aɪ æm goɪŋ tu go/	/aɪm gɔnə go/

In addition, there is one particular reduction, rarely written, which results in a very common spelling mistake among native speakers of English, usually interpreted as a grammatical error: *I should have* /aɪ ʃʊdəv/, *I could have* /aɪ kʊdəv/, *I might have* /aɪ maɪtəv/, which are frequently written *I should of, I could of, I might of* by native speakers. The possibility of writing *I should've, I could've, I might've* exists, but is rarely utilized.

In practically all of the above mentioned cases the careful, stressed, nonreduced pronunciation is unusual and unnatural in colloquial speech. The student should realize that he should neither produce it nor expect to hear it. He should be expressly trained to acquire the natural, normal pronunciation. If he doesn't, he may sound somewhat like Eliza Doolittle immediately after receiving her speech lessons from Professor Higgins in Shaw's *Pygmalion*.

Not all alternations in the form of the morphemes are based on the contrast of stressed vs. unstressed (or reduced) forms. Some of them occur in the stressed syllable in connection with certain patterns of English word formation. Thus the suffix *-ity* (used in the formation of nouns) produces the following vowel changes (examples quoted are from Weir and Venezky, pp. 43–44):

/e/ > /æ/	*humane/humanity*	*sane/sanity*
/i/ > /ɛ/	*supreme/supremity*	*extreme/extremity*
/aɪ/ > /ɪ/	*divine/divinity*	*senile/senility*
/o/ > /a/	*verbose/verbosity*	*morose/morosity*

The suffix *-ic* (used in the formation of adjectives) is associated with the same alternations (sometimes with change of stress):

/e/ > /æ/	*angel/angelic*	*state/static*
/i/ > /ɛ/	*meter/metric*	*athlete/athletic*

Noun derivation in *-ion* produces similar changes:

/aɪ/ > /ɪ/	*collide/collision*	*divide/division*
/i/ > /ɛ/	*convene/convention*	*discreet/discretion*

A change /u/ > /ə/ occurs with the *-tion* suffix in *reduce/reduction* and *assume/assumption*.

This type of alternation of the same morpheme appears in words of Latin origin. It is likely to cause difficulty in comprehension as well as in pronunciation (for example, *divine* pronounced /dɪvin/ on the analogy of /dɪvɪnəti/) and must be counteracted by exercises in which the different pronunciations of the same morphemes are contrasted: for example, *this is one **meter** long; we are using the **metric** system.*

(B) WORD FORMATION

Alternations such as *sane/sanity* (/sen/, /sænəti/) or *divine/divinity* (/dɪvɑɪn/, /dɪvɪnəti/) are part of the rather complex system of English word formation. Word formation is a historical process. If we say that the noun *arrival* is derived from the verb *arrive*, we state a historical fact. We know that the verb existed before the noun — which was created from the verb by the addition of the ending *-al*. Whether *arrive* existed before *arrival* or vice versa is of no particular interest to the learner of modern English. What is important is that the learner can see the relationship between *arrive* and *arrival*, and that he learns to identify *arrival* as a noun and *arrive* as a verb. To him the historical relationships expressed by word formation are transformational relationships existing in present day English. Knowing or being aware of these relationships will increase the pupil's passive vocabulary tremendously. Once he learns the pattern *arrive/arrival* he will be able to infer the meaning of *acquittal* from *acquit* or *refusal* from *refuse*. However, the pupil must be warned not to use his knowledge of the transformational relationships between word-classes to coin new words of his own. The limits and exact rules of transformational relationships are complicated and still ill-defined. For instance, *arrive/arrival* does not imply the possibility of *depart/*departal, remain/*remainal*.

In this section we shall present very briefly the most important types of word formation according to word classes: nouns, verbs, adjectives, adverbs. Under each word class we shall consider the following processes: **prefixation, suffixation, word formation by stress, word formation by "zero,"** and **compounding**.

By **prefixation** we mean the formation of words by adding at the beginning a prefix, a particle which has a specific identifiable meaning but which is not normally used as an independent word (= possible minimum utterance): for example, the *pre-* of *prefix* is a prefix.

Suffixation is derivation by a suffix, by the addition of a word final morpheme which is not normally an independent word: for example, the *-al* of *arrival* is a suffix.

Word formation by stress or **by "zero"** morphemes are processes quite characteristic of English. A very common stress pattern differentiating noun/verb is ′ ˘ for noun, ˘ ′ for verb: for example *récŏrd/rĕcórd, dígĕst/dĭgést*. Derivation by a "zero morpheme" is just another way of saying that in English many words can simply be switched from one word class to another without the addition of any prefix or suffix,

and without a change in stress. Except on the basis of historical knowledge, it is impossible to say which usage in this particular category was
first: for example, *we work* (verb) *hard* or *we finished the work* (noun).
The very frequent pattern in English of using the same word in two or
even more word classes without any formal morphological differentiation is often a source of bewilderment and confusion—especially for
native speakers of languages in which the word classes are clearly
marked by specific morphemes rather than by the particular slot in the
sentences as in English: *Where is the milk* (adjective modifier) *bottle?
Give me some milk* (noun)! *Did you milk* (verb) *the cow?*

Compounding is a process of creating new words from elements
which by themselves are also independent words. Here the character-
istically English process is the creation of compounds by simply putting
the original elements next to each other: *book + rack = bookrack*;
black + birds = blackbirds. (Note, however, that in the compound
the primary stress is on the first word: *blackbird* ´ `, but *black bird* ` ´!)

Two main types of compounds must be distinguished. One type is
like *bookrack* or *toothbrush*, in which the first word is used to modify
the second: in other words *book* of *bookrack* simply tells us what kind
of rack we are talking about. This kind of compound is usually quite
easily understood (if the words making up the compound are known).
In the other type of compound the meaning of the whole is not clear
from the meaning of the parts, because the kind of person or object
referred to is understood or implied but not mentioned. For example,
pickpocket refers to "the kind of person who *picks pockets*," and *under-
wear* refers to "garments which people *wear under* other clothing."
This kind of compound shares certain features with the so-called **idioms**
(expressions whose meaning cannot be inferred from the component
parts), and their meanings must be explained and learned just like those
of individual words.

One complicating and characteristic feature of English word formation is the fact that English has preserved the relationships between
word classes which existed in the languages from which English bor-
rowed so much of its vocabulary, especially French and Latin. Relations like *reduce/reduction, produce/production, divine/divinity,
sane/sanity* are characteristic of Latin word formation and were directly
imported into English. Many prefixes and suffixes are of French,
Latin, or Greek origins—imported into English and often used in
conjunction with words of different origins; for example, *anti* (against)
is of Greek origin and combines with the originally Italian *fascist* to
produce *antifascist*.

In our listing we shall consider only the most frequent of the various prefixes and suffixes. If prefixes are characteristic of several word classes they are arbitrarily listed in the noun class.

Nouns

1. *Prefixes*

ante- (before)	*ante*chamber, *ante*room
anti- (against)	*anti*fascist, *anti*alcoholic
auto- (self)	*auto*biography, *auto*harp
co- (together)	*co*defendant, *co*author
counter- (against)	*counter*revolutionary, *counter*spy
ex- (former)	*ex*-wife, *ex*-emperor
in- (negative)	*in*convenience, *in*fidelity, *in*ability

(Note the assimilation of *in-* to the following consonant: *in + legibility = illegibility*; *in + possibility = impossibility*.)

inter- (between, among)	*inter*action, *inter*dependence
mal- (badly)	*mal*function, *mal*practice
mis- (negative, badly)	*mis*deed, *mis*behavior
pre- (before)	*pre*conception, *pre*arrangement
re- (again)	*re*storation, *re*establishment, *re*capture, *re*gression
step- (related by marriage)	*step*father, *step*daughter
sub- (under, below)	*sub*division, *sub*group, *sub*way
super- (beyond, above)	*super*man, *super*highway, *super*star

2. *Suffixes*

-acy	*lunacy, piracy, efficacy*
-age	*bondage, orphanage, patronage*
-al (from verbs)	*arrival, withdrawal, dismissal, arousal*
-an, variant *-ian* (belonging or pertaining to)	*Elizabethan, republican, Parisian, Christian*
-ance (from verbs)	*acceptance, endurance*
-ence	*interference*
-ancy (-ency) (state of)	*permanency, relevancy, leniency, consistency, decency*
-ant (from verbs)	*consultant, defendant, contestant*
-ation, -ication (usually from verbs ending in *-ify*,	*justification* (justify), *purification* (purify), *centralization* (centralize), *neutralization*

-ize, -ate)	(neutralize), *contemplation* (contemplate), *accumulation* (accumulate), *accusation* (accuse), *annexation* (annex),
-dom (state, jurisdiction)	*Christendom, wisdom, freedom*
-er (agent, person from, usually from verb)	*commander, baker, boxer, singer, Londoner, Berliner*
-(e)ry (usually from noun)	*jewelry, ancestry* (ancestor), *treachery, robbery*
-ess (feminine suffix, of agency)	*waitress, temptress, millionairess*
-ette (diminution)	*kitchenette, dinette, roomette*
-ician (person with skill)	*physician, mathematician*
-ing (from verbs)	*finding, warning, surrounding*
-ism (system of religous or political ideas)	*fascism, paganism, Judaism*
-ist	*linguist, sophist, cartoonist, florist*
-ity (state, quality, usually from adjective)	*ability* (able), *capability* (capable), *chastity* (chaste), *scarcity* (scarce)
-ment (action, usually from verb)	*appeasement, judgment* (judge), *engagement*
-ness (state, condition, from adjective)	*darkness, bareness, tenderness*
-ship (state, condition, mainly from nouns)	*township, fellowship, trusteeship*
-th (θ) (quality, from adjective)	*length* (long), *width* (wide), *strength* (strong)
-ure (quality, action)	*mixture, rapture, closure*
-y (from verb)	*delivery, discovery*

3. *Stress changes*

Many derivations of nouns from verbs involve a shift in the stress pattern. If such a shift occurs, the heavy stress (primary stress) is usually shifted to the initial syllable.

ínterchange	(← verb ìnterchánge)
réprìnt	(← verb rèprínt)
récòrd	(← verb rĕcórd)
cóntèst	(← verb cŏntést)

cónvìct	(← verb cŏnvíct)
ínsùlt	(← verb ĭnsúlt)
tŕansfĕr	(← verb tŕansfér).

4. *Derivation without a change* (by a zero-morpheme)

Numerous examples of verbs and nouns with identical forms can be listed. In most cases the historical process derived the verbs from the nouns, so we shall list examples under the verb category. However, in quite a few cases — especially with older native words of the Anglo-Saxon stock of English — the derivational process was noun → verb: for example, *look, bite, fall, drink, sleep.*

5. *Compounding*

Here the most frequent type is probably the modification of the main noun (in second position) by another noun used as modifier: *countryman, clergyman, postman, rifleman, infantryman,* etc.

The lack of distinctions of gender (and sex) in English nouns gives rise to *girlfriend, boyfriend*; and — with the use of pronouns as first elements in the compound — *she-wolf, she-devil, he-goat,* and — with a slightly different meaning and an emphasis on masculinity — *he-man.*

In some instances of older compounds, the *-s* of the original genitive of the noun is preserved: *craftsman (craft + man), kinsman, woodsman.*

Modification of the noun by an adjective leads to such compounds as: *blackboard, bluebird, highschool, nobleman.*

Compound nouns of the type in which the object is implied but not mentioned are usually verb + adverb combinations and are related to verbs of the same type; for example, *dugout, takeoff, playback, fallout, countdown, blackout.*

Adjectives

1. *Prefixes*

Many of the prefixes mentioned with the nouns can of course also occur in adjectives. However, a few prefixes are typically adjectival.

a- (usually from a noun)	*ablaze, afire, aground, afoot*
a- (negative particle)	*asymmetric, acritical, asocial*
in- (see also **nouns** *in-*, negative particle)	*infrequent, inanimate, inaccurate*
un- (negative particle)	*unable, unspeakable, unfair, unclean*

2. *Suffixes*

-able (usually from verb)	*agreeable, desirable, acceptable, profitable, saleable*
-al (usually from noun)	*parental, accidental, global, cultural, essential* (essence)
-ic	*patriotic, domestic, basic, phonetic, linguistic*
-ical (*ic* + *al*)	*despotical, puritanical, nonsensical*
-an (see nouns)	*American, African*
-ian	*equestrian, Christian*
-arian	*humanitarian, utilitarian*
-ary (from nouns)	*elementary, stationary, complimentary*
-ate (from nouns)	*passionate, affectionate*
-ed (probably related to past participle ending *-ed*)	
(from nouns)	*jointed, checked, roofed, shelled*
(in the combination *well-. . . ed*)	*well-groomed, well-boned, well-behaved*
(in combination with other compounds)	*bare-legged, black-haired, heavy-handed, strong-headed*
-en (from nouns— made of . . .)	*wooden, silken, earthen*
-ful (from nouns)	*awful, fearful, lawful, wilful, merciful*
-ish (from nouns or adjectives)	*Swedish, Polish, Turkish, foolish, fiendish, hellish, boorish, sheepish*
-ive	*expensive, successive, native, competitive*
-less (without, from nouns)	*careless, meatless, lawless, fearless, doubtless.* (Note that the existence of an adjective derived by *-ful* often presupposes one derived by *-less*: *fearful/fearless, faithful/faithless*
-ly (from nouns or adjectives)	*friendly, orderly, fatherly, deadly, daily, nightly, yearly*
-ous (from nouns)	*ambitious* (ambition), *famous, dangerous, treacherous, glorious, industrious*
-eous, -ious (from nouns)	*erroneous* (error), *instantaneous, courteous, fallacious*
-some (from nouns)	*handsome, wholesome, troublesome*

| -y (from nouns) | *bloody, bony, leathery, windy, rainy,* |
| | *drizzly, sexy* |

3. *Stress changes*

Stress changes do not occur in formation of adjectives.

4. *Derivation without a change:* by a zero-morpheme

Derivation without a morpheme does not normally occur in the formation of adjectives, unless we consider combinations such as *chocolate drink, milk bottle,* as instances in which nouns (*milk, chocolate*) are used as adjectives. The type of expression in which a word other than an adjective becomes the modifier of the second part of the expression is rather frequent. It is doubtful whether the first part of the expression *girl friend* or *milk bottle* can really be considered an adjective. The fact that invariably the first element carries the main stress seems to indicate that the two words which form the expression have become completely one (that is, a compound) and that the first is no longer functioning as an adjective: the *blàck* of *blàck bírd* is an adjective, but *bláckbìrd* is simply a compound noun in which *black* is not genuinely used as an adjective.

In connection with the above mentioned adjectival or semi-adjectival use of other word classes as the first part of compound nouns, it is important to remember that this rather typically English way of compounding nouns may be quite confusing to the foreign student. In many cases the English compound **noun (1)** (used as modifier of another) plus **noun (2)** will be expressed in the foreign language as **noun (2) + preposition + noun (1)**; for example, English *coffee cup* is French *tasse à café,* while English *cup of coffee* is *tasse de café.* The result is that the foreigner may confuse the meanings and expressions: *coffee cup, teacup, soup dish* and *cup of coffee, cup of tea, dish of soup.* He may also misinterpret the relation between the first (modifying) and second (modified) noun of the English compound. In other words, *my girl friend* can be misunderstood as *friend of my girl* or even as *my friendly girl.* The exact meaning of combinations like *boyfriend, girl friend* and contrasts like *cup of tea* vs. *teacup* must be especially drilled in exercises (*this teacup is empty*; or *I just drank a cup of tea*).

5. *Compounding*

Adjectives formed by compounding are numerous. Invariably, the second part of the compound must be an adjective, or an *-ing* form or past participle used as an adjective.

Examples of compounds of the type **noun + adjective** are *homesick, carefree, footsore*. **Noun + -ing form** is a pattern found in words like *earthshaking, seafaring*. **Noun + past participle** is exemplified by *handmade, airborne*.

Compounds made up of **adjective + adjective** are *red-hot, light-blue, dark-brown, Franco-Italian, deaf-mute*. **Adjective + -ing form** is represented by *good-looking, hard-working*, etc. **Adjective + past participle** are the component parts of *frenchfried, newfound, readymade*.

Verbs

1. *Prefixes*

Many of the prefixes discussed under the heading of noun or adjective appear also with verbs. However, some are used primarily or exclusively in verb formation:

be-	*bewilder, bewitch, belittle* (One of the oldest prefixes in the English language. In many cases the word or root to which it has been prefixed no longer exists independently — so the native speaker feels that *be-* is no longer a derivational prefix but part of the stem itself, as in *believe, betray*.)
de- (take away, remove)	*deodorize, delouse, decode*
dis- (negative)	*disallow, disconnect, disassemble, discourage*
en- (put into)	*encircle, enamor, enrich, enlist, enslave*
ex- (out)	*express, exceed*
re- (again)	*repeat, reform, reappear*
trans- (across)	*translate, transform, transgress*

2. *Suffixes*

-ate	*create, separate, terminate*
-er	*quiver, glitter, flutter, jabber*
-en (usually from adjectives)	*lighten, darken, harden, ripen*
-fy	*glorify, verify, terrify, beautify*
-ize	*baptize, scandalize, spiritualize, modernize, capitalize, americanize*
-le	*dazzle, dwindle, giggle, rumble* (An old suffix; in most cases the word to which it has been added no longer exists independently.)

Finally we should also note that a voiced voiceless alternation in the pronunciation of the last consonant (v/f, $ð/θ$), sometimes with a change in the vowel sound, is also characteristic of the verb/noun relationship. For example:

strive (verb /straɪv/)	*strife* (noun /straɪf/)
prove (verb /pruv/)	*proof* (noun /pruf/)
grieve (verb /griv/)	*grief* (noun /grif/)
bathe (verb /beð/)	*bath* (noun /bæθ/)
clothe (verb /kloð/)	*cloth* (noun /klɔθ/)
breathe (verb /brɪð/)	*breath* (noun /brɛθ/)

3. *Stress changes*

The usual relation between nouns and verbs shown by stress changes has been discussed under the heading of nouns. If a stress change occurs in the shift from one category to the other, the noun has the primary stress on the first syllable, while the verb has the primary stress on the third. In disyllabic words, the verb has the primary stress on the second syllable.

Verb	*Noun*
ˋ ˬ ˊ	ˊ ˬ ˋ
run away	*runaway*
interchange	*interchange*
ˋ ˊ	ˊ ˋ
(ˬ)	(ˬ)
reprint	*reprint*
black out	*blackout*
convict	*convict*
digest	*digest*
record	*record*
insult	*insult*

4. *Derivation without a change:* by a zero-morpheme

English can shift words with great ease from the verb to the noun category and—more typically and even more frequently—from the noun to the verb category. The ease with which English can verbalize a noun is undoubtedly connected with the fact that English has comparatively few grammatical endings characteristic of nouns and verbs. The shift can thus be accomplished by simply utilizing a noun in the verb position. *The table* (noun) *is in the room*, but *we can table* (verb) *a motion. We sit in a chair* (noun), but *we chair* (verb) *a meeting.* Examples of noun → verb are very numerous. From the point of view of the student learning English, the noun = verb equation underlines the necessity of learning word order and function words as the important grammatical signals of English.

5. *Compounding*

Since nouns and verbs are so easily interchangeable, many compound nouns can also be used as verbs. Thus we find the **noun–noun** type noun compounds also used as verbs: for example, *spotlight, earmark.* The **adjective–noun** type is used verbally in *blacklist, soft-soap.*

Compounds in which the second part is actually a verb are also rather frequent:

Noun + verb:	*playact, spoon-feed, chain-smoke*
Adjective + verb:	*blindfold, dry-clean, double-park*

The type **preposition** (or **adverb**) **+ verb** is represented by such compounds as *outrun, outgrow, outvote; override, overrule, overtake; undercut, undermine, undersell, underpay.*

This latter type may create many problems in understanding as well as in correct usage. When combining verbs and prepositions, English distinguishes three different situations (which will be discussed later in more detail in connection with the teaching of syntactical and vocabulary problems):

1. **The compound verb** (for example, *undertake, overestimate, overtake*). The adverb (or preposition) is completely fused with the verb and functions simply like a prefix: as in *I undertook the task; the boat overtook us; we were overtaken by the car.*

2. **The two-part verb** (such as *take over, take up*). The preposition is separated from the verb, but it no longer functions as usual. For instance, if the noun object in the sentence is replaced by a pronoun, the preposition follows the pronoun, while normally a pronoun follows the preposition: for example, *under them, before me.* Thus we say: *He took over the whole class. He took it over* (not **over it*). Of course, it is also possible to use this word order with the noun object: *He took the whole class over.*

3. **The verb + preposition**. In this combination the preposition functions in a normal manner and is not (yet) part of the verb. The pronoun follows the preposition: for example, *he went over his notes*; *he went over them*; *he went under the bridge*; *he went under it*.

These three situations (compound verb, two-part verb, verb + preposition) pose a major problem: to *overcome* is not the same as to *come over*, and to *overtake* is not the same as to *take over*. Thus usages such as *he overtook the whole class* and *he took over the whole class* must be carefully compared and contrasted in special exercises.

Adverbs

1. *Prefixes*

a- (usually from nouns or adjectives)	*away, abreast, aground, ahead, apart, around, along*

2. *Suffixes*

-ly (from adjectives)	*noisily, wearily, gladly, hopefully*
-ward (from nouns)	*seaward, homeward*

3. *Change of stress*

   Not utilized.

4. *Derivation without a change:* by a zero-morpheme

   There are several cases in which adjectives and adverbs are identical.

   a. *fast*   (*A fast train runs fast*)
      hard   (*A hard worker works hard*)
   b. Adjectives derived by the suffix *-ly*: *nightly, yearly, hourly* (*the yearly statement; the statement arrives yearly*).
   c. Adverbs derived by the suffix *-ward*: *forward, backward, sideward* (*backward person; he moves backward*).
      But not *awkward/awkwardly*! The suffix *-ly* can be added to *-ward* if the latter does not have the meaning of "direction toward."

5. *Compounding*

   The most frequent compound adverbs are those utilizing *where, time(s)*, and *way(s)* as their second element: *anywhere, somewhere, nowhere; overtime, sometimes; sideways, crossways*, etc.

For most adverbs the regular derivation is the addition of the suffix -*ly* to the corresponding adjective. The main exceptions are the zero-morpheme formations (*fast, backward*) and the adverb *well*, which corresponds to the adjective *good*. The student may be tempted to introduce the -*ly* derivation in cases where it is not possible. For example, he might coin forms like **fastly* or **forwardly* or **goodly*. This tendency must be counteracted by exercises in which adjectival and adverbial uses are contrasted: *he is a good speaker*; *he speaks well*; or *this is a fast train*; *it runs very fast*.

The instances of **adjective = adverb** probably add an additional element of confusion to the problems created by the contrasting use of **adverb** vs. **adjective** after certain verbs (for example, *he appeared slow* vs. *he appeared slowly*) and by the substandard English use of adjective for adverb (for example, *this watch runs real good*). At any rate, special care must be taken so that the adjective = adverb equation (*the last man*; *he arrived last*; *the fast train*; *he ran fast*) is not extended to other adjectives. *A fast answer*; *he answers fast*, but *a quick answer*; *he answers quickly* (not *quick*!).

The adverbial suffix -*ly* also seems different from the other suffixes and prefixes discussed under word formation insofar as it has purely grammatical rather than both grammatical and lexical meaning. The addition of a suffix like -*or* (in *actor, instructor*) not only serves to mark the word as a noun—it also has a certain lexical meaning. It denotes *agent, a person performing an act*. The addition of a derivational morpheme like -*ous* (*advantageous, famous*) not only marks the words as an adjective—it also has a meaning such as *full of, made up of*. The addition of -*ly* to adjectives (*gladly, happily*) adds no new element of lexical meaning. Since it is used for word formation it was discussed in this section. From the point of view of the type of morpheme it represents, its discussion could also have been relegated to the following section.

(C)   THE GRAMMATICAL PARADIGMS

Some morphemes may be called stem or root morphemes. They form the backbone of the lexical meaning conveyed by a word. Others are the derivational morphemes discussed in the preceding section. They have some aspects of lexical meaning but serve primarily the function of assigning a word to a specific word class. **Grammatical morphemes** are morphemes which serve the exclusive function of indicating grammatical relationships. For the purpose of establishing a linguistic analysis of a language we can also classify words according to the grammatical morphemes with which they combine. All words which are capable of combining with the same grammatical morphemes can be assigned to the same grammatical class. A listing of all the forms which can be created by combining a stem with grammatical morphemes is called a **paradigm**. Words which combine with the same grammatical morphemes are said to belong to the same **paradigmatic class**. For example, a form like *laugh* can combine with the grammatical morphemes *-ing* (*laughing*); *-s* (*he laughs*); *-ed* (past tense: *he laughed*); *-ed* (past participle: *he has laughed*). The listing *laugh, laughing, laughs, laughed, laughed* is the paradigm of the word *laugh*. Words like *step* or *kick*, which can take the same endings as *laugh*, are quite clearly identified as belonging to the same paradigmatic class as *laugh* — namely the class of **verbs**. From the point of view of classification according to grammatical endings, English has four main paradigmatic classes: **nouns, adjectives, (personal) pronouns**, and **verbs**.

1. Nouns

English nouns are capable of combining with two grammatical morphemes: most important, with the one that indicates the plural (*table/tables*), and also, less frequently, with the morpheme that indicates possession and which is the only other morpheme for noun inflection remaining in the language: *the man's attitude, the boy's room; the men's attitude, the boys' room.*

By far the most frequent and thus "regular" plural morpheme is represented by the alternation of /s/, /z/, /əz/ which has been discussed already: /s/ appears after voiceless consonants (*caps, hats, cliffs*); /z/ after voiced consonants and vowels (*dogs, cabs, ladies, shoes*); /əz/ after /z/, /s/, /ʒ/, /ʃ/, /ǰ/, /č/ (*noses, horses, dishes, garages*).

These plural formations (just like the minor orthographic irregularities connected with them: *-y/-ies, lady/ladies*; or *o/oes, potato/potatoes*) must be practiced — preferably in sentences in which the change singular ⇒ plural is also accompanied by a change in the verb: *the dog barks ⇒ the dogs bark; the cat is brown ⇒ the cats are brown; the dog was barking ⇒ the dogs were barking.*

A minor variation of the regular patterns involves the words in which the change to the plural is also accompanied by a voicing of the stemfinal consonant:

thief	/θif/	*thieves*	/θivz/
wife	/waɪf/	*wives*	/waɪvz/
mouth	/maʊθ/	*mouths*	/maʊðz/
oath	/oθ/	*oaths*	/oðz/
house	/haʊs/	*houses*	/haʊzəz/

The irregular patterns of plural formation comprise the following:

a. the use of *-en* /ən/ in *ox/oxen, child/children,* and *brother/ brethren* (the latter only in the special meaning of *people belonging to the same group or sect*);

b. the use of a zero-morpheme in *sheep/sheep; deer/deer; fish/fish* (although *fishes* also occurs); *swine/swine*;

c. the use of various Greek or Latin plurals in borrowings from those languages: *alumna/alumnae; alumnus/alumni; crisis* /kraɪsɪs/, *crises* /kraɪsɪz/; *criterion/criteria*;

d. the use of a vowel change in the stem of some very common nouns: *man/men* (/mæn/, /mɛn/); *woman/women* (/wʊmən/, /wɪmən/); *foot/feet* (/fʊt/, /fit/); *goose/geese* (/gus/, /gis/); *tooth/teeth* (/tuθ/, /tiθ/), *mouse/mice* (/maʊs/, /maɪs/).

The pupil must practice the irregular plurals because, once he has learned the regular plural formation, he is likely to extend it to words which take the irregular formation. For example, he may be tempted to formulate plurals like **oxes* or **childs.*

The major and most persistent problems affecting the plural of nouns are of a general syntactical nature and are not a matter of learning the forms. They will be discussed in subsequent chapters.

The **possessive** morpheme appears in four forms: /z/ after voiced consonants or vowels: *John's book, Joe's hat;* /s/ after voiceless consonants: *Jack's book, Bert's cap;* /əz/ after the sibilants (/s/, /z/, /ʃ/, /ʒ/, /č/, /ǰ/): *Rich's car, Rose's dress, the judge's decision;* and finally, a zero-morpheme after the plural morpheme /s/, /z/: *the boys' room.* Note, however, that the zero-morpheme is indicated in spelling by the use of an apostrophe.

The use of the possessive morpheme seems fairly restricted to human beings or at any rate animate beings; in addition, the prepositional phrase with *of* is often used in such expressions as *friends of John's* or *friends of mine.* At any rate the main problem for the foreign student (extension of the possessive form to inanimates, or the use of the prepositional phrase instead of the possessive form) is a syntactical rather than a morphological one.

2. Adjectives

The only grammatical morphemes with which English adjectives can combine are those of the comparative and superlative: -er /ər/ and -est /əst/: big, bigger, biggest; thin, thinner, thinnest. This paradigm occurs primarily with one-syllable adjectives and those two-syllable adjectives ending in a vowel sound; this entails no particular morphological problems. Note that with some adjectives ending in -ng the stem is pronounced slightly differently when the -er and -est endings are added: strong /strɔŋ/, long /lɔŋ/, young /yəŋ/; but stronger /strɔŋgər/ longer /lɔŋgər/, younger /yəŋgər/. Also, the comparative and superlative often show some orthographic changes: for example, a change of y to i (happy, happier), a doubling of the last consonant after /ɪ, ɛ, æ, ʊ, ɔ, ə/ (thin/thinner, big/bigger, fat/fatter), or the disappearance of a silent e (late/later).

The exceptions to the regular formations and the morphological difficulties are caused by two types of adjectives: those which form their comparative and superlative on a stem different from the one used for the positive form; and those which do not belong to the paradigmatic class of adjectives using the -er/-est morphemes, but which form their comparative and superlative by the use of more and most.

Adjectives with Special Stems for Comparative and Superlative

The adjectives basing their comparative and superlative on special stems are:

good	better	best
bad	worse	worst
little	less	least
much	more	most
far	farther	farthest
	(further)	(furthest)

These irregular comparatives and superlatives are characteristic of a few—very important—words. The general tendency of the language has been toward the elimination of these irregular forms; for example, the formerly quite common comparative and superlative of *old — elder, eldest —* has become rare. The old comparative and superlative of *late — latter, last —* have either become rare or changed in meaning (*latter*), or the meaning has become restricted (*last*). The normal paradigm of *late* is now *later, latest.* Yet *better/best, worse/worst, less/least* are still firmly entrenched (except that *lesser*, adding the *-er* morpheme to *less*, exists with a different meaning). The irregular comparatives and superlatives must be taught in exercises contrasting them with the regular formation: *Charlotte is a pretty girl; she is prettier than her sister; she is the prettiest girl in the family; she is also a good student; she is a better student than all the others; she is the best student in the class.*

Adjectives Using more *and* most *for Comparative and Superlative*

Most adjectives of two or more syllables (except two-syllable adjectives ending in a vowel sound) form their comparative and superlative with *more* and *most.* There are a few one-syllable adjectives which follow this pattern rather than adding the usual *-er* and *-est* endings: *real, more real, most real; right, more right, most right.* There are also a few two-syllable adjectives with which either pattern is possible: for example, *handsome, clever.*

The problem is to teach the student that a lesson can be *easier* than another but that it cannot be **difficulter;* or that a book can be *cheaper* than another but that it cannot be **expensiver.* In other words, the formations with *-er/-est* must be contrasted with those using *more* and *most.* The best procedure is to introduce the *-er/-est* pattern first because it affects many of the most frequently used adjectives. After it has been mastered, the comparative and superlative forms with *more* and *most* can be introduced.

To some extent, the strategy of presenting *-er, -est* vs. *more, most* will be influenced by the native language of the learner. For example, the native speaker of German (whose language tends to form all comparatives and superlatives by suffixes corresponding to *-er, -est*) will have little difficulty with the English *-er, -est* formation and will tend to overextend them to other adjectives. Spanish, on the other hand, forms practically all comparatives **and** superlatives (except a few irregular ones) by the function word *más*, which corresponds to English *more;* therefore the Spanish speaker will have the inclination to overuse *more.* For Spanish-speaking students, the *more, most* formation should be postponed until the *-er, -est* formation is well understood.

English adjectives (unlike those of many other languages, such as

Spanish and French) do not show any inflection for either number or gender. As a matter of fact the only noun modifiers of English which do have a singular/plural distinction are *this/these* and *that/those*. In line with their native speech habits, some students may attempt to produce **plural adjectives**: *these *beautifuls girls* or *the girls are *beautifuls*. Considerable practice may be necessary to form the habit of pluralizing the noun but **not** the adjective which modifies it.

3. Pronouns

The English pronouns furnish a good example of an instance in which a paradigm comprises words which, according to substitution criteria, have to be assigned to very different classes. The concept of *I*—the morpheme meaning *first person*—appears in the subject pronoun *I*. It also reappears in the object pronoun *me*, in the possessive determiner *my*, and the possessive pronoun *mine*. Even though *I* and *me* are not similar in form, we can say that they somehow contain different variants of the morpheme meaning first person and that *I*, *me*, *my*, *mine* form a paradigm. The same reasoning can be applied to the other pronouns, and we can establish a paradigm class which looks as follows:

I	*me*	*my*	*mine*
you	*you*	*your*	*yours*
he	*him*	*his*	*his*
she	*her*	*her*	*hers*
it	*it*	*its*	*its*
we	*us*	*our*	*ours*
they	*them*	*their*	*theirs*
who	*whom*	*whose*	*whose*

Memorization of paradigms has been a favorite tool of language teachers for centuries. Generations of language students have spent many hours conjugating Latin verbs (*amo, amas, amat*, etc.) or declining nouns (*populus, populi*). One of the authors of this book distinctly remembers having to memorize *I, me, my, mine* when starting to learn English at the age of twelve. Perhaps in no other case does the memorization of a paradigm seem more pointless than in learning the English pronouns. The real problem is not learning the forms but acquiring their correct use in syntax once they have been learned.

Some of the confusion in usage of the forms of the pronoun paradigm consists simply in overextending the dominant regular patterns to situations in which they do not apply. Here the mistake of the foreign learner is often the same as the nonstandard use of the native speaker: since *me, him, her, us, them, whom* are the only remnants of a subject/object contrast in English (it no longer exists with the nouns or with *it* and *you*), it is tempting to confuse these forms with the corresponding subject forms.

This confusion is particularly frequent with native speakers whenever the subject/object relation is not clearly marked by the object's appearing immediately after the verb. In the construction *it is . . .* , the object pronouns *me, them* are often used instead of *I* or *they*. As a matter of fact, *it is me* is now the more frequent usage, and it is questionable whether one should insist that the foreign student learn *it is I*. The same confusion occurs with the word *whom* where again the object is not in its usual postverbal or postprepositional slot (*John, who you met yesterday, will be here soon*; *who are you talking to?*). Also, after prepositions and with double pronouns object and subject forms are used indiscriminately: *you and me know this*; *he did this for you and I*. To what extent the foreign learner of English should be allowed to imitate this type of usage is debatable. The best path to follow is probably to teach the official standard but not to spend too much time correcting the nonstandard colloquial usage when it occurs. The only exception to this strategy is perhaps the form and use of *whom* which can be omitted completely from the student's active vocabulary if the subject/object distinction is not taught. The forms *me, him, her, us, them* have to be taught in any case, since their obvious subject/object distinctions are maintained by practically all native speakers.

Other confusions within the pronoun paradigm are comparatively minor. One—also used in nonstandard native speech—consists of the attempt to formulate what seems a very badly needed plural of *you* (*yous*). (Note the southern U.S. use of *you all* to denote plurality in the second person.)

Another confusion common among foreign learners is the mix-up of possessive adjectives (determiners) and possessive pronouns (*mine book* instead of *my book*—especially with native speakers of German—or *theirs books*). The latter confusion is facilitated by the fact that for some forms (*his, its*) the determiners and pronouns are identical and that for others (*her, hers*) the pronouns look like plural forms of the determiners. (We discussed above the tendency of some speakers to try to create plural adjectives.)

Another confusion arises for speakers of languages (such as French, Spanish) in which the possessive adjectives agree in gender with the nouns they modify. The learner will thus use *his* and *her* not according to the sex of the possessor but according to the gender of the corresponding modified noun in his language. *His table* becomes *her table* because *mesa* (= *table*) is feminine in Spanish, and *her brother* becomes *his brother* because *hermano* (= *brother*) is masculine.

The above mentioned confusions must be counteracted by various types of exercises. An obviously useful one is the question/answer type.

To Practice Possessive Adjectives

> *Is this **my** book?   Yes, this is **your** book.*
> *Is this **your** book?   Yes, this is **my** book.*
> *Is this **Charles's** book?   Yes, this is **his** book.*
> *Is this **Clara's** book?   Yes, this is **her** book.*
> *Are these **John's** and **Charles's** books?*
> > *Yes, these are **their** books.*

To Practice the Possessive Pronouns

> *Is this **my** book?   Yes, it is **yours**.*
> *Is this **Charles's** book?   Yes, it is **his**.*

To Practice the Object Case

> *Does Charles like **you**?   Yes, he likes **me**.*
> *Does Charles like **Mary**?   Yes, he likes **her**.*
> *Does Charles like **John**?   Yes, he likes **him**.*

Another type of exercise in which the entire paradigm can be practiced in a syntactical context consists of sentences contrasting the use of *I*, *me*, *my*, *mine*, etc.:

*I am a student. **My** parents sent **me** this book. It is **mine**.* Upon the cue *Charles*, a student repeats the pattern by saying: *He is a student. **His** parents sent **him** this book. It is **his**.* On the cue *Mary*: *She is a student. **Her** parents sent **her** this book. It is **hers**.*

4. Verbs

From the morphological point of view English verbs have only five forms: (1) a simple form (*laugh*); (2) the *-ing* form (*laughing*); (3) the third person singular present (*laughs*); (4) the past tense (*laughed*); and (5) the past participle (*laughed*).

The *-ing* form is always regular. The third person singular is practically always regular. Minor irregularities occur only with the irregular verb *be* (*is*), the verb *have* (*has*), the verb *do* (*do* /du/, but *does* /dəz/), and the verb *say* (*say* /se/, but *says* /sεz/).

The really complicated morphological problem arises with forms (4) and (5), the past tense and the past participle. Here we can distinguish one regular or dominant type, formed by adding the ending *-ed*, which is pronounced:

> /d/   after voiced consonants and vowels
> (*rubbed, stirred, enjoyed*)
>
> /t/   after voiceless consonants
> (*laughed, stepped*)
>
> /əd/   after *t* and *d*
> (*seated, fitted*)

Thus we can say that the normal or regular formation consists of: (a) having no change in the stem vowel; (b) adding the suffix *-ed* (/d/, /t/, /əd/). Irregular formations can be classified according to whether they violate either rule (a) or (b) or both (a) and (b). There are approximately 130 irregular verbs in English and, no matter how we classify or present them, the student has to learn the most important ones. A specific classification or grouping in presentation may facilitate learning somewhat. Nevertheless the acquisition of the forms remains primarily a task of memorization and intensive practice.

Below we will summarize the most important classes or types of irregular verb formation. In our classification we shall distinguish the formation of the **past** participle (**PP**) and of the past tense (**PT**) and describe the formation according to the stem (**S**) and the ending (**E**). The symbol ∅ stands for "no change" or "no ending."

CLASS 1.   **PT (S: ∅; E: ∅); PP (S: ∅; E: ∅):**
bet, burst, cast, cost, cut, hit, hurt, let, put, quit, rid, set, shed, shut, split, spread, thrust, wet. (Example: *bet, bet, bet*; /bεt, bεt, bεt/.)

CLASS 2. **PT (S: ɪ → ə/; E: ∅); PP (S: /ɪ → ə/E: ∅):**
cling, dig, fling, shrink, sling, slink, spin, sting, stink, string, swing, win, wring. (Example: *cling, clung, clung;* /klɪŋ, kləŋ, kləŋ/.)

CLASS 3. **PT (S: /i → ɛ/; E: /t/,); PP (S: /i → ɛ/; E: /t/,):**
(In both past tense and past participle, the vowel change occurs in pronunciation, but not always in orthography.)
creep, deal, feel, keep, leap, mean, sleep, sweep, weep. (Example: *deal, dealt, dealt;* /dil, dɛlt, dɛlt/.)

CLASS 4. **PT (S: /i → ɛ/; E: ∅); PP (S: /i → ɛ/; E: ∅):**
bleed, breed, feed, lead, meet, plead, read, speed. (Example: *bleed, bled, bled;* /blid, blɛd, blɛd/.)

CLASS 5. **PT (S: /ɪ → æ/; E: ∅); PP (S: /ɪ → ə/; E: ∅):**
begin, drink, ring, sing, sink, spring, swim. (Example: *swim, swam, swum;* /swɪm, swæm, swəm/.)

CLASS 6. **PT (S: /aɪ → o/; E: ∅); PP (S/aɪ → ɪ/;E: ən/):**
drive, ride, rise, smite, strive, write. (Example: *write, wrote, written;* /raɪt, rot, rɪtən/.)

CLASS 7. **PT (S: ∅; final *d* of stem → *t*; E: ∅); PP (S: ∅; final *d* of stem → *t*; E: ∅):**
bend, build, lend, rend, send, spend. (Example: *spend, spent, spent;* /spɛnd, spɛnt, spɛnt/.)

CLASS 8. **PT (S: /i → o/; E: ∅); PP (S: /i → o/; E: /ən/):**
freeze, speak, steal, weave. (Example: *steal, stole, stolen;* /stil, stol, stolən/.)

CLASS 9. **PT (S: /aɪ → aʊ/; E: ∅); PP (S: /aɪ → aʊ/; E: ∅):**
bind, find, grind, wind. (Example: *find, found, found;* /faɪnd, faʊnd, faʊnd/.)

CLASS 10. **PT (S: /o → u/; E: ∅); PP (S: ∅; E: /n/):**
blow, grow, know, throw. (Example: *grow, grew, grown;* /gro, gru, gron/.)

CLASS 11. **PT (S: /ɛ → ɔ/; E: ∅); PP (S: /ɛ → ɔ/; E: /n/):**
bear, swear, tear, wear. (Example: *bear, bore, borne;* /bɛr, bɔr, bɔrn/.)

CLASS 12.   **PT (S: /e → ʊ/; E: ∅) PP (S: ∅, E: /ən/):**
take, shake, foresake. (Example: *shake, shook, shaken*; /ʃek, ʃʊk, ʃekən/.)

The above classifications do not give an exhaustive presentation of the irregular formations. They represent only the major classes which can be grouped together to facilitate the student's learning of the forms. There are still more irregular verbs, which form at best classes of two (for example, *sit, sat, sat*; *spit, spat, spat*; or *bring, brought, brought*; *think, thought, thought*). Approximately thirty verbs do not fit into any class, because they do not agree with any other verb in all three factors on which the classification is based, that is, the stem vowel, past tense, and past participle (for example, *catch, caught, caught*; *buy, bought, bought*; *teach, taught, taught*, which agree in the **PT** and **PP** forms but not in the stem vowel of the simple form).

Three verbs are in unique classes: *do* (*do*, /du/; third person present: *does*, /dəz/; **PT**: *did*; **PP**: *done*); *have* (*have*, /hæv/; third person present: *has*, /hæz/; **PT, PP**: *had*, /hæd/); and of course the verb *be*, which is morphologically the richest and most irregular of the English verbs, having the forms *am, are* (*I am*; *you, we, they are*), a third person present *is*, the **PT** forms *was, were* (*I, he was*; *you, we, they were*), and a **PP** *been*.

There is a strong temptation to extend the dominant *-ed* type of past tense/past participle formation to the irregular verbs or to confuse irregular formations. Even native speakers will sometimes get confused in the formation of the past tense and past participles. Especially among young children forms like *I *cutted my finger* or *he *brang me the book* (*bring → *brang* on the analogy of *sing → sang*) are not uncommon. For the native speaker, just as for the foreign learner, the acquisition of forms like *cut* (past tense) or *brought* is ultimately a matter of practice.

Since the problem involved is primarily one of simply recalling the forms when producing the past participle or past tense of the verb, simple rote memorization—even out of context—will certainly not hurt. However, the best practice consists of having the student change verbs from one form or tense to another, preferably in some sort of pattern practice which furnishes a conversational context and, at the same time, practice in the correct use of the forms involved. For example:

TEACHER: *Did you find* (simple form) *your car keys?*

STUDENT: *Yes I found* (past tense) *them.*
TEACHER: *Did you read the book?*
STUDENT: *Yes I read it.*

Or:

TEACHER: *Did you see* (simple form) *the dean yesterday?*
STUDENT: *No, I did not see* (simple form) *him. I have never seen* (past participle) *him.*
TEACHER: *Did you speak to the president?*
STUDENT: *No, I did not speak to the president. I have never spoken to him.*

Before leaving the discussion of verb morphology, we reiterate that the auxiliary verbs *can, should, must, will, may, might* represent a class by themselves—morphologically as well as syntactically. They do not combine with the *-ing* ending. They do not have the *-s* ending in the third person singular, nor are they ever followed by *to* preceding the main verb (occasionally a foreign student may produce forms like he **cans to speak,* or he **wills to spell* in analogy to the *-s* ending of main verbs). They do not form a past participle. Some grammars present the forms *could, should, would* as the past tense of *can, shall,* and *will.* With the exception of *could,* which does in one usage at least represent the past tense of *can* (*today I can do this; yesterday I could not*), and more rarely *would,* these forms are typically not used as past tenses. Thus, to treat them as past tenses morphologically only increases the problems encountered with their actual syntactical usage, which will be considered in the following chapters.

CHAPTER VI

Teaching Syntactical Patterns

(A) BASIC STRUCTURES AND GENERAL PROBLEMS

We stated earlier that the major means of communicating grammatical meaning are **word order**, **inflection**, **derivation**, and **function words**. Languages employ these grammatical devices in various ways. Some languages give priority to word order, others rely heavily on derivation or inflection.

English undoubtedly places its heaviest reliance on word order and only minimal reliance on inflection. This clearly makes English, at least as far as comprehension is concerned, a very difficult language for native speakers of languages (such as Russian) which place their main reliance on grammatical endings and attach little or no significance to word order. However, confusion and difficulty caused by English word order may be even greater for students whose languages use word order in a way different from English: for example, subject, object, verb instead of subject, verb, object.

Since word order is so important in English, it is not surprising that probably the most frequent syntactical mistakes involve some sort of confusion of English word order and the imposition of foreign word order upon English. The speaker of Spanish, which places most modifying adjectives after the noun, may say *the boys intelligent* instead of *the intelligent boys*. The German who, while placing the finite verb in second position, puts the rest of the verb at the end of the sentence, may produce the sentence *he has with the boys spoken*.

Because of the paramount importance of word order in English it is quite important to present the elements of the English sentence by positions — according to the **slots** which they fill. Visual presentation — lining up sentences so that substitutable elements are presented in columns — is particularly important in teaching English syntax.

The basic type of English sentence can be presented as having four slots or positions.

Type I:

1. SUBJECT (Noun Phrase)	2. VERB	3. OBJECT (Noun Phrase)	4. ADVERB
as in:	*Charles*	*speaks*	*English*	*well*
or:	*Robert*	*met*	*his uncle*	*yesterday*

As we shall show later, other more complex sentences can be considered expansions of the same sentence type. Note that the position of each slot does not change even if we expand each element. For example:

My good friend/is making/excellent progress/this year.

In addition to the sentence type mentioned above (1. Subject, 2. Verb, 3. Object, 4. Adverb), we can distinguish three other basic constructions, which differ from Type I according to the kind of verb utilized in the sentence.

Type II:

1. SUBJECT	2. VERB (*be*)	3. PREDICATE	4. ADVERB
Charles	*is*	*here*	*today*
Charles	*is*	*in Vienna*	*today*
Charles	*is*	*happy*	*today*
Charles	*is*	*a good boy*	*today*

Sentences of Type II are formed with the verb *be* followed by a construction referred to as a **predicate**, which may be either an expression of location (*here, in Vienna*), an adjective (*happy*), or a noun phrase (*a good boy*).

Type III:

1. SUBJECT	2. VERB	3. COMPLEMENT	4. ADVERB
Charles	*looks*	*ill*	*today*
The milk	*tastes*	*fresh*	*today*

The characteristic feature of Type III is that the verb is followed not by an object but by a complement which modifies the subject of the sentence.

Type IV:

1. SUBJECT	2. VERB	3. OBJECT, PREDICATE, COMPLEMENT	4. ADVERB
The leaves	*fall*	$\emptyset$	*in the autumn*
My head	*aches*	$\emptyset$	*terribly*

In sentences of Type IV the third slot must stay empty. These sentences are formed with verbs which cannot be followed by a complement, a predicate, or any kind of an object.

The initial attack on syntactical patterns must be concerned with impressing upon the student the importance of the position of the four slots of the basic sentence types. The more complex constructions of English can be derived from the basic ones by operations of expansion or transformation. The most important of those operations will be discussed in the following sections of this chapter. The difficulties encountered by the student will vary according to his native language. We have already mentioned the imposition of native word order upon English as the chief danger. Another important source of error is the possibility of misapplying an English expansion or transformation operation: for example, a student may produce *I *am knowing the rule* (from *I know the rule*) on the basis of *I am working* (from *I work*). Or he may treat an English auxiliary verb like a normal verb: *I *have must go home*; *I must *to go home* (by analogy to *I have decided to go home, I decided to go home*). A third major source of error is the inability to gauge the exact meaning or appropriateness of a construction. In such cases the construction used by the student may be perfectly correct or possible but may simply not fit or express the desired meaning: for example, the distinctions between *I went* and *I have gone*, or between *I go* and *I am going*, are often difficult to grasp. The student's inability to see the contrast between the forms mentioned may lead to sentences like **yesterday I have gone to school at six o'clock*, or **I am studying for two hours every day.* (instead of *I study*). We shall point out the most difficult constructions and typical sources of errors in the subsequent discussion.

(B)   THE NOUN PHRASE

1. Basic Uses and Expansions

The noun phrase, the nucleus or center of which is a noun, is one of the basic elements of the English sentence. It can be used as the subject of any sentence: *my good old friend lives in Vienna*. It can be the predicate of a sentence after the verb *be*: *Charles is my good old friend*. It can appear after prepositions in the predicate: *Charles lives in good old Vienna*. It may be a direct object or object of a preposition: *he knows my good old friend*; *he speaks with my good old friend.*

The noun, the nucleus of the noun phrase, can be added to or expanded in different ways. The most frequent expansion is the addition of an adjective or adjectives: *a man* → *a good man* → *a good, intelligent man.*

Any number of adjectives can be added to a noun. They are placed before the noun and they do not agree with the noun by morphological ending. The statements in the last sentence may seem superfluous to the native speaker of English, but there are many languages in which the normal position of the modifying adjective is after the noun and in which adjectives take plural endings (for example, Spanish). Speakers of such languages are sometimes tempted to produce noun phrases such as *the intelligents student, *the students intelligents. By and large, however, adjectives in the English noun phrase offer no major problem.

The noun phrase may also be expanded by adding to it any adverb or expression of location that can be used as a predicate in sentence type II:

The boy is from Vienna.   → *The boy from Vienna . . .*
The boy is here.   → *The boy here . . .*
That man is with my uncle. → *The man with my uncle . . .*

2. Determiners

The major difficulty concerning the English noun phrase is the use of the system of determiners. In our first chapter we defined determiners as the article *the* and all words which can be substituted for the article. This definition must now be supplemented by the consideration that there are several types of determiners and that some (*the, this, my*) are mutually exclusive, while others are not. In other words, once the article *the* has been used it is not possible to use *this* or *my* in the same noun phrase (for example, *the this man, *my this boy), while it is quite possible to say *my three most interesting students*, putting several determiners (*my, three, most*) next to each other.

The groups into which the determiners of English are divided are summarized in the table below. The columns represent the sequence in which the determiners may occur before the noun. We shall deal with two broad problems which are particularly difficult for the foreign student—the choice of number (singular vs. plural) in verb agreement, and the choice of article (*the*, *a*, *an*, or no article).

ENGLISH DETERMINERS

	Determiners				Postdeterminers		
Prede-terminers	Pre-articles	Articles	Demon-stratives	Posses-sives	Cardinal Number	Ordinal Number	Compara-tive, Super-lative
all of	*all*	*a, an*	*this*	*my*	*one*	*first*	*more*
some of	*only*	*the*	*these*	*your*	*two*	*second*	*most*
most of	*most*	*∅*	*that*	*his*	*three*	*third*	*fewer*
much of	*just*	*any*	*those*	*her*	*etc.*	*etc.*	*fewest*
several of		*every*		*its*			*less*
many of		*each*		*our*			*least*
the rest of		*some*		*their*			
a lot of							
(a) few of							
(a) little of							

a. Predeterminers and Number Agreement

Predeterminers are groups of words which must stand first in noun phrases. They are made up of determiners and all contain the word *of* as last element. In spite of the use of the preposition *of* as part of the predeterminers, it is best to consider them as one grammatical unit which is used to modify the noun which is the **center** or main word of the noun phrase that follows. In phrases like *all of the milk* or *all of the boys*, *all of* is a modifier of the following noun; the following noun is the center or **head** of the construction. If predeterminers are used, number agreement depends on the following noun, and the verb becomes singular or plural according to the noun used after the predeterminer:

All of   **the milk**   *is spoiled.*

center (singular)

All of   **the boys**   *are spoiled.*

center (plural)

The rest of   **the milk**   *is spoiled.*
↑
center (singular)

The rest of   **the boys**   *are spoiled.*
↑
center (plural)

The construction **predeterminer + noun (phrase)** should be distinguished quite carefully from the construction **noun phrase + of + noun phrase**. In the latter case the noun of the first noun phrase is of course the center or head of the construction and governs singular/plural agreement.

The   **principles**   *of his work are interesting.*
↑
center (plural)

The   **principle**   *of his works is interesting.*
↑
center (singular)

In our definition of "predeterminer" we have **not** included any construction followed by a prepositional phrase preceded by *of*, in which verb agreement is not determined by the noun in the prepositional phrase. For example, *each (of)*, *every one (of)*, *two grams (of)* are nouns or pronouns followed by a prepositional phrase, but they are not predeterminers:

Each   *of my friends is here.*
↑
Center (singular)

Two   **grams**   *of butter are enough.*
↑
Center (plural)

In actual usage a number of nouns or pronouns used frequently before prepositional phrases starting with *of* are evidently in the process of becoming predeterminers, because many speakers tend to make the singular/plural agreement with the noun in the prepositional phrase: for example, *a number of the books* **are** *missing* (not *is missing*).

It is important for the student of English as a foreign language to distinguish predeterminers from nouns or pronouns followed by *of*. If he is not aware of this distinction, the student will be puzzled about the logic of saying *a few* (which seems to be a singular) *of my friends are* (plural) *here*, but *some* (which seems to imply plural) *of the milk is* (singular) *spoiled*.

Aside from the use of *some* vs. *any* (to be discussed in connection with the interrogative and negative) the student faces two major problems in connection with the determiner system: (1) the choice of singular versus plural (and with it the choice of *many*, (*a*) *few* vs. *much*, (*a*) *little*); and (2) the choice of *the* vs. *a* or zero (omission of the determiner).

b. Count and Mass Nouns and Number Agreement

The singular/plural choice hinges primarily on the understanding of the all-important contrasts between **count nouns** on the one hand and **mass** and **abstract** on the other. The first category comprises things, objects, ideas which can be counted—and can thus be put into the plural: *two tables, three chairs, four books, five friends, six ideas—one table, one chair*. The mass or abstract category comprises all concepts which cannot be counted—and thus cannot be used in the plural: *silver, gold, butter* (mass nouns); *honesty, blindness, knowledge* (abstract nouns). It is impossible to say **one silver, *one honesty, *two knowledges*. This categorization, while obvious to the native speaker, is not at all clear to many non-natives. Mistakes such as *I bought *three inks* (perhaps meaning three bottles of ink) or *I admired his *honesties* (after all, he was honest all the time—not just once) are quite common.

The awareness of count vs. mass/abstract noun must be established by exercises contrasting their usage. Best are exercises in which *much* or *a little* is used to signal the mass/abstract noun and contrasted with the use of *a few* or *many* with count nouns; for example:

TEACHER: *He doesn't have many friends.*
            Energy.
STUDENT: *He doesn't have much energy.*
TEACHER: *Books.*
STUDENT: *He doesn't have many books.*
TEACHER: *Sense.*
STUDENT *He doesn't have much sense.*
TEACHER: *He has a few friends.*

Energy.
STUDENT: *He has a little energy.*
TEACHER: *Books.*
STUDENT: *He has a few books.*
TEACHER: *Sense.*
STUDENT: *He has a little sense.*

Note that the use of *a few, a little* as opposed to *few, little* without *a* is essentially a difference of affirmative vs. negative meaning. For example, *he has a few friends* is an affirmative view of the situation — that is, he does have some — while *he has few friends* is a negative view, equivalent to *he doesn't have many friends.*

Unfortunately, the distinction mass noun (not used in the plural, modified by *much, a little*) versus count noun (used in the plural, modified by *many, a few*) is not always quite so clear-cut. There are many words which can be used both as a mass moun and as a count noun:

MASS NOUN	COUNT NOUN
I drank a lot of coffee.	*I ordered two coffees.*
I ate too much cake.	*Give me two cakes.*
You are using too much paper.	*I bought two papers.*
He doesn't have much hair.	*He has a few gray hairs.*
Much of his verse is bad.	*I memorized two verses.*
He drinks too much Coke.	*He drank three Cokes.*
He eats a lot of fruit.	*Apples and pears are my favorite fruits.*

In all of the above cases the distinction between the mass noun and the count noun use is that the latter refers to a countable finite category: the *coffee* of *I ordered two coffees* (a usage generally restricted to restaurant and cafeteria situations) is a countable portion of coffee and not the mass category. The distinction between the mass and count use must be made clear to the student. At the same time he must also be warned that the double use of both mass and count nouns applies to a limited category of words and cannot be extended beyond the specific usages learned by the student.

c. Collective Nouns and Number Agreement

Another possible singular/plural confusion arises in connection with **collective** nouns, those which are morphologically singular, but are used as plurals: *the people are leaving; the police are here*. In the case of some collectives there is a hesitation between singular and plural even among native speakers: *the class don't know the answer* vs. *the class doesn't know*. The most frequently used collective, and the one which is also likely to present the biggest problem to the non-native, is the word *people*. It is always used as a morphological singular, but with plural agreement when it has the meaning of *persons*:

Many people (persons) understand English.

At the same time the student must also be told that *people* acts like any regular count noun if it is used in the meaning of *nation*:

The peoples (nations) of Europe are not yet united.
The Swiss are a people (nation) that has succeeded in avoiding wars.

Note that certain nationality words, such as *French, English, Swiss, Spanish* (that is, those ending in a sibilant sound), are also used as collective nouns when referring to the people as a whole; for example, *the English are our friends.*

d. The, A (An), or No Article

The problem of choosing among *the, a (an)*, or no article is one of the most complicated for most learners. It is relatively easy only for speakers of German and other Germanic languages in which the use of the definite and indefinite articles corresponds—in a very general way at least—to that of English. But many languages (for example, the Romance languages) use the definite and indefinite articles on a basis quite different from that which determines their use in English, and many languages use neither definite nor indefinite articles (for example, Russian, Japanese). For speakers of such languages the obligatory choice between *the, a* or no article is a puzzling problem indeed.

What makes the problem and its presentation even more complicated is the fact that the exact use and meaning of the articles (including $\emptyset$) cannot always be explained in precise grammatical terms and often depend on the specific context in which an utterance is used. The decision as to whether or not, or how, to use an article depends upon a grasp of concepts which are completely strange and foreign to speakers of languages which do not use articles or use them very differently. Only the main principles governing the use of the articles in English can be explained here.

The main use of the definite article in English is to refer to a specific noun – a noun that has just been mentioned or a noun that is thought of as specific in a particular context: *going down the street I met several children*. **The** *children* (they are now the specific children I met) *were dirty. . . .* Some examples of nouns which are thought of as specific in a context (even though they have not been mentioned previously) are:

> *Please close **the** window and turn on **the** heater!*

It is understood that there are a window and a heater in the room. So the speaker can refer to **the** *window* and **the** *heater*. Possibly an idea like *there are a window and a heater in the room* was on the speaker's mind before he uttered the sentence – but there was no need to express that thought.

In the abovementioned use, the definite article by itself is sufficient to establish the fact that we are referring to a specific person, idea, or object. It is thus often referred to as the **article of complete determination**. In the other main use, the so-called **article of incomplete determination**, the article alone is not sufficient to express the idea of specificity; another element is needed – usually a prepositional phrase or a relative clause:

> *Where is **the** book (which) I lent you?*
> *Is this **the** man from the German department?*
> *I am studying **the** philosophy of Plato.*
> *When you get to the theater talk to **the** man at the desk.*

In the above cases, the definite article could not be used without the following relative clause or prepositional phrase. They are the elements which produce the specific reference. In terms of transformational grammar the article of incomplete determination can be explained exactly like the article of complete determination: the relative clause or the prepositional phrase which follows the noun can be derived from a sentence which contains the noun and which precedes the sentence in which the definite article is used. In other words *where is the book which I lent you?* can be explained as having been generated from the sentences:

> (1) *I lent you a book.* (2) *Where is the book?*

The other examples given can be explained similarly.

> *A man is (here) from the German department. Is this the man?*
> *Plato wrote philosophy. I am studying the philosophy (of Plato).*
> *A man is at the desk. Talk to the man when you get to the theater.*

In addition to the idea of **specificity** as expressed by the definite article *the*, there are two additional concepts—**indefiniteness** and **generalization**.

Indefiniteness is illustrated in sentences such as: *I am drinking milk* (indefinite quantity); *I am eating an apple* (not a specific one); *I am eating apples* (indefinite number).

Generalization (statement made about a category as a whole) is illustrated in statements such as: *milk is a very healthy food*; *the apple is the best fruit produced in this country*; *apples are my favorite food*.

The following table summarizes the most typical ways in which the ideas of specificity, indefiniteness, and generalization are expressed in English:

		Specificity	*Generalization*	*Indefiniteness*
Mass Nouns	Singular	*the*	no article	no article
	Plural	—	— —	— —
Count Nouns	Singular	*the*	*(the)*	*a*
	Plural	*the* ·	no article	no article

Additional examples of each usage:

Specificity

Mass nouns:	*I like the coffee from Brazil.*
	The coffee that comes from Brazil is the best.
Count nouns:	*Where is the pencil I lent you?*
	Where are the pencils I lent you?
	He gave me a pen and a pencil. Well, I lost the pencil and I had to write with the pen.

Generalization

Mass nouns:	*Coffee is very expensive in the United States.*
	Milk is now quite a bit cheaper.
	I do like coffee, but I don't like milk.
Count nouns:	*The pencil was not invented until the nineteenth century.*
	Pencils were not invented until the nineteenth century.
	Pencils are very expensive, pens are a lot cheaper.

Indefiniteness

Mass nouns: *Are you drinking **coffee** or **milk**?*
                     *Please give me **coffee**.*

Count nouns: *Could you lend me **a pencil**?*
                     *Don't write with **a pen**, write with **a red pencil**.*
                     *My secretary uses **pens** and **pencils** as if they*
                         didn't cost anything.
                     *For dinner we are eating **tomatoes** and **cucumbers**.*

The concepts of specificity, generalization and indefiniteness and the corresponding usages must be contrasted in special exercises:

Indefiniteness → Specificity

> *I need **a pencil**. Where is **the pencil** I lent you?*
> *I need **a notebook**. Where is **the notebook** I lent you?*
> *I need **pencils**. Where are **the pencils** I lent you?*

Generalization → Specificity

> *I am studying **philosophy**, especially **the philosophy** of Plato.*
> *I am studying **history**, especially **the history** of the United States.*

Generalization → Indefiniteness

> *I like **coffee**; that's why I am drinking **coffee** right now.*
> *I like **pears**; that's why I am eating **a pear** right now.*
> *I like **eggs**; that's why I am eating **eggs** right now.*

The mistakes made by the student may range from complete confusion of *a, the,* or lack of articles to some very systematic errors due to usage in the native language. For example, the use of the definite article for generalization in the Romance languages accounts for typically Spanish or French mistakes such as: *I study *the philosophy,* or *the water is necessary to sustain life.*

The abovementioned rules do not account for all the English uses of the article. The following are some of the additional ones:

1. Generally speaking, English does not use an article with proper names, that is, names of persons, cities, countries, states, etc. For example, ***Mary** is my friend*; ***Professor Jones** teaches history*; ***New York** is a big city*; ***Canada** is in North America*; ***Mt. Hood** is in Oregon*; ***Chicago** is on Lake Michigan.*

However, this general rule does not hold in the following cases: names of rivers (*the Mississippi is our longest river*); names of mountain ranges (*the Alps are in Switzerland and Austria*); oceans (*the Pacific is the largest ocean*); names of countries which have a plural form (*the United States, the Netherlands*). Furthermore, in cases where specificity is indicated, the article may be used even with proper names with which it is not normally used: *I know two girls named Mary Jones; the Mary Jones in my history class has blond hair. The state of Maine has a town called Paris, named after the Paris in France.* This usage follows that explained previously in discussing nouns with post-modification.

When surnames are used in the plural to denote a family, *the* is required: *The Browns are our neighbors.*

2. Names of languages follow the general rule for proper names; that is, no article, unless they precede the word *language*, in which case they function as adjectives, and the rule does not apply: *English is a difficult language; the English language is difficult.*

Words denoting the people of a particular nation often coincide with the name of the language spoken there. When these words have a plural form (*German, Germans; Italian, Italians*), the singular form is used without the article for the language, while the plural form, with or without the article, refers to the people. However, certain nationality words ending in sibilant sounds (such as *French, English, Spanish*) have no plural forms. Therefore, the use of the word without an article for the language is normal, while the use of the article is mandatory when referring to the people:

> *Professor Jones teaches Spanish.*
> *The Spanish are not the only people who speak Spanish.*
> *Italian is a musical language.*
> *Italians usually like music.*
> *The Italians are friendly people.*

3. Articles are not used with names of sports and games: for example: *John likes to play football; tennis is a popular sport; Steve likes to play chess.* However, if words such as *football, baseball,* etc., are used to refer to the objects used in the game, the normal rule for count nouns applies: *you can't play football without a football.*

Note that with names of musical instruments the article may be used or omitted: *do you play (the) piano? Mary plays (the) violin.*

*Tommy is learning to play (**the**) **clarinet***. When any of these terms for sports, games, or musical instruments are used before another noun (that is, as adjectives), the basic rule applies: *I went to **the football game**; **the chess board** is in the closet; let's sit on **the piano bench***.

4. The article is omitted in certain fixed expressions such as *go to school, go to church, go to bed, stay in bed, go to town*. Most of the words used in such expressions are count nouns and therefore the omission of the article is not accounted for according to the basic rule. Note that the expressions *go to school, go to church* refer to attending the specific activities which are typical for those locations. It is possible to use *go to the church, go to the school* when reference is to the building rather than the function: for example, *the children **go to school** every day; Mrs. Jones went **to the school** to attend a committee meeting; we **go to church** every Sunday; on Thursdays I **go to the church** for choir practice*.

3. Nominalization

The most typical English way of converting a verb into a noun is the use of the *-ing* form, or gerund. A persistent and common error is the use of the simple form of the verb or of *to* + verb (equated by the student with the **infinitive**) where only the *-ing* form is permissible.

The student must be taught that the verb form used after prepositions is the *-ing* form, not the form (*to*) + verb: *without paying attention*, not **without to pay attention*. Drills impressing correct English usage on the student can be substitution drills in which the prepositions are changed upon cues by the teacher:

TEACHER: *He left after saying goodbye.*
Without.
STUDENT: *He left without saying goodbye.*
TEACHER: *Before.*
STUDENT: *He left before saying goodbye.*

In other types of drills students can be asked to combine sentences by using prepositions:

TEACHER: *He left, but he didn't say goodbye.*
STUDENT: *He left without saying goodbye.*
TEACHER: *He said goodbye. Then he left.*
STUDENT: *He left after saying goodbye.*

Simple gerunds may be either count or mass nouns: *wrestling* (mass noun) *is a sport*; *the bill was passed after two* **readings** (count noun). Many of the gerund forms present problems because they may be used either as count nouns or as mass nouns, with slightly different meanings: *his* **teaching** (mass noun) *is excellent*; *it is difficult to understand his* **teachings** (count noun); *his* **writing** (mass noun) *is illegible*; *we have read several of his* **writings** (count noun).

In addition to simple gerunds, English also uses more complicated gerund constructions, in which the gerund is accompanied by an expression of the subject or object of the action. The derivation of such gerunds from declarative sentences has been studied in detail by transformational grammarians. While their exact classification need not concern us here, we can use the derivational processes in exercises teaching the meaning and use of these *-ing* constructions:

> *Charles* (1) **sang** (2) *the songs* (3) *beautifully* (4).
> *His* (1) *beautiful* (4) **singing** (2) *of the songs* (3) . . .
>
> *The rioters* (1) **shouted** (2) *the slogans* (3) *loudly* (4).
> *The rioters'* (1) *loud* (4) **shouting** (2) *of the slogans* (3) . . .
>
> *They* (1) **questioned** (2) *the prisoner* (3) *mercilessly* (4).
> *Their* (*the*) (1) *merciless* (4) **questioning** (2) *of the prisoner* (3) . . .

In the above examples, note that the *-ing* forms are preceded by either a determiner or a possessive form corresponding to the subject of the sentence from which the construction is derived; that the object of the original sentence becomes the object of the preposition *of*; and that the manner adverbial (*-ly* adverb) of the original sentence becomes an adjective preceding the *-ing* form.

When the verb is used with the auxiliary *have*, the adverb cannot be changed to an adjective:

John (1) **has missed** (2) *the English class* (3) *frequently* (4).
John's (1) **having missed** (2) *the English class* (3) *frequently* (4) *may cause him to fail the course.*

He (1) **has answered** (2) *my question* (3) *correctly* (4).
His (1) **having answered** (2) *my question* (3) *correctly* (4) *surprises me.*

Mary (1) **has studied** (2) *French* (3) *for many years* (4).
Mary's (1) **having studied** (2) *French* (3) *for many years* (4) *impressed her friends.*

When adverbial expressions other than those of manner are used, the sequence of sentence elements remains the same:

John (1) **traveled** (2) *to Europe* (3) *by ship* (4).
John's (1) **traveling** (2) *to Europe* (3) *by ship* (4) *was unexpected.*

The guests (1) **arrived** (2) *at midnight* (3).
The guests' (1) **arriving** (2) *at midnight* (3) *was annoying.*

Mary (1) **met** (2) *her friend* (3) *in Washington* (4).
Mary's (1) **meeting** (2) *her friend* (3) *in Washington* (4) *was a surprise.*

A general statement in which *it* anticipates the verb can be converted to a sentence using an -*ing* form in subject position:

It (1) *is* (2) *difficult* (3) **to learn** (4) *English* (5).
Learning (4) *English* (5) *is* (2) *difficult* (3).

It (1) *is* (2) *important* (3) **to speak** (4) *clearly* (5).
Speaking (4) *clearly* (5) *is* (2) *important* (3).

It (1) *is* (2) *interesting* (3) **to teach** (4) *foreign students* (5).
Teaching (4) *foreign students* (5) *is* (2) *interesting* (3).

Another **verb → noun** transformation which occurs with sufficient regularity to be performed as an exercise by the student is the formation of a nominal of agency:

John (1) **writes** (2) *music* (3) *quite successfully* (4).
John (1) *is a successful* (4) **writer** (2) *of music* (3).

That company (1) **produces** (2) *books* (3) *very efficiently* (4).
That company (1) *is a very efficient* (4) **producer** (2) *of books* (3).

The agency transformation derives nouns which are animate or are considered animate; they are also all count nouns (therefore, *John is a writer*).

(C)   THE VERB PHRASE

In the discussion of the verb phrase we will deal only with those aspects most likely to cause difficulty for the foreign student: (1) the basic types of verbs and their constructions; (2) the modifications of the basic forms (which leads to the **tense** system of English); (3) the connections between verb phrases (*I begin to write*); and (4) the use of adverbs.

1. Basic Types of Verbs

As we have pointed out previously, the verb occupies the second slot of the basic English sentence and belongs to one of four basic types: Type I, verbs which can be followed by objects, Type II, the verb *be* followed by a predicate; Type III, verbs followed by a subject complement (an adjective)—for example, *he looks good*; and Type IV, verbs which are not followed by either an object or a complement—for example, *my head aches*—but may be followed by an adverb (*my head aches terribly*).

Depending on his native language, the student may confuse these four basic types in various ways and assign an expression to the wrong pattern. He may use Type I instead of Type IV (**my head aches to me*), or he may assign a sentence to Type IV instead of Type III.

>**He seems_____intelligently,* instead of
>*He seems intelligent_____.*

In teaching Type II, the verb *be* followed by a predicate, certain English usages must be drilled; for example, the use of words such as *cold, hot, hungry, thirsty,* and expressions of age, which in many languages (for instance, the Romance languages) are expressed with the verb *have.* For example:

TEACHER:	STUDENT:
John is hungry.	*John is hungry.*
Cold.	*John is cold.*
Thirsty.	*John is thirsty.*
Twenty years old.	*John is twenty years old.*

In addition, the various uses of *it is* (*it's*) for expressing time, weather, season, distance, identity, etc., must be practiced:

It's eight o'clock.	*It's far from here.*
It's Monday.	*It's thirty-five miles to San Francisco.*
It's July.	*It's a short distance from here.*
It's summer.	*It's Mary on the telephone.*
It's cloudy.	*It's the mailman at the door.*

Verbs of Types III and IV can usually also appear as Type I when followed by a preposition. However, they must be learned in groups and differentiated from one another according to whether they are followed by an adjective or an adverb. For example:

TYPE III	TYPE IV
He seems intelligent.	*My head aches terribly.*
He appears cold.	*John sleeps soundly.*
She looks pretty.	*The music played softly.*
He became angry.	*He laughs easily.*
He grew tall.	*They spoke softly.*
They remained silent.	*He walks slowly.*
It tasted good.	*They listened carefully.*
The music sounds beautiful.	*She smiled sweetly.*

Verbs of Types III and IV can be effectively practiced in substitution exercises:

TEACHER:	STUDENT:
He seems kind.	*He seems kind.*
Good.	*He seems good.*
Intelligent.	*He seems intelligent.*
Answered.	*He answered intelligently.*
Angrily.	*He answered angrily.*
Look.	*He looks angry.*
Speak.	*He speaks angrily.*
Carefully.	*He speaks carefully.*
Seem.	*He seems careful.*
Listened.	*He listened silently.*
Remained.	*He remained silent.*
Calm.	*He remained calm.*
Spoke.	*He spoke calmly.*

However, the major problems of verbs arise in connection with those of Type I (verbs followed by nouns), which may be divided into various subclasses; confusion among these subclasses is quite common. The most frequent constructions of Type I (with some examples of the verbs which occur in each type) are:

a. Verb + Noun:

> *He broke the dish.*
> *She answered the question.*

(Many verbs can occur in this construction, as well as in one or more of the others.)

b. Verb + Noun + Preposition + Noun:

(1) **Verb + noun +** *to* or *for* **+ noun**

    1.1 Convertible to **Verb + Noun + Noun**:

        *She **gave** the book to Charles > She **gave** Charles the book.*

        (**Verbs +** *to*: *give, sell, read, tell, teach, send,* etc.)

        *He **bought** a book for me > He **bought** me a book.*

        (**Verbs +** *for*: *buy, get, make, fix, bake, fry,* etc.)

    1.2 Not convertible:

        *She **explained** the lesson to Charles.*

        (**Verbs +** *to*: *explain, repeat, announce, introduce,* etc.)

        *She **answered** the question for Charles.*

        (**Verbs +** *for*: *answer, open, close, pronounce,* etc.)

(2) **Verb + noun + other preposition + noun**:

    Not convertible:

        *He **expected** a letter from John.*

        *She **heard** a rumor about John.*

        (*Hear, receive, expect,* etc.)

c. Verb + Noun + Noun:

(1) Not convertible to any other type:

    1.1 *They **elected** John president.*

        (*Elect, choose, name,* etc.)

    1.2 Adjective can be substituted for second noun:

        *She **considered** Charles a genius.*

        *She **considered** Charles intelligent.*

        (*Consider, think, call,* etc.)

(2) Conversion from Type I-b-1.1:

        *She **baked** John a cake < She **baked** a cake for John.*

        *She **gave** John a book < She **gave** a book to John.*

(3) One additional verb which must be noted here because of its
    frequent occurrence is *ask*:

        *She **asked** him a question.*

        *She **asked** him a favor.*

    (*Ask* may be converted to Type I-b using the preposition *of — she*
    asked *a favor* **of** *him —* but this is relatively rare.)

The errors committed by the foreign student may be of various
types. For one, he may simply use the wrong construction on the basis
of his native language habits. For example, in French, *obey* (*obéir*) is
followed by a preposition; therefore, the French speaker may say

*I obey *to the teacher*, just as he may say *I am asking a question *to you* on the basis of the French construction in which the verb meaning *ask* must be followed by the preposition meaning *to*.

Another problem is created by the fact that while the examples for Type I-c have a superficial similarity, they differ as follows: Type I-c-1.1 cannot be converted to any other type; Type I-c-1.2 cannot be converted, but it is possible to substitute an adjective for the second noun; verbs of type I-c-2 can be converted to I-b-1.1 with either *to* or *for*. On the basis of this surface similarity the student may make certain kinds of errors. He has learned, for example, that both *she gave the book to Charles* and *she gave Charles the book* are possible sentences. He may therefore be tempted to change *she bought Charles the book, she asked Charles a question* to *she bought the book *to Charles, she asked a question *to Charles*. In a similar way, the student may also be tempted to change Type I-b-1.2 to Type I-c: *She explained *Charles the lesson.*

The best way to counteract this tendency is to avoid practicing the seemingly identical constructions in the same exercise. Constructions like *she gave Charles the book* and *she bought Charles the book* should not be taught together. Instead, the constructions with prepositions should first be practiced in separate exercises, followed by transformation exercises demonstrating that these different constructions can be transformed into the **noun + noun** type. For example:

TEACHER:	STUDENT:
Us. He explained the problem.	*He explained the problem to us.*
Me. She described her work.	*She described her work to me.*
Charles. She introduced me.	*She introduced me to Charles.*
The class. I announced the test.	*I announced the test to the class.*
The police. He reported the accident.	*He reported the accident to the police.*

Or:

TEACHER:	STUDENT:
I gave the book to Charles.	*I gave the book to Charles.*
Sent.	*I sent the book to Charles.*
Read.	*I read the book to Charles.*
Letter.	*I read the letter to Charles.*
Wrote.	*I wrote the letter to Charles.*
Gave.	*I gave the letter to Charles.*

Bicycle.	*I gave the bicycle to Charles.*
Sold.	*I sold the bicycle to Charles.*

Then:

TEACHER:	STUDENT:
Answer with complete sentences, using the construction without **to** *wherever possible:*	
Did she give the book to Charles.	*Yes, she gave Charles the book.*
Did she sell the car to Charles?	*Yes, she sold Charles the car.*
Did she explain the lesson to Charles?	*Yes, she explained the lesson to Charles.*
Did she teach the lesson to Charles?	*Yes, she taught Charles the lesson.*
Did she repeat the instructions to Charles?	*Yes, she repeated the instructions to Charles.*
Did she read the story to Charles?	*Yes, she read Charles the story.*
Did she introduce her sister to Charles?	*Yes, she introduced her sister to Charles.*
Did she write a letter to Charles?	*Yes, she wrote Charles a letter.*

The construction requiring *for* can be practiced similarly:

TEACHER:	STUDENT:
Mary. I answered the question.	*I answered the question for Mary.*
Tommy. I opened the door.	*I opened the door for Tommy.*
Me. The bank cashed a check.	*The bank cashed a check for me.*
John. I bought a gift.	*I bought a gift for John.*
The class. The teacher pronounced the word.	*The teacher pronounced the word for the class.*

Then:

TEACHER:	STUDENT:
Did you buy a book for Mary?	*Yes, I bought her a book.*
Did you answer a question for Mary?	*Yes, I answered a question for her.*
Did you bake a cake for Mary?	*Yes, I baked her a cake.*
Did you open the window for Mary?	*Yes, I opened the window for her.*

Did you fry some eggs for Mary?	*Yes, I fried her some eggs.*
Did you close the door for Mary?	*Yes, I closed the door for her.*

For some students the surface similarity of types I-c-1.1 and I-c-1.2 may also cause problems. It must be made clear to the student that in construction I-c-1.2 the second noun (which may be replaced by an adjective) is merely descriptive of the preceding noun (*Charles* = *genius*) and does not allow the same types of transformations as construction I-c-1.1. For example, in I-c-1.1 the second noun can appear as the subject of a related passive sentence (*a president was elected*); in I-c-1.2 it cannot (**a genius was considered*). Again, it is important not to practice types I-c-1.1 and 1.2 with the rest of the **verb** + **noun** + **noun** constructions (such as *they gave the student the book*), but to drill it in exercises which make the meaning and special nature of the construction quite clear; for example:

TEACHER:	STUDENT:
Is Charles a genius?	*No, but they call him a genius.*
Is Charles a liar?	*No, but they call him a liar.*
Is Charles stupid?	*No, but they call him stupid.*

In other exercises the teacher can cue the verb to be used in the reply:

TEACHER:	STUDENT:
Is John their leader?	
Consider.	*They consider him their leader.*
Is John their president?	
Elect.†	*They elected him their president.*
Is John their friend?	
Call.	*They call him their friend.*
Is John chairman of the committee?	
Name.†	*They named him chairman of the committee.*
Is John captain of the team?	
Choose.	*They chose him captain of the team.*

---

†(Note that in this exercise verbs of Type I-c-1.1 require the use of a past form in the response, while those of Type I-c-1.2 do not.)

Another problem is created by the fact that very often the same verb may be used in several of the different construction types. For example, we can say *the door gave* or *the bank closed* using the verbs *give* and *close* in constructions without object (Type IV). However, if we say *he gave the book to his friend*, we are using *give* in the construction **Verb + Noun + to + Noun** (Type I-b-1.1). And in the sentence *he closed the window for his friend* we use *close* in the construction type **Verb + Noun + for + Noun** (I-b-1.2). In each of the two construction types the verbs appear with a different meaning. This switching of meaning according to the construction type in which a verb appears is one of the most confusing aspects of English, interfering with correct production and also—especially in the initial stages of learning—with the student's comprehension. Therefore, the various meanings of the same word in different constructions must be contrasted for the student in special exercises. For example:

> *My coffee got cold.* (Type III)
> *I got a letter.* (Type I-a)
> *I can get you a ticket.* (Type I-c-2)

Closely connected with and similar to the abovementioned problems (caused by different meanings for the same verb in different types of constructions) is the use of the so-called two-part verbs, which must be contrasted with the use of **verb + prepositional phrase**, and **verb + adverb**. The following cases must be quite clearly distinguished:

1. The verb and the preposition form a unit which must be considered as a single verb, and may not be separated:

> (a) *We talked about the problem.   We talked about it.*
>   *He looks like his mother.   He looks like her.*
>   *He called on my parents.   He called on them.*

> (b) *The man talked to Charles.   He talked to him.*
>   *They listened to the music.   They listened to it.*
>   *She looked at the book.   She looked at it.*

In group (a) above, the preposition modifies the meaning of the verb, or creates a new meaning; for example, *talk about = discuss; look like = resemble; call on = visit*. In group (b), however, the meaning of the verb itself is not affected by the preposition, and the preposition is required only when a noun follows; for example, in the sentences *John talks slowly* and *I talked to John* the basic meaning of *talk* (communicate orally) is the same. On the other hand, *talk + about* implies the additional meaning of exchanging ideas or discussion.

2. The verb and the preposition still form a single unit, particularly in meaning, but the preposition can be separated from the verb by the noun in a statement:

> *They filled out the forms.   They filled the forms out.*
> *He put on his coat.   He put his coat on.*
> *He got across the idea.   He got the idea across.*

In the above examples, the placement of the preposition either before or after the noun is optional. However, if a pronoun is used, it must precede the preposition:

> *He put on his coat.*⎫
> *He put his coat on.*⎭   but: *He put it on.*

In this respect, this class of verbs is quite different from the ones mentioned under (1) above, where the pronoun always stands in exactly the same position as the noun:

> *He talked about the problem.   He talked about it.*

3. The preposition which follows the verb is not connected with the verb, but forms part of a prepositional expression with the following noun:

> *He lived in Austria.*
> *He walked down the street.*
> *He traveled by train.*
> *He sat on the chair.*

In cases like those above, a pronoun would normally replace a noun in exactly the same position (*He sat on the chair*; *he sat on it.*) The preposition could never be put after the noun which depends on it.

4. The verb is followed by a preposition (or an adverb) which is not followed by another noun:

> (a) *The rain let up.*
> *The fire went out.*
> *The engine blew up.*

> (b) *He jumped down.*
> *He came in.*
> *He drove away.*

The combinations in group (a) form a single meaning unit; they are two-part verbs. The adverbs in group (b), however, are not part of the verb, and the fact that some adverbs can also be used as prepositions (*in the house*) adds to the difficulties of the student.

Students often are confused by the situations just described: 1(a) nonseparable two-part verb; 1(b) verb requiring preposition only when object follows; 2. separable two-part verb; 3. verb + prepositional expression; 4. verb plus preposition or adverb. The result is that often the wrong expression is used, or the wrong transformation applied: *did he talk about the problem? *Yes, he talked it about.* To avoid this type of mistake, the categories discussed above must be clearly distinguished.

The nonseparable two-part 1(a) verbs such as *look like, talk about, call on* should be learned and treated throughout as single vocabulary items. Visual aids can be employed to impress upon the student that they form one unit. The visual help may include use of identical colors, underlining, etc., or boxes drawn around the nonseparable items:

He $\boxed{looks\ like}$ *his father.*

We $\boxed{talked\ about}$ *the problem.*

Verbs in this group should be practiced with two purposes in mind: (1) to establish their meanings; and (2) to emphasize their nonseparable character:

TEACHER:	STUDENT:
Does Mary resemble her father?	*Yes, she looks like him.*
Did John visit his friend?	*Yes, he called on him.*
Did the boys discuss their project?	*Yes, they talked about it.*

Verbs in group 1(b) may be practiced in exercises showing their use with and without prepositions:

TEACHER:	STUDENT:
The sunset is beautiful. Come and look!	*I'm already looking at it.*
Don't you want to listen to the new record?	*I'm listening now.*
Does the teacher smile at the students?	*Yes, she always smiles.*
Does Bob talk a lot?	*He talks to me a lot, but not to others.*

Separable two-part verbs can be distinguished from the nonseparable ones by a dotted line drawn between the two parts; for example:

$$He \boxed{called \vdots up} \; his \; friend.$$

Or some other device, such as partly identical underlining, may be used:

$$He \underline{called} \; \underline{up} \; his \; friend.$$

The optional placement of the noun object and the obligatory placement of the pronoun object must be drilled in exercises such as:

TEACHER:	STUDENT:
*Did he **call up** Mary?*	*Yes, he **called** Mary **up**.*
*Did he **put on** his coat?*	*Yes, he **put** his coat **on**.*
*Did you **fill out** the form?*	*Yes, I **filled** the form **out**.*

followed by:

TEACHER:	STUDENT:
*Did he **call up** Mary?*	*Yes, he **called** her **up**.*
*Did he **put on** his coat?*	*Yes, he **put** it **on**.*
*Did you **fill out** the form?*	*Yes, I **filled** it **out**.*

Another very serious problem is created by the fact that a number of English verbs combine with many different prepositions or adverbs to form two-part verbs with a variety of meanings, and that quite often a verb can combine with the same preposition or adverb in two or more of the various constructions discussed above.

To give complete lists of the possible two-part verb combinations would go beyond the scope of this discussion. However, as an illustration of the magnitude of the problem, the sample sentences below will demonstrate the most important uses of just one verb — *get* — both in nonseparable two-part combinations and in two-part separable combinations:

Get in nonseparable combinations:

> *I **get up** in the morning.*
> *Let's **get on** the bus.*
> *Let's **get on** with the work.*
> *Charles does not **get on** with those people.*
> *He **gets along** with them.*
> *The criminal **got off** free.*

> *Let's **get in**.*
> *Let's **get out**.*
> *Let's **get out** of the car.*
> *Charles manages to **get around** his parents.*
> *John will **get over** his cold in a few days.*
> *The criminal **got away**.*
> *She will not be able to **get away** with this behavior.*
> *He works just enough to **get by**.*
> *We will **get back** in time for the movies.*
> *Let's **get together** at three o'clock.*
> *He can't **get down** the stairs unassisted.*

Get in separable combinations:

> *When will you **get** Charles **up**?*
> *I can't **get** the medicine **down**.*
> *Let me **get** the message **down** on paper.*
> *I cannot **get** these shoes **on**.*
> *He'll **get** the letter **off** by tomorrow.*
> *The publisher will **get** this book **out** by spring.*
> *Let's **get** this exam **over** with.*
> *When will we **get** the book **back**?*
> *I'll try to **get** a meal **together** by eight.*

The above partial list shows that many two-part verb combinations exist in both separable and nonseparable form, typically with very different meanings: *he **got off** the bus* (nonseparable); *he **got** the letter **off*** (separable). In addition, the preposition used as part of the two-part verb may also be used as part of a prepositional phrase in conjunction with the same verb: *he **got off** the fence*.

Two-part verb combinations present a major problem in comprehension because understanding a sentence depends on the correct interpretation of the preposition or its place in the sentence. They present an even larger problem in correct production, since the high degree of similarity among expressions such as *get up, get on, get off* is likely to prove confusing to the student.

Probably the best way of treating the problem is **not** to spend a great deal of time in specifically contrasting expressions like *get out, get in, get off* or *make up, make out, make off* in the initial phases of instruction. Such contrasting is only likely to confuse the student and leave him with the awareness that words like *make up, make out, make off* mean very different things—but which means what? After different two-part verbs or different uses of similar two-part verbs have been introduced at spaced intervals, special exercises can be introduced to eliminate difficulties and confusions and to contrast the different meanings of the separable vs. nonseparable uses; for example: *he gave up smoking* vs. *he gave up in the last round.*

Also, the pronoun replacement in the separable and nonseparable two-part verbs, as well as in the preposition + noun combinations, must be drilled in special exercises:

Turn	*the television*	*on!*	*Turn*	*it*	*on!*
Put	*your coat*	*on!*	*Put*	*it*	*on!*
Get	*the letter*	*off!*	*Get*	*it*	*off!*

But:

Get on	*the train*	*!*	*Get on*	*it*	*!*
Look at	*the book*	*!*	*Look at*	*it*	*!*
Get off	*the table*	*!*	*Get off*	*it*	*!*

2. The Verb and its Modifications (The System of Tenses)

The English verb has only two basic tenses: a **past tense** (*I bought, I laughed*) and a tense usually referred to as **present** but which perhaps should be called a **nonpast** (*I buy, I laugh*). The term nonpast seems preferable in many ways, because normally the use of this tense does **not** imply that an action is going on at the present moment, but rather that it is a repeated or habitual action; for example, the conversational exchange: *do you buy your suits at Macy's?; yes, I buy them there all the time* does not imply that the action of buying is going on at that moment. Rather, it implies that the interlocutor *has bought* and *will continue to buy* his suits at Macy's. *I buy* contrasts simply as nonpast with *I bought*—which relegates the action to the past: *last year I bought two suits at Macy's; I liked them very much* (past)—*so I still buy my suits there* (nonpast).

The other tenses of English are created by modification of the two basic tenses through auxiliaries. Thus the **past modification** consists of replacing the simple (nonpast) forms of the verbs with the corresponding form of *have*, while the verb that is being replaced becomes a past participle. Thus, the past modification of the nonpast forms the **perfect tense**, and the past modification of the past produces the **past perfect**.

Nonpast   **Perfect**
He speaks ⇒ *He has spoken*
Past   **Past Perfect**
He spoke ⇒ *He had spoken*

Perhaps the best way to approach the meaning of the English perfect tense is to point out that it is a past modification of the present tense. In other words, relevance to the present time is indeed the main characteristic of the tense: **it implies that an action is relevant to the present** and **that the exact time at which it happened in the past is irrelevant.**

A: *Have you done your homework?*
B: *Yes, I have done it.*

A is inquiring whether B is at present a person who at some time in the past (just when does not matter) has done his homework. B is replying that indeed he **is** a person who has done his homework.

Note, however, that the past tense immediately replaces the perfect if the time of the past event becomes relevant.

A: *Have you done your homework?*
B: *Yes, I have done it. I did it between four and five o'clock.*

Or:

A: *When did you do your homework?*
B: *I did it while I was in school.*

The past tense rather than the perfect will thus normally be used in a question beginning with *when* (since the question makes the exact time of the action relevant) and it is also normally used in statements which contain a specific reference to a past time: *yesterday*; *last year*; *last June*; *in 1965*; *I spoke to him yesterday*; *I studied in Vienna in 1965*.

If the statement makes reference to a time not yet completed (*today*, *so far*, *this year*, *not yet*), the use of the perfect is more likely: *I have visited him twice this month*; *I have not yet read his book.*

The contrasting uses of the past and the perfect can be drilled in exercises such as the following:

TEACHER: *Have you spoken to Robert?*
STUDENT: *Yes, I have (spoken to him).*
TEACHER: *When did you speak to him?*
STUDENT: *I spoke to him at six o'clock.*
TEACHER: *Have you read his book?*

STUDENT: *Yes, I have (read it).*
TEACHER: *When did you read it?*
STUDENT: *I read it last night.*

The use of the past perfect is somewhat difficult to explain to some foreign students (except for speakers of some European languages such as French and German), particularly because it can frequently be replaced by the simple past: *yesterday I saw Bill; before that I had spoken to Jack; (before that I spoke to Jack).* Specifying that an action took place before another action, event, or time in the past does not always seem relevant to speakers of some Oriental languages, for example.

The past perfect may be practiced by setting up a hypothetical point in the past and having the students make sentences referring to actions previous to that point; for example:

TEACHER: *You left your country six months ago. Tell about your activities before you left, using words such as **study**, **pack**, **attend**, **obtain**.*
STUDENT: *Before I left home I had studied English for three months. I had packed my clothes. I had attended the university. I had obtained a visa.*

Another modification which is likely to cause trouble for many students is the **progressive**, the replacement of a verb form by the corresponding form of *be* and the *-ing* form of the verb that is being replaced:

Progressive form

He writes	⇒ *He is writing*
He wrote	⇒ *He was writing*
He will write	⇒ *He will be writing*
He has written	⇒ *He has been writing*
He had written	⇒ *He had been writing*

Since many languages do not have special forms for the progressive aspect of the verb, distinctions such as *he writes* vs. *he is writing* or *he wrote* vs. *he was writing* are difficult for many students to grasp. The exact differences between the progressive and nonprogressive forms are often quite subtle, and the exact meaning of the progressive modification is still a matter of contention and debate among grammarians. Perhaps the best way of approaching the meaning of the progressive form is to emphasize the meaning of the *-ing* form used in the progressive tenses: **the *-ing* form refers to an action which—at the moment referred to by the speaker—has already started but is not yet finished**. In other words, it does indeed represent the action **in progress.**

I am writing a letter to my friend stresses the point that *I have started writing the letter* and that *I am still doing it*. In that sense, *I am writing* is the real present tense of English—as opposed to *I write*, which, as mentioned earlier, simply asserts that the action is not entirely in the past: *what do you usually do if you are bored?; I write to my friend*. It is only the present progressive which really refers to an action going on at the present moment: *what are you doing right now?; I am writing a letter.*

The present progressive can also be extended to refer to an activity occurring **within a time period including the present moment** (though not actually **at** the present moment), but not yet completed:

> *This year **I'm studying** history and anthropology.*
> *This term John **is working** on his dissertation.*

In a similar way, the past progressive refers to an action which had started but was not yet completed at a given moment. We can contrast a sentence such as *when he phoned I was writing a letter* with a statement like *whenever I felt bored I wrote to my friends*. It is only in the first of these statements that the progressive can be used to convey the idea of noncompletion.

A very special problem arises in connection with the use of the progressive modification of a past modification:

> *I have written* → *I have been writing*
> *I had written* → *I had been writing*

By combining both the past and progressive modifications in forms such as *I have been studying English for two months* or *he has been reading about this for a long time*, the English language is capable of expressing both the past and the progressive aspect of an action— the facts that: (1) **an action has (had) started**; and (2) **is (was) still in progress**. Most languages demand a clear-cut distinction between present and past. Thus to most students forms like the ones quoted above: (*I have been writing, I have (had) been studying*) are quite confusing. Since the action of *I have been studying* refers to an action still in progress, it seems logical to many speakers that a "present tense" (*I study* or *I am studying*) should be used.

The uses of the progressive and past progressive must be drilled in special exercises which make clear the particular meanings implied in the progressive forms. For example:

Simple verb forms (nonpast) vs. present progressive:

TEACHER:	STUDENT:
Do you play soccer?	*Yes, I play soccer.*
Are you playing soccer now?	*No, I am not playing soccer; I am studying English.*
Do you speak Spanish?	*Yes, I speak Spanish.*
Are you speaking Spanish now?	*No, I am not speaking Spanish; I am speaking English.*

Present progressive vs. perfect progressive:

TEACHER:	STUDENT:
Are you studying English?	*Yes, I am studying English.*
When did you start?	*Two months ago. I have been studying English for two months.*
Are you going to X. University?	*Yes, I am going to X. University.*
When did you start?	*A year ago. I have been going to X. University for a year.*

A further problem is created by the fact that there are some verbs — typically verbs expressing states such as *be, know, believe, need, see, like, love, hate, understand* — which are not used in the progressive forms, or at least are used only rarely and with special meanings. Since these verbs denote states rather than actions, there is no need to use them in a modification which emphasizes that the action has started but is not completed. Normally we would not say *I am knowing the truth* or *he is being intelligent*, since *know* and *be* already indicate progressive action or lack of completion. However, the foreign student must be trained not to transfer the progressive tense modification to such verbs. The use of the progressive with some verbs and the lack of such use with others must be contrasted:

TEACHER:	STUDENT:
*Are you **studying** English?*	*Yes, I **am studying** English.*
*Do you **know** your assignment?*	*Yes, I **know** it quite well.*
*Are you **repeating** these sentences?*	*Yes, I **am repeating** these sentences.*

*Do you **understand** these sentences?*	*Yes, I **understand** them.*
*How long **have** you **been studying** here?*	*I **have been studying** for two months.*
*How long **have** you **known** me?*	*I **have known** you for two months.*
*How long **have** you **been following** my course?*	*I **have been following** it for two months.*
*Since when **have** you **understood** my English?*	*I **have understood** it since the beginning.*
*How long **have** you **been living** in the dorm?*	*I **have been living** there for three months.*
*How long **have** you **been** in New York?*	*I **have been** in New York for five months.*

In addition to the past and progressive modifications, English has an array of modal auxiliaries available which can be used to express various aspects of the verb. The English verbal auxiliaries (*must, can, may, might, should*, etc.) offer various and often serious problems to the learner. Only the most important can be discussed in this context.

One of the important stumbling blocks connected with the modal auxiliaries of English is that they are not subject to further tense modification. It is impossible to apply a past or future modification to words like *can, must*, etc. We cannot say: **I will must* or **I have could*. Since in many languages the equivalents of the verbs *must, can*, etc., are expressed by verbs capable of being put into the various tenses, the peculiar manner in which English must work its way around this restriction is often puzzling to the foreigner. In addition, most of the modals lack even a distinctive past tense (*must* has no corresponding simple past), so again English must work its way around the absence of such a form (by using an expression like *had to*). While some modals do have a past form (*could, should* are morphologically the past tenses of *can, shall*), these past tenses do not always have the meaning of a past and are best taught as separate forms **not** related to their nonpast forms.

The following table summarizes in very brief form the main modal auxiliaries of English and the ways which are used to express time differentiations with them.

All the modals in the table can be used with future as well as present meaning (remember that the simple form is a nonpast rather than a

Modal (Nonpast)	Main Meaning	Past Form	Future Modification going to	Perfect Modification with have	Past Modification of Dependent Verb
1. can He can speak (He is able to speak)	ability	could He could speak (He was able to speak)	(He is going to be able to speak)	— (He has been able to speak)	He can have spoken
2. must He must speak (He has to speak)	necessity, obligation	— (He had to speak)	(He is going to be able to speak)	(He has had to speak)	— He must have spoken (supposition)
3. will He will speak	volition, intention (futurity)	— (He would speak) (He would not speak)	—	—	He will have spoken
4. may He may speak	permission, possibility	—	—	—	He may have spoken (possibility only)
5. might He might speak	possibility	—	—	—	He might have spoken
6. should He should speak	advisability, obligation (felt by speaker)	—	—	—	He should have spoken
7. would He would speak	contrary to fact	—	—	—	He would have spoken
8. could He could speak	possibility, ability (contrary to fact)	—	—	—	He could have spoken
†9. ought to He ought to speak	obligation, advisability	—	—	—	He ought to have spoken
‡10. shall He shall speak	(futurity) (command)	—	—	—	He shall have spoken

†Ought is the only one of the modals after which to is used before the main verb.
‡See discussion in text.

present): *I can come tomorrow*; *I must study tomorrow*; *I may go home next week*; *I could help you tomorrow* (*if you need help*); *I should visit my family next month.*

Since the use of *would* as a past of *will* is very limited (*he says he will speak today, although he would not speak yesterday*), only *can* should be taught as having a past form, *could*: *he can answer the question*; *yesterday he couldn't answer the question*; *he could speak Spanish when he was a child, but he can't anymore.* This past tense *could*—frequently occurring in the context *used to be able to*: *John could* (*used to be able to*) *ski before he had the accident*—should be presented to the student quite separately from the form *could* (number 8 in the table) which refers to a **contrary to fact** condition in the present or future: *I could help you* (*if I had the money*). If a student is confused by the two distinct meanings of *could*, they can be contrasted in special exercises. One possible way of teaching the contrast is to cue sentences by the paraphrase *be able*. For example:

TEACHER: *Yesterday Charles **wasn't able to answer** the question.*
STUDENT: *Yesterday Charles **couldn't answer** the question.*
TEACHER: *Charles **would be able to help** me if I wanted him to.*
STUDENT: *Charles **could help** me if I wanted him to.*
TEACHER: *Yesterday we **weren't able to understand** the lecture.*
STUDENT: *Yesterday we **couldn't understand** the lecture.*
TEACHER: *If we knew French we **would be able to understand** him.*
STUDENT: *If we knew French we **could understand** him.*
TEACHER: *Charles **used to be able to speak** French when he was a child.*
STUDENT: *Charles **could speak** French when he was a child.*

If a specific reference to the future is desired, *I'll be able* may be used.

The modal *must* has no past tense, and necessity in the past must be expressed by *had to*. This can be practiced in simple exercises involving a shift from present to past:

TEACHER: *We **must work** carefully today.*
STUDENT: *Yes, we **must**; we **had to work** carefully yesterday, too.*
TEACHER: *We **must study** hard this year.*
STUDENT: *Yes, we **must**; we **had to work** hard last year, too.*
TEACHER: *We **must do** our homework this week.*
STUDENT: *Yes, we **must**; we **had to do** our homework last week, too.*

TEACHER: *You **must go** to the bank tomorrow.*
STUDENT: *Yes, I **must**; I **had to go** to the bank yesterday, too.*

The past of *must* (= *had to*) must be differentiated from *must* + *have* + past participle, which denotes supposition and not obligation or necessity. *Must* may denote supposition even if it is applied to the simple verb form: *Robert must work very hard* may mean obligation (= *Robert has to work very hard*), but it can also imply supposition (*Robert probably works very hard*). However, if *must* is applied to a past modification or to a progressive, it invariably implies supposition. For example, *Robert must be working very hard* and *Robert must have worked very hard* imply supposition, not necessity or obligation. The meaning of *must* + **progressive** or *must* + **past modification** must be made clear in special exercises.

An exercise to practice *must* + **progressive**:

TEACHER: *Robert did not come to class. Why?*
*I suppose he **must be working**.*
TEACHER: *Robert is absent today.*
Visit his family.
STUDENT: *I suppose he **must be visiting** his family.*
TEACHER: *Robert is not coming to school today.*
Feel sick.
STUDENT: *I suppose he **must be feeling** sick.*

An exercise to practice *must* + **past modification**:

TEACHER: *Robert got a bad grade on the test.*
*He **must have made** many mistakes.*
TEACHER: *Robert failed the course.*
Play too much football.
STUDENT: *He **must have played** too much football.*
TEACHER: *Robert dropped the course.*
He had other interests.
STUDENT: *He **must have had** other interests.*

Another problem connected with the use of *must* is the use of negation. The negation used together with *must* applies not to *must* but to the main verb. Thus *I must not leave* must be interpreted as *I must $\boxed{not\ leave}$*. It establishes the obligation to *not leave*, not the lack of obligation to leave: *I must $\boxed{not\ leave}$ = I must $\boxed{stay}$*.

The meaning of *must $\boxed{not + \textbf{verb}}$* can be drilled in exercises in which the student is asked to replace $\boxed{not + \textbf{verb}}$ by an equivalent expression. (for example, as above — $\boxed{not\ leave}$ = *stay*).

TEACHER: *Robert must* $\boxed{not\ leave}$ *home.*
STUDENT: *Robert must* **stay** *home.*
TEACHER: *He must* $\boxed{not\ speak}$.
STUDENT: *He must* **be silent.**
TEACHER: *Robert must* $\boxed{not\ forget}$ *the lesson.*
STUDENT: *He must* **remember** *the lesson.*

Negation + *have to* is used to express the meaning of lack of obligation. The contrast between *must not* and negation + *have to* can be made clear in special exercises:

TEACHER: *Use* **does not have to work** *or* **must not work** *in response to the following statements:*
Robert is rich.
STUDENT: *He* **does not have to work.**
TEACHER: *Robert is sick.*
STUDENT: *He* **must not work.**
TEACHER: *Robert understands his assignments very quickly.*
STUDENT: *He* **does not have to work.**
TEACHER: *Charles has been in an accident.*
STUDENT: *Charles* **must not work.**

The uses of *shall* and *will* form a rather complex and confusing picture. The original meaning of *shall* was tied to the notion of obligation, while that of *will* implied volition. These original meanings have been preserved to varying degrees in various uses. Perhaps the main point is that the expression of futurity no longer employs *shall*. The rule still found in many grammar books — that the future is expressed by *shall* in the first person and *will* in the second and third person — is pure fiction in present-day usage. In practice the use of *shall* is limited to some rather rare and special cases (especially invitation to joint action when acquiescence is anticipated: *shall we dance? shall we leave?*), and futurity may be expressed in all persons by the unstressed contracted form of *will* (*I'll leave tomorrow*) and even more typically by the phrase *going to* (*I'm going to leave tomorrow*), which is the normal way of expressing futurity in English. It is essential that this form be made clear to the student, especially to those who have had some previous instruction in English and have been taught that the future is formed with *shall* and *will*.

Since the pattern *present tense form of* **be** + **going to** + *simple form of verb* is unfamiliar to most foreign students, it must be thoroughly drilled in exercises which make clear its meaning as well as its form. A conversion exercise is one means of accomplishing this:

TEACHER: *Change each of the following statements to the future, using the word* tomorrow:
I ***drink*** *coffee every day.*
STUDENT: *I* ***am going to drink*** *coffee tomorrow.*
TEACHER: *John* ***is doing*** *his homework now.*
STUDENT: *John* ***is going to do*** *his homework tomorrow.*
TEACHER: *The students* ***arrived*** *yesterday.*
STUDENT: *The students* ***are going to arrive*** *tomorrow.*

In addition, the colloquial reduced form of *going to* [gɔnə] must be drilled for purposes of comprehension.

The form *should* is used in all persons to denote obligation or advisability and is nearly synonymous with *ought to*. Beginning students may learn the form in exercises in which the forms are used as replacements for each other, contrasting the use of *to* after *ought* with its absence after *should*, and in which the sense of obligation is made clear by the context:

TEACHER: *John is lazy.*
Study.
STUDENT: *John* ***should study***.
John ***ought to study***.
TEACHER: *Charles is not getting enough practice.*
Speak English at home.
STUDENT: *Charles* ***should speak*** *English at home.*
Charles ***ought to speak*** *English at home.*

Could and *would* are probably practiced most effectively in conjunction with a **contrary to fact** *if* clause.

TEACHER: *Charles cannot answer. He has not prepared his lesson.*
Charles ***could answer***, *if he had prepared his lesson.*
TEACHER: *John cannot understand. He does not know enough English.*
STUDENT: *John* ***could understand***, *if he knew enough English.*

Or:

TEACHER: *John does not understand. We speak too fast.*
            *John **would understand**, if we spoke slowly.*
TEACHER: *Charles doesn't speak English. He hasn't learned it.*
STUDENT: *Charles **would speak** English, **if** he had learned it.*
TEACHER: *Charles doesn't read his assignment. He is not interested
            in it.*
STUDENT: *Charles **would read** his assignment, **if** he were interested
            in it.*

May and *might* both express potentiality and can be used in exercises in which they are interchanged in that particular meaning.

TEACHER: *Charles is not in school.*
            Be sick.
STUDENT: *He **may be** sick.*
            *He **might be** sick.*
TEACHER: *Charles is late.*
            Be in trouble.
STUDENT: *He **may be** in trouble.*
            *He **might be** in trouble.*
TEACHER: *John has lots of money.*
            Help his friend.
STUDENT: *He **may help** his friend.*
            *He **might help** his friend.*

May not only indicates potentiality or possibility; it is also used quite frequently to indicate permission. Therefore, a sentence such as *John may help his friends* is ambiguous; it can mean *there is a possibility that John will help his friends*, or *John has permission to help his friends*. The student can be told that ambiguity can be largely avoided by using *might* for the meaning of possibility rather than *may*.

The meaning of permission is inapplicable if the verb used with *may* is either in the progressive or in the past modification. Permission is normally not given for an action which has already taken place or which is thought of as taking place already: *John **may have helped** his friends* and *John **may be helping** his friends* can only imply possibility. On the other hand, the use of the interrogative will normally restrict the meaning to permission. *May John help his friends?* is clearly an inquiry as to whether John has permission to help.

Another problem in connection with the modals concerns the lack of future forms, and the restricted use of such past forms as do exist. It must be made clear to the non-native that the modals *should, could, would* in most cases do not represent past tenses any more than *can, will, must* are truly present, and that all of them usually refer to a state which is nonpast. They are often used with clear time reference to the future: *I must speak with you tomorrow*; *you should see him tomorrow*; etc.

English makes up for the lack of a past by applying the past modification not to the modal but to the verb used with the modal:

> **Nonpast:** *I should speak to him.*
> **Past:** *I should have spoken to him.*

This English practice proves to be confusing to speakers of languages such as Spanish, French, or German, in which the idea denoted by the modal is expressed by a verb which is capable of the past modification:

> **Present** English: *I* ⬚*ought*⬚ *to write.*
> Spanish: ⬚*Debería*⬚ *escribir.*
> **Past** English: *I ought to* ⬚*have written*⬚*.*
> Spanish: ⬚*Habría debido*⬚ *escribir.*

The English usage can be practiced in exercises in which the student is asked to transform statements to the past:

TEACHER: *Today **I should prepare** my lesson.*
　　　　Yesterday.
STUDENT: *Yesterday **I should have prepared** my lesson.*

Another peculiarity of the English modals—a peculiarity which they share with the auxiliaries *have* and *be*—is their use in **echo responses:**

TEACHER:	STUDENT:
May we go home?	*Yes, you may.*
Could you help me?	*Yes, I could.*
Are you sick?	*Yes, I am.*
Has he arrived?	*Yes, he has.*
Do you know the answer?	*Yes, I do.*
Do you know the answer?	*No, I don't.*
May I leave?	*No, you may not.*

This particular feature of the auxiliaries and modals can easily be practiced in exercises which—like the examples above—consist of teacher–student exchanges approximating the normal conversational question–answer situation.

3. The Verb + Verb Structure (Use of the -ing Form)

We have already stressed the fact that in English the modal auxiliaries cannot be considered to be in the same class as real verbs. The construction **auxiliary + verb** (*I can speak*) is quite different from the construction **verb + verb** (*I begin to speak*) and should not be confused with it. Since in many languages the meanings conveyed by the English modals are expressed by verbs, the confusion of **auxiliary + verb** and **verb + verb** constructions is a fairly common error. For example, *I can speak* is expressed in Spanish by *puedo hablar*; *I like to speak* by *quiero hablar*. Speakers of Spanish will thus often produce sentences such as **I like speak* (in analogy to *I can speak*) or, even more typically, sentences such as **I can to speak* (in analogy to *I like to speak*). The latter mistake is often reinforced by grammars which tell the student that the English infinitive (corresponding to the Spanish infinitive *hablar*) is *to speak*. Actually it makes little sense to designate a form like *to speak* as an infinitive. The student should simply be told that *to* is the preposition used in the construction which connects verbs, while no preposition is used for the modal modification.

Since confusion between the **verb + verb** and the **auxiliary + verb** constructions usually persists, it is necessary to contrast them in special exercises:

TEACHER: *We prefer to study English.*
           Like.
STUDENT: *We like to study English.*
TEACHER: *Can.*
STUDENT: *We can study English.*
TEACHER: *Begin.*
STUDENT: *We begin to study English.*
TEACHER: *Must.*
STUDENT: *We must study English.*

In another construction, the subject of the dependent verb is not the same as the subject of the main verb: *I expected John to send the letter* or *I persuaded John to send the letter*. Transformational grammarians have pointed out that at least two possible constructions are hiding behind this **verb + noun + verb** structure. In the construction *I expected John to send the letter*, the entire phrase *John to send the letter* is the object of the verb *expected*: $\boxed{I\ expected}\,\boxed{John\ to\ send\ the\ letter}$. In the sentence *I persuaded John to send the letter*, the noun *John* is actually the object of *persuaded* as well as the subject of *send the letter*: $\boxed{I\ persuaded}\,\boxed{John}\,\boxed{to\ send\ the\ letter}$. The difference between the two constructions can be demonstrated in various ways. For example, it is possible to say *what I expected was that John would send the letter*, but a sentence like **What I persuaded was that John send the letter* would not be possible. The two construction types (*expect, want* + **noun** + *to* + **verb** and *tell, persuade* + **noun** + *to* + **verb**) do not usually present any problem to the foreign student and may be taught without differentiating between them. Occasionally students of some language backgrounds (French, Spanish, German), who have comparatively little difficulty with the *tell, persuade* type of construction, will be tempted to use subordinate clauses with the *want, expect* type: **I want that John send the letter* instead of *I want John to send the letter*.

A special problem is presented by verbs such as *let, make, have, see, hear, watch, feel* which are followed by a noun plus another verb without the preposition *to*: *I let him answer*; *I made him go*; *I had him speak*; *I saw him fall*. Special drill is necessary to counteract the student's tendency to use *to*:

TEACHER: *Did John leave? Yes, we let him leave.*
          Did John speak?
STUDENT: *Yes, we let him speak.*

Or the drill may contrast this construction with the one using *to*:

TEACHER: *We persuaded John to leave.*
          Let.
STUDENT: *We let John leave.*
TEACHER: *Asked.*
STUDENT: *We asked John to leave.*
TEACHER: *Made.*
STUDENT: *We made John leave.*
TEACHER: *Told.*
STUDENT: *We told John to leave.*
TEACHER: *To return.*

STUDENT: *We told John to return.*
TEACHER: *Let.*
STUDENT: *We let John return.*

We must also consider another peculiarity of English, which is the frequent use after another verb of the *-ing* form of the verb rather than the *to* + **simple verb** construction. In other words, English often uses a nominalization of the verb rather than the verb itself: *I began to write = I began writing.* What proves confusing to the student is that some English verbs (*begin, continue, like, neglect, prefer, start, try*) can be used with a following *-ing* form as well with the *to* + **verb** construction. However, with many other verbs (*admit, avoid, consider, deny, enjoy, finish, keep (on), recall, regret, suggest*), only the nominalized *-ing* form is possible. Thus sentences like **I enjoy to speak* are a very common mistake on the part of the student. A series of special drills is necessary in which the verbs requiring the construction with *-ing* are first singled out and practiced, and then contrasted with those that can also be used with *to* + **verb**, as well as those taking only *to* + **verb**. Such drills can take various forms.

A simple substitution drill can be used to contrast verbs requiring the *-ing* and *to* forms:

TEACHER:	STUDENT:
I enjoy playing tennis.	*I enjoy playing tennis.*
Skiing.	*I enjoy skiing.*
Playing football.	*I enjoy playing football.*
Swimming.	*I enjoy swimming.*

TEACHER:	STUDENT:
I intend to play tennis.	*I intend to play tennis.*
Study.	*I intend to study.*
Watch television.	*I intend to watch television.*

In other types of drills the student can be forced to choose between the *-ing* and *to* forms:

TEACHER:	STUDENT:
Take a trip this summer — planned.	*I planned to take a trip this summer.*
Go to Europe — wanted.	*I wanted to go to Europe.*
Travel by plane — enjoyed.	*I enjoyed traveling by plane.*
Smoke cigarettes — stopped.	*I stopped smoking cigarettes.*

A few verbs, such as *stop, remember,* have one meaning when followed by the *-ing* form and a different meaning when used with *to* + simple form:

He stopped speaking (stopped the activity of speaking).
He stopped to speak (stopped some other activity in order to speak).
He remembers answering my letters (he remembers that at some time in the past he answered my letters).
He remembers to answer my letters (he does not forget to answer my letters).

These verbs must be pointed out to the student to avoid confusing them with the *begin, continue* type, which has the same meaning with either construction.

Further complications arise concerning the **verb** + *to* + **verb** and **verb** + *-ing* constructions if the subject of the second verbal is not the same as the subject of the main verb. As pointed out before, the **verb** + **noun** + **verb** construction uses the noun or an object pronoun to express the subject of the second verb: *I want John (him) to study English.* Since the *-ing* form used after the main verb is a nominal, the possessive of the noun or a possessive adjective must be used to express the subject of the second action: *I like John's singing (I like his singing).* These contrasting usages can be practiced in the following manner:

TEACHER:	STUDENT:
John is singing. Want.	*We want John to sing.*
Enjoy.	*We enjoy John's singing.*
Expect.	*We expect John to sing.*
Appreciate.	*We appreciate John's singing.*

Verbs of perception such as *hear, notice, watch, see, feel, smell* can often be used with either the *-ing* form or the simple form of the verb (without *to*). However, the noun or object pronoun, rather than the possessive, is used to express the subject of the second verb. Thus the above drill could be continued:

TEACHER:	STUDENT:
Heard.	*We heard John sing (singing).*
Watched.	*We watched John sing (singing).*

Another type of error the foreign student may make is extension of the **verb** + *to* + **verb** or the **verb** + *-ing* construction to cases where a subordinate clause is required; for example: *I hope that John is studying*

English; *I think that John is studying English* (not **I hope John to study English* or **I think John studying English*). Words such as *think*, *hope* can be drilled with their respective constructions and can then be included in contrastive drills with verbs demanding the other construction types:

TEACHER: *Hope.*
STUDENT: *We hope that John is going to sing.*
TEACHER: *Want.*
STUDENT: *We want John to sing.*
TEACHER: *Think.*
STUDENT: *We think that John is going to sing.*

4. The Use of Adverbs

The main problem connected with the use of adverbs concerns their position in the sentence. We have stated previously that the place of the adverb or adverbial expression in the typical English sentence is the fourth position in the sequence:

1. NOUN PHRASE   2. VERB PHRASE   3. NOUN PHRASE   4. ADVERB
   (subject)   (object)
   My friend   *talked to*   *your brother*   *last night.*

The three most common types of adverbial modification are expressions of **manner**, **place**, and **time**. Adverbs of manner are typically those formed from adjectives by adding the *-ly* ending (*slowly*, *carefully*, *correctly*); those of place and time may be single words (*here*, *there*; *yesterday*, *now*) or phrases (*in the library*, *at school*; *last night*, *in July*). The basic sequence of these adverbial expressions within the fourth position is (a) manner, (b) place, (c) time:

1. SUBJECT	2. VERB	3. OBJECT
John	*wrote*	*the report*
Mary	*sang*	*the song*

4. ADVERBIALS		
(a) MANNER	(b) PLACE	(c) TIME
carefully	*at school*	*yesterday*
beautifully	*at the concert*	*last night*

These adverbial positions may be practiced in expansion drills:

TEACHER: *He spoke to his teacher.*

> *Yesterday.*
STUDENT: *He spoke to his teacher yesterday.*
TEACHER: *In the office.*
STUDENT: *He spoke to his teacher in the office yesterday.*
TEACHER: *Very politely.*
STUDENT: *He spoke to his teacher very politely in the office yesterday.*

Another way to practice adverbial positions is to ask the student to expand a sentence in response to a series of *how, when, where* questions (choice of adverbs may be left to the student, or the adverb can be cued by the teacher):

TEACHER: *Did he talk to his teacher?*
STUDENT: *Yes, he talked to him.*
TEACHER: *How?*
> *Very politely.*
STUDENT: *He talked to him very politely.*
TEACHER: *Where?*
> *In the office.*
STUDENT: *He talked to him very politely in the office.*
TEACHER: *When?*
> *Yesterday.*
STUDENT: *He talked to him very politely in the office yesterday.*

In a variation of this type of drill adverbials of time and place can be written on the board. The student is then asked to use two of them to construct a sentence with a verb suggested by the teacher:

yesterday	*at the office*
last week	*in Florida*
two days ago	*at the bank*
last year	*downtown*

TEACHER: *Cash a check.*
STUDENT: *I cashed a check at the bank last week.*
TEACHER: *Have an accident.*
STUDENT: *He had an accident downtown yesterday.*
TEACHER: *Take a vacation.*
STUDENT: *He took a vacation in Florida last year.*

The basic sequence is not always followed, however: adverbs of manner, place, and time are sometimes transposed to the position before the subject. This transposition is most frequent with the adverb or adverbial of time, and is used primarily for the purpose of emphasis. If a sentence contains several adverbs, the transposition is sometimes used to lighten the load of adverbial expressions at the end of the sentence:

1.   2.   3.   4a.   4b.   4c.
Robert wrote his report quickly in the library last night.
Last night Robert wrote his report quickly in the library.

Adverbs of manner are also sometimes used at the beginning of the sentence for stylistic effect:

He tiptoed up the stairs slowly and quietly.
Slowly and quietly he tiptoed up the stairs.

The main error that the student is likely to make is to interpolate the adverb between the verb and the object—the one position where it is almost impossible to use adverbs in English: *The boy wrote carefully his homework.* This error is best counteracted by substitution exercises or the abovementioned question/answer type of exercises in which the student is asked to supply his own adverbs:

TEACHER: *How did Charles do his homework?*
STUDENT: *He did his homework very carefully.*

There are a few adverbs of manner which do not end in *-ly* (the typical ending of most adverbs of manner): *well* (the adverb of *good*), *fast*, *hard*. These adverbs can be practiced in exercises of the following type:

TEACHER: *He is a good student. How does he study?*
STUDENT: *He studies well.*
TEACHER: *He is a fast walker. How does he walk?*
STUDENT: *He walks fast.*
TEACHER: *He is a hard worker. How does he work?*
STUDENT: *He works hard.*

In English there is a class of adverbial expressions (usually ending in *-ly*) which are not adverbs of manner modifying the verb, but which must be considered as sentence adverbials, because they modify the sentence as a whole. These sentence adverbials (*certainly, usually, surely, normally, definitely, generally, ordinarily, possibly*) normally cannot occupy the position of the adverb of manner. It is possible to say:

1.　　2.　　　3.　　　4.

John finished his work completely

but not:

*John finished his work certainly.

However, a few of the adverbs in this group also occasionally occur as adverbs of manner, with a slightly different meaning:

> **Normally** *John is very dependable.*
> *He reacted quite* **normally**.
> **Surely** *you didn't expect that to happen.*
> *He climbed the rocky path* **surely** *and carefully.*

Note that the sentence adverbials are often used at the beginning of the sentence:

> *Certainly John finished his work.*

Although a degree of flexibility exists, for purposes of emphasis, the sentence adverbials occur most frequently in the following positions:

1. Immediately before the main verb (and after any auxiliary) in an affirmative sentence:

> *He certainly speaks well.*
> *I definitely expect him today.*
> *He will surely be here by six o'clock.*
> *He can certainly come today.*
> *He has definitely agreed to help.*

2. Before the auxiliary in negative sentences:

> *He generally doesn't arrive before nine o'clock.*
> *He certainly won't come tomorrow.*

If the main verb is a form of *be* in the present or simple past, the sentence adverbial occurs:

3. Usually after (occasionally before) the form of *be* in affirmative sentences:

> *He is certainly clever.*
> *He was definitely the best student in that class.*

4. Before the form of *be* in negative sentences:

> *He certainly isn't very friendly.*
> *She definitely wasn't here last night.*

In interrogative sentences, the sentence adverbial occurs immediately before the main verb, unless the main verb is *be*, in which case it follows the subject:

> *Does John generally work late on Fridays?*
> *Is John generally late to class?*

The most effective way to practice the sentence adverbials is in question-and-answer exercises which make it clear that they refer to the sentence as a whole. The students may be instructed to respond first with the sentence adverbial at the beginning of the sentence, then rephrase their response with the adverbial in an appropriate position within the sentence:

TEACHER: *Is it certain that Robert finished his homework?*
STUDENT: *Certainly Robert finished his homework.*
          Robert certainly finished his homework.
TEACHER: *Is it definite that John is coming tomorrow?*
STUDENT: *Definitely John is coming tomorrow.*
          John is definitely coming tomorrow.
TEACHER: *Is it obvious that Mary is the best student?*
STUDENT: *Obviously Mary is the best student.*
          Mary is obviously the best student.
TEACHER: *Is it usual for you to work until midnight?*
STUDENT: *Usually I work until midnight.*
          I usually work until midnight.

Other exercises may concentrate on the various positions of the sentence adverbials using direct questions and specifying an affirmative or negative response:

TEACHER: *Answer affirmatively:*
          Does John generally speak well?
STUDENT: *Yes, John generally speaks well.*
TEACHER: *Does he ordinarily answer correctly?*
STUDENT: *Yes, he ordinarily answers correctly.*
TEACHER: *Do you definitely plan to go to the concert?*
STUDENT: *Yes, I definitely plan to go to the concert.*

TEACHER: *Answer negatively:*
Does Mary normally finish her work on time?
STUDENT: *No, Mary normally doesn't finish her work on time.*
TEACHER: *Does she generally enjoy her classes?*
STUDENT: *No, she generally doesn't enjoy her classes.*

Or:

TEACHER: *Answer affirmatively:*
Can you usually get to class on time?
STUDENT: *Yes, I can usually get to class on time.*
TEACHER: *Will John certainly come to the party?*
STUDENT: *Yes, John will certainly come to the party.*
TEACHER: *Answer negatively:*
Will the students definitely take the test tomorrow?
STUDENT: *No, they definitely won't take the test tomorrow.*
TEACHER: *Can the boys usually go to the football game?*
STUDENT: *No, they usually can't go to the football game.*

Or:

TEACHER: *Answer affirmatively:*
Was Mary definitely the smartest in your class?
STUDENT: *Yes, Mary was definitely the smartest in our class.*
TEACHER: *Is John generally prompt?*
STUDENT: *Yes, John is generally prompt.*
TEACHER: *Answer negatively:*
Is Charles generally late to class?
STUDENT: *No, Charles generally isn't late to class.*
TEACHER: *Was the rumor definitely true?*
STUDENT: *No, the rumor definitely wasn't true.*

There is another class of adverbs which cannot be used in the fourth position: the so-called **frequency words** or **preverbs**, which normally stand immediately before the main verb in both the affirmative (after the auxiliary) and negative (after *not*) patterns:

Bill	*always arrives on time.*
Bill has	*always arrived on time.*
He doesn't	*always arrive on time.*
He can't	*always arrive on time.*
He hasn't	*always arrived on time.*

However, when the main verb is *be* in the present or simple past, the frequency adverb follows the form of *be* in the affirmative sentences and follows *not* in negative patterns:

> *Mary is* | *always prompt.*
> *Mary was* | *always prompt.*
> *Mary isn't* *always prompt.*

In interrogative sentences the preverb retains its position immediately before the main verb, unless the main verb is *be* in the present or simple past. In the latter case it remains in its position after the subject:

> *Does Bill always arrive on time?*
> *Can Bill always arrive on time?*
> *Is   Bill always   on time?*

Preverbs, like adverbials of time, are sometimes placed at the beginning of the sentence for emphasis: *sometimes I wonder why he did that.*

The adverbs of the preverb group include *sometimes*, *occasionally*, *frequently*, *often*, *usually* (which also occurs as a sentence adverbial), *always*, and a few with negative meaning (*rarely*, *seldom*, *never*, *hardly ever*) which will be discussed separately. The special position of the preverbs can be drilled in various types of exercises; for example, substitution drills:

TEACHER: *John speaks English to his friend.*
            Always.
STUDENT: *John always speaks English to his friend.*
TEACHER: *Sometimes.*
STUDENT: *John sometimes speaks English to his friend.*
TEACHER: *Answer negatively:*
            Often.
STUDENT: *John doesn't often speak English to his friend.*
TEACHER: *Usually.*
STUDENT: *John doesn't usually speak English to his friend.*

Question-and-answer type exercises can be used:

TEACHER: *Does John always eat lunch in the cafeteria?*
STUDENT: *Yes, he always eats lunch in the cafeteria.*
TEACHER: *Can you always answer correctly?*
STUDENT: *No, I can't always answer correctly.*
TEACHER: *Is Mary sometimes late to class?*
STUDENT: *Yes, Mary is sometimes late to class.*

TEACHER: *Do you often have fish for breakfast?*
STUDENT: *No, I don't often have fish for breakfast.*

In a less controlled type of drill the student can be asked to formulate sentences using phrases suggested by the teacher and a frequency word of his own choice:

TEACHER: *Eat breakfast in the morning.*
STUDENT: *I sometimes eat breakfast in the morning.*
TEACHER: *Walk to school.*
STUDENT: *I often walk to school.*

In another variety of less controlled drill the teacher suggests the frequency word, but the student chooses the rest of the reply:

TEACHER: *What do you usually do when you are tired?*
STUDENT: *I usually go to bed.*
TEACHER: *Where do you often spend your vacation?*
STUDENT: *I often spend my vacation in Florida.*

One more group of adverbs which must be discussed includes those which have a negative meaning and therefore may never be used with negative verb forms. The meanings of the adverbs in this group deal with frequency (*rarely, seldom, hardly ever, never*) or degree (*hardly, barely, scarcely*). Their position in the sentence follows the pattern of the frequency words, and therefore they may also be considered preverbs:

John		*seldom*	*goes*	*to the movies.*
He		*rarely*	*studies.*	
He		*hardly ever*	*writes*	*to his mother.*
He	*will*	*never*	*finish*	*this course.*
He	*is*	*never*		*on time.*
He	*is*	*seldom*		*in class.*
Mary	*can*	*hardly*	*understand*	*him.*
She		*scarcely*	*knows*	*him.*
He		*barely*	*passed*	*his exam.*
He	*is*	*hardly*		*literate.*
His writing	*is*	*barely*		*legible.*

It is advisable to clarify for the foreign student what is meant by **negative meaning** by defining these adverbials with equivalent expressions using *not* or *never*, thereby emphasizing that they cannot be used with a negative verb form:

> *never = not at any time; not ever*
> *seldom = not often*
> *rarely = almost not ever; almost never*
> *hardly ever = almost never*
> *hardly* ⎫
> *scarcely* ⎬ *= almost not at all; not well; not very much*
> *barely* ⎭

These meanings, as well as the sentence positions, can be practiced in exercises of the following types:

TEACHER: *Rephrase the following negative statement, substituting the suggested negative word:*
John doesn't often go to the movies.
Seldom.

STUDENT: *John seldom goes to the movies.*

TEACHER: *He doesn't ever study.*
Never.

STUDENT: *He never studies.*

TEACHER: *He is almost never in class.*
Rarely.

STUDENT: *He is rarely in class.*

TEACHER: *He doesn't usually come on time.*
Hardly ever.

STUDENT: *He hardly ever comes on time.*

Or:

TEACHER: *I don't know Mary very well.*
Hardly.

STUDENT: *I hardly know Mary.*

TEACHER *He almost didn't pass his exam.*
Barely.

STUDENT: *He barely passed his exam.*

TEACHER: *He is almost illiterate (= not literate).*
Hardly.

STUDENT: *He is hardly literate.*

Or:

TEACHER: *Answer negatively, using the suggested word:*
Does John often go to the movies?
Seldom.

STUDENT: *John seldom goes to the movies.*

TEACHER: *Does John often go to the movies?*
Often.
STUDENT: *John doesn't often go to the movies.*
TEACHER: *Is Mary frequently late to class?*
Rarely.
STUDENT: *Mary is rarely late to class.*
TEACHER: *Is Mary always late to class?*
Always.
STUDENT: *Mary isn't always late to class.*

Finally, mention must be made of the interrogative frequency word *ever*, which occurs only in questions, except for negative statements in which *not ever = never*; or *hardly ever = almost never*:

*Does he **ever** come on time?*
*No, he **doesn't ever** come on time.*
*Is he **ever** in class?*
*He is **hardly ever** in class.*

Questions with *ever* can be answered with any appropriate frequency word and may be practiced in question-and-answer drills:

TEACHER: *Answer affirmatively using the suggested word:*
Do you ever go the movies?
Sometimes.
STUDENT: *I sometimes go to the movies.*
TEACHER: *Are you ever at home in the evening?*
Often.
STUDENT: *I'm often at home in the evening.*
TEACHER: *Does John ever have dinner at a restaurant?*
Occasionally.
STUDENT: *John occasionally has dinner at a restaurant.*
TEACHER: *Answer negatively:*
Do you ever play chess?
Never.
STUDENT: *I never play chess.*
TEACHER: *Does he ever go to the theatre?*
Often.
STUDENT: *He doesn't often go to the theatre.*
TEACHER: *Is John ever late to dinner?*
Seldom.
STUDENT: *John is seldom late to dinner.*

(D) THE SUBORDINATE CLAUSE

Relatively speaking, the subordinate clauses of English offer few problems. Unlike many other languages, English usually retains the word order of the main clause in the subordinate clause and does not use special subjunctive forms. As a matter of fact, the problem encountered by the foreign student often consists of his trying to introduce into English some of the intrinsically more complicated features of his native language. Not all the possible types of subordinate clause or problems connected with them can be taken up here. However, we shall point out the main features of the English subordinate clause structure under the headings of (1) **noun and adverbial clauses**; (2) **adjectival (relative) clauses**; and (3) **problems connected with the use of tenses.**

1. Noun and Adverbial Clauses

Noun and adverbial clauses are best thought of as sentences which have been put into another sentence as a replacement for a noun (or noun phrase) or an adverb (or adverbial phrase). For example, we can replace the noun phrase of the sentence

I know | *the whole truth* | *.*

by

I know | *that this has really happened* | *.*

Or we can replace the adverbial expression of

He came | *in spite of his fatigue* | *.*

by

He came | *although he was very tired* | *.*

Noun clauses can serve the same functions as noun phrases in the basic sentence types. Thus, in the sentence type **NP + V + NP + (Adv)** noun clauses can function as the subject:

| *What you are saying* | *makes little sense.*

Or as the object:

We all understand | *what he is saying* | *.*

In the sentence type **NP + be + predicate** noun clauses can again function as subjects:

| *What you are saying* | *is very interesting.*

Or as predicates:

> *His answer was* $\boxed{\textit{that we should leave immediately}}$.

The use of independent noun clauses is well taught in an exercise which requires the student to fit a statement into a main clause, replacing the word *this* or *that* used in a cue question. For example:

> *Charles was sick.   Did you know **that**?*
> *No, I didn't know **that Charles was sick**.*

There are several problems to be considered in connection with this process of fitting dependent clauses into main clauses.

If the dependent noun clause is derived from a declarative statement, it is introduced by *that*. But *that* may be omitted if the noun clause is used as the object of a verb:

> *I know (that) he has come in time.*

Or as a predicate:

> *The fact is (that) he has come in time.*

Or as a subject of a sentence using the verb *to be* introduced by *it*:

> *It is fortunate (that) he has come in time.*

The omission of *that* is not possible in all cases, namely if the noun clause is the subject in a **NP + VP** sentence:

> $\boxed{\textit{That he has come in time}}$ *makes me very happy.*
> *It makes me very happy* $\boxed{\textit{that he has come in time}}$.

Or if it is subject of a **(NP)** + *be* + **predicate** sentence which does not begin with *it*:

> $\boxed{\textit{That he has come in time}}$ *is a fact.*

The student who is trained to omit *that* in the noun clause or who simply notices that the native speaker omits *that*, may be tempted to leave it out in cases in which it is required, and thus produce sentences such as **he has come makes me very happy*. Therefore, it is preferable to train the beginning student to use *that* in all cases, because the use of *that* is always acceptable and the omission may not be.

When the dependent clause is derived from a question, two distinct situations exist:

1. When the question word is the subject of the sentence, the

dependent clause takes the same form as the main clause from which it is derived:

> *What has happened?*
> *I do not know* ⌐*what has happened*⌐ .
> *Who is the best student?*
> ⌐*Who is the best student*⌐ *is a debatable question.*

2. When the question from which the dependent clause is derived is of the type in which the subject is not a question word (for example, *has he finished? where is he going?* with inverted word order), the normal declarative word order must be reestablished in the dependent clause:

> *Where is he going?*   *I don't know where he is going.*
> *What will he do?*   *I don't know what he will do.*

The characteristic features of the English question will be discussed in the next section of this chapter.

Considerable practice is necessary to teach the student **not** to import the word order of the independent question into the dependent clause or vice versa. The practice can take the form of questions asked by the teacher, to which the student replies by making them dependent on an expression such as *I don't know:*

TEACHER: *Why has Charles left?*
STUDENT: *I don't know why he has left.*
TEACHER: *Whom will Charles visit tomorrow?*
STUDENT: *I don't know whom Charles will visit tomorrow.*
TEACHER: *Why is he studying English?*
STUDENT: *I don't know why he is studying English.*

A special situation exists when the question uses a form of the auxiliary *do* (*does, did*), which disappears from the indirect question. This must be pointed out and practiced:

TEACHER: *What does Charles study?*
STUDENT: *I don't know what he studies.*
TEACHER: *Where did he go?*
STUDENT: *I don't know where he went.*
TEACHER: *When do they work?*
STUDENT: *I don't know when they work.*

The reverse operation—changing dependent questions into direct ones—can take the form of so-called **directed dialogue practice**. The teacher tells the student to ask a question:

TEACHER: *Ask your neighbor when he came to school this morning.*
STUDENT: *When did you come to school this morning?*
TEACHER: *Ask your neighbor whom he talked to before class.*
STUDENT: *Whom did you talk to before class?*

The use of *whether* in dependent questions (derived from questions not introduced by question words) can be practiced in both types of exercises:

TEACHER: *Has Charles left?*
STUDENT: *I don't know whether Charles has left.*
TEACHER: *Did Charles leave?*
STUDENT: *I don't know whether Charles left.*

Or:

TEACHER: *Ask your neighbor whether he can speak English.*
STUDENT: *Can you speak English?*
TEACHER: *Ask your neighbor whether he speaks English.*
STUDENT: *Do you speak English?*

A special problem also arises in connection with the use of noun clauses as subjects in the **NP** + *be* + **adjective** type of sentence: *that he has told the truth is obvious*. Here the pronoun *it* must be used when the noun clause is postposed, as is normal in colloquial usage:

*It is obvious **that he has told the truth**.*

The *it* of the above sentence merely anticipates the following noun clause, which is the subject of the predicate *is obvious*. The *it* vanishes if the noun clause is put in initial position. Some students, however, tend to retain the *it* (**that he has told the truth, it is obvious*) even if the noun clause comes first. Even more typically, some students will omit the rather "superfluous" *it* (**is obvious that he has told the truth*) under the influence of the **noun clause first** construction and/or their native language (for example, Spanish), which does not require any word paralleling the English *it* in the corresponding construction. Exercises drilling the use of *it* may include switching from the **noun clause first** to the *it* construction:

TEACHER: *That he hasn't come is quite regrettable.*
STUDENT: *Yes, it is quite regrettable that he hasn't come.*

TEACHER: *That he won't help us is clear.*
STUDENT: *Yes, it is clear that he won't help us.*

The student may also be asked to use expressions of his choice, such as *it is obvious, it is clear, it is desirable,* in response to statements made by the teacher:

TEACHER: *We study too much.*
STUDENT: *It is obvious that we study too much.*
TEACHER: *We know English.*
STUDENT: *It is desirable that we know English.*

The main problems caused by adverbial clauses are not primarily of a syntactical nature. The problem is rather one of clear comprehension of the meaning of the function word introducing the clause: *so that, in order that, because, after, when, whenever.* Some of these problems will be presented under the heading of vocabulary.

2. Adjectival (Relative) Clauses

Adjectival clauses can be explained best as derived from main clauses in which the noun modified by the adjectival clause has also been used:

$\boxed{Robert}$ *is my friend.*
$\boxed{Robert}$ *teaches English at the university.*

The second clause (*Robert teaches English at the university*) is then embedded in the first:

$\boxed{Robert, who}$ *teaches English at the university, is my friend.*

If the noun to be modified does not correspond to the subject of the adjectival clause, the word order of the adjectival clause will no longer correspond to the one of the main clause from which it is derived, since the relative pronoun must stand at the beginning of the relative clause:

Robert is my friend.
You know Robert very well.
Robert, whom you know very well, is my friend.

If the sentence from which the adjectival clause is derived contains the noun to be modified in the possessive form, the relative pronoun *whose* is used in the adjectival clause:

> *Robert is my friend.*
> *You know* $\boxed{Robert's \,\, \boxed{work}}$ *very well.*
> *Robert,* $\boxed{whose \,\, \boxed{work}}$ *you know very well, is my friend.*

In the above case, both the possessive relative pronoun and the noun modified by it move to the beginning of the sentence. The result is the unusual (and for many students quite confusing) situation that the noun object actually precedes the subject of the relative clause.

The explanation given for the relative clause suggests the best type of exercise in which it can be practiced—the combination of two sentences into one:

TEACHER: *Robert is my friend. He teaches English at the university.*

STUDENT: *Robert, who teaches English at the university, is your friend.*

TEACHER: *Mr. Smith is also my friend. We talked about him yesterday.*

STUDENT: *Mr. Smith, about whom we talked yesterday, is also your friend.*

TEACHER: *Mr. Jones is a very good teacher. His son was in our class yesterday.*

STUDENT: *Mr. Jones, whose son was in our class yesterday, is a very good teacher.*

TEACHER: *Mr. Jones speaks very good Spanish. We met his wife yesterday.*

STUDENT: *Mr. Jones, whose wife we met yesterday, speaks very good Spanish.*

The use of *who, whose* vs. *which, of which* does not represent a major problem. In most cases the choice of the one or the other is quite clear; *who, whose* for human beings, *which* for animals and animate objects. However, the position of *of which* (which does not correspond to the position of *whose*) may cause problems.

> *The man **whose mother** you know is not Mr. John.*

But:

> *The book **of which** you know **the content** is quite dull.*

Or:

> *The book **the content of which** you know is quite dull.*

The use of *that* in relative clauses may also cause some problems: (1) the relative pronoun *that* cannot be used after prepositions; (2) it should not be confused with the demonstrative *that* /ðæt/ (it is pronounced /ðət/ and does not form a plural *those*!); (3) it is used only in **restrictive relative clauses** — clauses which do not simply supply **additional** information about the noun they modify, but which are **necessary**, since they supply **essential** information without which the thought would be incomplete: *I don't understand the idea that you mentioned yesterday.* Since the use of other pronouns is also possible in restrictive clauses, the concept of restrictive vs. nonrestrictive is probably not too crucial in the teaching of English as a foreign language. (The main reason for teaching the concept is to establish the rules of punctuation. Restrictive clauses are not separated by commas from the noun they modify, but nonrestrictive clauses are.) Mistakes such as the use of *that* after prepositions (**the book about that I told you* instead of *the book about which I told you*) are more serious.

The correct use of *that* and the restrictions applied to its use can be practiced in exercises in which the teacher uses *which* or *who* as the relative pronoun and the student is asked to replace them with *that* whenever possible:

TEACHER: *This is the idea which you suggested to us.*
STUDENT: *This is the idea that you suggested to us.*
TEACHER: *This is the idea about which we talked yesterday.*
STUDENT: *This is the idea about which we talked yesterday.*

The possibility of omitting the relative pronoun altogether is also a characteristic and (for the student) often puzzling feature of English: *the man (whom) we met yesterday is my uncle.* The option of omitting the pronoun is used only in the restrictive type of clause. It can be practiced by asking the student to restate relative clauses without a relative pronoun whenever possible. Since omission of the pronoun is an option rather than a must, there is no need to emphasize this type of exercise for the beginning student.

Omission of the relative pronoun is not possible after prepositions. But *that* as well as other relative pronouns can be omitted if the preposition remains after the verb.

The idea that we talked about yesterday is really quite good.
The idea_____we talked about yesterday is really quite good.

The general tendency in modern English is indeed to use the preposition after the verb: *the man we talked about* rather than *the man about whom we talked*; *the chair we sat on* rather than *the chair on which we sat.*

Putting the preposition at the beginning of the dependent clause is possible (and in many grammars this is taught as the desirable construction) even in cases in which the verb and the preposition can be considered nonseparable units: $\boxed{speak\ to}$, $\boxed{talk\ about}$, $\boxed{care\ for}$, as well as in constructions in which the preposition is quite independent of the verb (for example, *visit **with a friend**, live **in a city***):

> *the man to whom he spoke = the man he spoke to*
> *the city in which he lived   = the city he lived in*

Anticipation of the preposition is not possible with separable two-part verbs such as *cut off, fill out*:

> *the form which we filled out ≠ *the form out which we filled*

According to a well-known anecdote, this feature of English was utilized by Winston Churchill when an eager editor of one of his speeches changed one of the relative clauses from the **verb + preposition** type to the construction in which the preposition and relative pronoun precede the verb. Sir Winston is said to have crossed out the correction with the comment: "This is the kind of nonsense up with which I shall not put."

At any rate, the problem of **verb + preposition** or nonseparable two-part verb vs. separable two-part verb affects the possible placement of the preposition in the relative clause and may prove confusing to the student. Since the trend of colloquial English is toward using the preposition after the verb and such a construction is possible in practically all cases, it may in fact be advisable to emphasize this type of construction with the beginning student.

A typical exercise for practicing this construction consists of questions which the student answers with responses requiring a relative clause:

TEACHER: *Did you live in this house?*
STUDENT: *Yes, this is the house we lived in.*
TEACHER: *Did you speak to this man?*
STUDENT: *Yes, this is the man we spoke to.*
TEACHER: *Did you fill out this form?*
STUDENT: *Yes, this is the form we filled out.*

3. Problems Connected with the Special Use of Tenses

Here we shall discuss briefly some English usages which are puzzling to the student because they involve the use of the past tense in contrary-to-fact statements, after expressions implying wish or desire, and after the expression *it's time*:

> *If I had money, I could buy a car.*
> *I wish I had a car.*
> *It is about time (that) you had a car.* (= *It's time for you to have a car.*)

Historically, these usages are explained by the fact that the past tense used in those constructions was originally a past subjunctive, which, for all practical purposes, eventually merged with the indicative. It seems extremely doubtful that the student should be taught that English has a subjunctive.

The few visible remains of the subjunctive in English are:

a. The use of the simple verb form (rather than verb form + third person singular ending) in expressions of desire or wish (command form): *long live* (not *lives*) *the king! so be* (not *is*) *it!*

b. The use of the simple verb form for the third person singular in some subordinate clauses after verbs of **desiring**:

> *We desire that every student know the answer.*
> *The director insists that his assistant understand the issues.*

This particular usage is literary rather than colloquial and is rather rapidly disappearing from anything but the most artificial kind of speech.

c. The use of the form *were* (instead of *was*) as the singular past tense of *be* in contrary-to-fact statements.

> *If I were rich, I would help you.*
> *I wish he were here.*

Here too, the indicative *was* is replacing the subjunctive *were* in colloquial usage.

Thus, with the possible exception of *were* (first and third person), no special subjunctive form must be taught; however, the student must get practice in the seemingly puzzling use of the past tense in the contrary-to-fact and "wishing" subordinate clauses.

Practice in contrary-to-fact *if* clauses (present and past) can be given in exercises in which the teacher describes a situation and asks the student to respond with the corresponding contrary-to-fact construction:

TEACHER: *Mr. Smith has no money. He cannot buy a car.*
STUDENT: *If Mr. Smith had some money, he could buy a car.*
TEACHER: *Mr. Smith had no money. He could not buy a car.*
STUDENT: *If Mr. Smith had had some money, he could have bought a car.*

Other expressions requiring the use of the past in contrary-to-fact situations may be practiced in exercises which consist of a student using a fixed expression like *it's time that* or *I wish* in response to a statement by the teacher:

TEACHER: *Mr. Pereda doesn't know any English.*
STUDENT: *He wishes he knew some English.*
TEACHER: *Mr. Gomez does not own a car.*
STUDENT: *He wishes he owned a car.*
TEACHER: *Mr. Gomez does not study English.*
STUDENT: *It's about time he studied some English.*

(E) TRANSFORMATIONS

We shall now consider a series of grammatical operations which require a fairly extensive regrouping or change of the normal declarative sentence patterns. The transformational operations usually described in generative transformational grammars include: (1) the **question transformation**; (2) **negation**; (3) the **passive**; (4) the **emphasis transformation.**

1. The Question Transformation

The following rules summarize the question transformation of English:

a. If the question contains an auxiliary but does not contain a question word, it is formed from the statement by putting the auxiliary verb (either modal auxiliary, or *have*, *be*) at the beginning of the sentence:

STATEMENT: *Robert has spoken to him.*
QUESTION: *Has Robert   spoken to him?*
STATEMENT: *Robert is   sick.*
QUESTION: *Is   Robert   sick?*
STATEMENT: *Robert can speak French.*
QUESTION: *Can Robert   speak French?*

b. If the statement from which the question is formed does not contain an auxiliary verb, the auxiliary verb *do* is used in the tense, person, and number of the main verb, placed at the beginning of the sentence, and the main verb is replaced by the simple verb form:

STATEMENT: *Robert speaks French very well.*
QUESTION: *Does Robert speak French very well?*
STATEMENT: *They   understood you very quickly.*
QUESTION: *Did   they   understand you very quickly?*

c. If a question word is used, then the question word or the phrase containing the question word is put at the beginning of the sentence immediately before the auxiliary verbs:

STATEMENT: *Charles saw his aunt.*
QUESTION: *Whom did Charles see?* (referring to *aunt*)
STATEMENT: *Charles understood the answer.*
QUESTION: *What did Charles understand?* (referring to *answer*)
STATEMENT: *Charles met his friend's uncle.*
QUESTION: *Whose uncle did Charles meet?* (referring to *friend's*)
STATEMENT: *Charles put on his yellow sweater.*
QUESTION: *Which sweater did Charles put on?* (referring to *yellow*)

d. If the question refers to the subject of the sentence, rules (a) and (b) above do not apply and the normal declarative word order is retained.

STATEMENT: *Charles worked very hard.*
QUESTION: *Who   worked very hard?* (referring to *Charles*)
STATEMENT: *Charles' brother speaks French quite fluently.*
QUESTION: *Whose brother speaks French quite fluently?* (referring to *Charles*)

The best exercises for the practice of the question transformation consist in having the student turn statements into questions:

TEACHER: *Mr. Jimenez studies medicine.*
STUDENT: *Does Mr. Jimenez study medicine?*

Or in directing the student to ask questions for successive elements of a sentence on the chalkboard:

Mr. Jimenez met Mr. Smith's uncle in the library.

TEACHER: (points to *Mr. Jimenez*)
STUDENT: *Who met Mr. Smith's uncle in the library?*
TEACHER: (pointing to *Mr. Smith*)
STUDENT: *Whose uncle did Mr. Jimenez meet in the library?*
TEACHER: (points to *uncle*)
STUDENT: *Whom did Mr. Jimenez meet in the library?*
TEACHER: (points to *in the library*)
STUDENT: *Where did Mr. Jimenez meet Mr. Smith's uncle?*

A possible source of error is confusing the different question words (*what, which, which one, who, whom*). The difference between *who* (*whom*), referring to persons, and *what*, referring to objects or animals, is usually grasped fairly easily. Confusion between *what* and *which* tends to be a somewhat more persistent problem, because both of them can be used as noun modifiers:

What book did you read?
Which book did you read?

The substitution of *which* for *what* tends to be carried over to the pronominal use (**which are you reading?* for *what are you reading?*). Special practice is also needed to teach the use of *which* (*one*) (in a question which seeks alternatives) for persons as well as for things:

TEACHER: *Mr. Smith speaks French and Spanish. Which (one) does he speak better? Respond according to this model to the following statement:*
Mr. Smith knows German and French.
STUDENT: *Which (one) does he know better?*
TEACHER: *Mr. Smith likes Mary and Jane.*
STUDENT: *Which (one) does he like better?*

The confusion between *who* (subject) and *whom* (object) is such a frequent feature in colloquial English that many textbooks have given up the effort of explaining the difference or at least insisting upon it in teaching English to the foreign student. Another feature of collo-quial English discussed and sometimes disapproved of in some text-books is the placement of the preposition at the end of the sentence rather than at the beginning before the question word:

Who(m) did your sister talk to?

rather than

To whom   did your sister talk?

As pointed out previously, the more normal usage and the general trend of colloquial English is to put the preposition at the end of the sentence. Just as in the case of the relative clause (where the problem of **preposition first** vs. **preposition last** also applies), it seems preferable to teach the use of the preposition at the end of the sentence, not only because this corresponds to colloquial usage but also because it will help the beginning student to avoid the error which results from misinterpreting two-part verbs as **verb + preposition**. Thus it is possible to say:

What did he sit on?

Or:

What did he cut up?

The habit of regularly using the preposition at the end will help the student to avoid the impossible:

*Up what did he cut?

2. Negation

The following rules characterize negation:

a. A positive statement is made negative by putting the negative (*not*) after the auxiliary verb (modal or *have, be*).

POSITIVE: *Charles can   speak Spanish.*
NEGATIVE: *Charles cannot speak Spanish.*
POSITIVE: *Charles has   seen my friend.*
NEGATIVE: *Charles has not seen my friend.*

b. If the positive statement does not contain an auxiliary verb, the auxiliary *do* is used in the tense, person, and number of the main verb, which is replaced by the simple verb form and preceded by *not*:

POSITIVE: *Charles   speaks Spanish.*
NEGATIVE: *Charles does not speak Spanish.*

POSITIVE: *Charles*   *saw our friend.*
NEGATIVE: *Charles did not   see our friend.*

Note that if the verb *have* is used in the meaning of *own*, rather than as an auxiliary, either rule (a) or rule (b) may be applied; however, the pattern with *do* is much more frequent.

POSITIVE: *Charles has   a lot of   money.*
NEGATIVE: *Charles hasn't much   (a lot of) money.*
                    Charles does not have a lot of   money.

The best exercises for the practice of the negation transformation consist of having the student negate positive statements or having him give negative answers to positive questions. These exercises can also be used to practice the sometimes troublesome switch from *somebody, something, someone* to *anybody, anything, anyone* (optional in the interrogative and mandatory in the negation transformation). For example:

TEACHER: *Make the following sentence negative:*
                 We found something.
STUDENT: *We didn't find anything.*
TEACHER: *We saw somebody.*
STUDENT: *We didn't see anybody.*

The student must also be taught the possible use of *anybody, anything, anyone* in a positive sentence (*anybody can do this*) as well as the use of *nobody, nothing, no one* as simple negatives not requiring a negative verb form (*I know nobody at that place; nothing will help you*). The use of *anybody, anything* as the subject of a positive sentence is practiced best in question-and-answer exercises in which the student is asked to give an affirmative answer using *anything, anybody, anyone*. For example:

TEACHER: *Can anybody learn English, if he works hard?*
STUDENT: *Oh yes, anybody can learn English, if he works hard.*
TEACHER: *Can anyone take this course?*
STUDENT: *Oh yes, anyone can take this course.*

The use of *nobody, nothing, no one* can be practiced in restatement exercises. The teacher uses negative sentences with *anybody, anything, anyone*, and the student restates them using *nothing, nobody, no one*:

TEACHER: *Mr. Pereda does not know anything.*

STUDENT: *Mr. Pereda knows nothing.*
TEACHER: *I don't know anybody who can help us.*
STUDENT: *You know nobody who can help us.*

3. The Passive

The following processes are involved in the transformation of a sentence into the passive:

a. The object of the transitive verb (*see, hit, talk to*) becomes the subject of the sentence.

b. The verb is replaced by the corresponding form of the verb *be* plus the past participle of the main verb.

c. The original subject of the sentence is used after the verb, preceded by the preposition *by*:

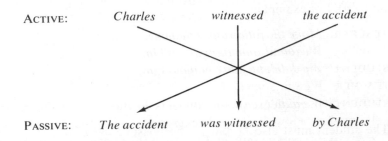

ACTIVE: *Charles has   witnessed   the accident.*
PASSIVE: *The accident has been witnessed by Charles.*

The main passive transformation errors committed by students result from their inability to recognize situations in which such transformations are possible in English. Basically the transformation can be applied to: (A) the object of any transitive verb (including verbs such as *talk to, care for,* which we considered as nonseparable units); and (B) the objects of separable two-part verbs.

(A) *He cared for his parents (he cared for them).*
   His parents were cared for by him.
(B) *He got the letter off in time (he got it off in time).*
   The letter was gotten off in time.

The transformation cannot be applied to the objects of prepositions. It is possible to make the object of the verb *talk to* the subject of a passive sentence (*the teacher talked to Charles* may be transformed to *Charles was talked to by the teacher*); however, the sentence *Charles traveled to New York* cannot be similarly transformed to **New York was traveled to by Charles*.

The formation of the passive voice can be practiced in conjunction with the explanation of the problem of **transitive verb** (*care for*) vs. separable **two-part verb** (*get off, fill out*) vs. **verb + preposition + object**. The teacher can ask the students to transform sentences into the passive whenever possible:

TEACHER: *They cared for Charles.*
STUDENT: *Charles was cared for.*
TEACHER: *They took care of him.*
STUDENT: *He was taken care of.*
TEACHER: *They took him to the hospital.*
STUDENT: *He was taken to the hospital.*
TEACHER: *They filled out his registration.*
STUDENT: *His registration was filled out.*
TEACHER *They did not leave without him.*
STUDENT: *They did not leave without him.*

The specific problems of the students in their use of the passive depend on their native language background. One of the main purposes of the passive construction in English is to convey action without naming the actor: *English is spoken in most of the world* or *the invitation has been sent out.* Some foreign languages (such as Spanish) use a reflexive to convey the same concept (*se habla español = Spanish is spoken*). Obviously, the student must be taught to avoid this construction in English. The concept of **action without actor** can also be conveyed in English by the use of the pronoun *you* (not as a second person, but as a general reference: *you never can tell what's going to happen*) or of the pronoun *they* (in general reference, not referring to specific persons: *in England they drink a lot of tea*). To impress these usages on the student, the teacher can cue passive sentences by sentences using the impersonal *they* or vice versa:

TEACHER: *In the United States they consume a lot of beer.*
STUDENT: *A lot of beer is consumed in the United States.*
TEACHER: *Coffee is served with meals.*
STUDENT: *They serve coffee with meals.*

4. The Emphatic Transformation

In some grammars of Spanish, German, or French for speakers of English we can find the statement that Spanish *hablo* (German *ich spreche*, French *je parle*) corresponds to English *I speak, I am speaking, I do speak*. This equation expresses the fact that these languages (like many others) lack not only the English progressive form but also the English way of emphasizing the action by replacing the verb by the corresponding form of *do* (+ simple form of the verb):

We met Charles.

(Emphatic:) *We did meet Charles.*

He understands English.

(Emphatic:) *He does understand English.*

This use of *do* for emphasis may prove confusing to the student who meets the use of *do* + **verb** primarily in the negation and interrogative transformations. It can be practiced in drills in which the student is asked to use *do* (with emphatic stress on *do*!) in positive statements in response to negative cues:

TEACHER: *Mr. Perez does not speak English.*
STUDENT: *Oh yes, Mr Perez **does** speak English.*
TEACHER: *You don't really like this class.*
STUDENT: *Oh yes, we **do** like this class.*

English also possesses a construction which can be interpreted as putting emphasis not on the verb but on the noun phrase: the use of *myself, yourself, himself* to reinforce a noun or pronoun.

***She herself** spoke to the emperor.*

*She spoke to **the emperor himself**.*

The use or meaning of this construction offers no particular problem. However, the use of *myself, yourself*, etc., for emphasis can be easily confused with the use of the same forms to indicate reflexive action (action performed by the subject upon itself):

I washed myself. (reflexive action)
I myself washed the socks. (emphasis)
I washed the socks myself. (emphasis)

The grammatical signal distinguishing the reflexive use from the emphatic is that the reflexive pronoun is the object of the verb and, like any other object, appears in the object slot:

He washed the socks.
He washed himself.

The emphatic pronoun is more mobile, but it usually appears either immediately after the noun which is being stressed or at the end of the sentence.

Emphatic construction vs. reflexive construction can be practiced in question-and-answer exercises in which the student is asked to put the emphatic pronoun immediately after the noun or pronoun which it reinforces:

TEACHER: *Did John wash the dishes himself?*
STUDENT: *Yes, John himself washed the dishes.*
TEACHER: *Did the child wash himself?*
STUDENT: *Yes, the child washed himself.*
TEACHER: *Did Mary drive the car to school herself?*
STUDENT: *Yes, Mary herself drove the car to school.*
TEACHER: *Did you hurt yourself when you fell?*
STUDENT: *Yes, I hurt myself when I fell.*
TEACHER: *Did Jane bake the cake herself?*
STUDENT: *Yes, Jane herself baked the cake.*
TEACHER: *Did she cut herself when the knife slipped?*
STUDENT: *Yes, she cut herself when the knife slipped.*

In practicing the form *by* + *-self*, it must be pointed out that in addition to lending emphasis this pattern implies that the action was performed by the subject alone, to the exclusion of others:

TEACHER: *In the following exercise answer with a* by + -self *construction:*
Did you do your homework without any help?
STUDENT: *Yes, I did it by myself.*
TEACHER: *Did John go to the concert alone?*
STUDENT: *Yes, he went there by himself.*
TEACHER: *Did Mary's sister help her clean the house?*
STUDENT: *No, Mary cleaned it by herself.*
TEACHER: *Does Jane have a roommate?*
STUDENT: *No, she lives by herself.*

Note that *I drove to school myself* must be distinguished from *I drove to school by myself.* The former merely states that the subject did the driving; the latter makes it clear that he was alone.

The student's problem in distinguishing the reflexive construction from the emphatic construction is primarily caused by the fact that his native language may use completely different constructions for these very different ideas (French, Spanish, German use *moi-même, yo mismo, ich selbst* for emphatic *myself*, and reflexive pronouns *me, me, mich* for the reflexive *myself*). The problem of comprehension and production is further compounded by the different construction types and the different uses for the reflexive in the student's native language. English *I shave every morning* corresponds to a Spanish construction in which the reflexive is mandatory and precedes the verb: *yo me afeito cada mañana* (**I myself shave*). In many instances the native language uses a reflexive where English does not: English *I get up*; Spanish *me levanto*: **(I) myself get up*. As a result, the student may misunderstand English emphatic constructions as reflexives; or, even more typically, he may use (or rather misuse) reflexive constructions which may be misunderstood as emphatic constructions by the speaker of English. A Spanish speaker saying **I myself bathed* (*yo me bañé*) or **I myself went* (*yo me fui*) is most likely translating from his native language and is merely expressing *I took a bath* or *I went away* without wanting to emphasize the subject. Awareness of the emphatic construction and practice of the reflexive will help the student avoid this type of error.

CHAPTER VII

Teaching Vocabulary Problems

(A) IDIOMS; DIFFICULT CONSTRUCTION TYPES

In the area of vocabulary perhaps even more than in any other aspect of language learning, the specific problems of the student depend on the contrast between his native language and the language to be learned. In this chapter we shall confine ourselves to a classification of problems and to emphasizing the most typical difficulties for which the teacher must be on the lookout.

Many students and teachers often make the statement that English is a very **idiomatic** language and that much, perhaps most, of the difficulty of English lies in its **idioms** rather than its grammar. Indeed, there may be a great deal of truth in this statement — though it becomes meaningful only if **idiom** is carefully defined. Frequently a foreign student will have a tendency to regard as idiomatic any expression which conflicts with the usage and/or structure of his native language. A Spanish speaker who normally conveys the meaning of *I like the book* by *me gusta el libro* (*the book is pleasing to me*) may consider the expression *I like* ... an idiom. From this point of view most or practically all of English is idiomatic — simply because it is not like Spanish. A somewhat more precise and linguistic definition of **idiom** applies the term only to any expression the meaning of which cannot be inferred from the meaning of its component parts. In this category belong the many expressions which have acquired specialized figurative meanings, expressions which are familiar and clear to the native but which may be quite opaque to the foreigner. One of the authors of this book remembers the uncomprehending look on the face of a foreign student (whose English was actually quite fluent) when he was told: *"When Professor_____was told that his theory would not hold water, he really hit the ceiling."* Obviously the meaning of this type of idiom must be explained to the student, who otherwise will not understand, and in some cases may misinterpret, the meaning of the English expression.

In some instances the idiomatic nature of an expression is caused not by figurative use but rather by the type of construction as such. Expressions such as *I would rather ...* or *you had better ...* belong in this category. Since the difficulty is connected with the grammatical pattern, response or restatement exercises can be used to drill this kind of idiomatic expression:

TEACHER: *Restate the following according to this model:*
Mr. Smith prefers to stay home. He would rather stay home.
Mr. Smith prefers to speak English.
STUDENT: *He would rather speak English.*
TEACHER: *Mr. Smith prefers to study in California.*
STUDENT: *He would rather study in California.*

Or:

TEACHER: *Restate the following according to this model:*
Mr. Smith ought to study for his test. He'd better study for his test.
Mr. Smith ought to stay home.
STUDENT: *He'd better stay home.*
TEACHER: *He ought to talk to his friend about the test.*
STUDENT: *He'd better talk to his friend about the test.*

(B) SIGNIFIER INTERFERENCE

Any linguistic unit from the morpheme level up is composed of a "**signifier**" (the sounds which make up the acoustic aspect of the word) and a "**signified**" (the meaning with which the sounds are associated). Vocabulary problems can have their origin in the meaning part of the expression, or they can originate in the signifier, in the sounds themselves. Usually the trouble caused by the signifier is one of two types of confusion: (1) the confusion can arise within English; or (2) it can arise from a similarity between English and the student's native langauge. The first type of confusion presents a major problem for **all** students of English as a foreign language, and two main categories may be distinguished within it.

1. Same Word in Different Constructions

One source of confusion is the use of the same word in different types of constructions. The very common words *have, do,* and *there* may be used to illustrate the problem.

English *have* may be utilized as a main verb with the meaning of *possess, own: Charles has a car = Charles owns a car. Have* is also the auxiliary verb used for the past modification: *Charles buys a car = Charles has bought a car.* It is also used to express **obligation** in the expression *have to: Charles has to buy a car.* A final and very frequent usage is the expression of **causation**: *Charles had his brother buy the car.* The confusion which can arise from these different meanings of *have* is obvious:

> *Charles had bought his brother a car.*

vs.

> *Charles had his brother buy a car.*
> *Charles had to have his brother buy a car.*

These meanings must be clearly differentiated, preferably in restatement exercises:

Charles must buy a car = Charles has to buy a car.
Charles told his brother to buy a car = Charles had his brother buy a car.

The passive construction after the causative *have* may prove to be even more confusing, because it is often differentiated only by word order from the use of *have* in the past modification:

> *He has his hair cut*   vs.   *He has cut his hair.*
> *He had a suit made*   vs.   *He had made a suit.*

Again, restatement exercises can be used to drill the causative construction:

TEACHER: *Restate the following sentences according to this model:*
He told them to make him a suit = He had a suit made.
He told them to send him the book.
STUDENT: *He had the book sent.*

TEACHER: *He told them to prepare dinner.*
STUDENT: *He had dinner prepared.*

Just like *have*, the verb *do* can be used as a regular main verb: *Charles does his homework = Charles prepares his homework.* This use of *do* is quite different from its use as an auxiliary in the negation, interrogative, and emphatic transformations, and in truncated answers to questions (*Did he do his homework? Yes, he did*). In addition, even the main verb *do* has several meanings according to whether or not it is used with an object (*he does his homework*) or without it, with adverbial expressions (*he is doing well in English*; *this won't do at all*; *this will do nicely*).

The confusion must be prevented by exercises which make clear the specific meanings of *do* according to the construction type being used. The transformations (question, negation, emphatic) discussed in the previous chapter will take care of the auxiliary *do*. The main verb *do* can be practiced in restatement exercises:

TEACHER: *This answer is not satisfactory = It won't do.*
         This car is not satisfactory.
STUDENT: *It won't do.*

Or:

TEACHER: *Robert is a good student in French = He is doing very well in French.*
         Charles is a good student in English.
STUDENT: *He is doing very well in English.*

The word *there* is used as an adverb in sentences such as *the book is over there* or *there is the book* (with emphasis on *there*, and the speaker pointing in the direction of the book). However, in a sentence such as *there are many books in the library*, *there* is not functioning as an adverb indicating place or location. It is merely part of an expression indicating existence. The so-called ***there*-transformation** can be applied to any English sentence of the type **noun** (indefinite) + *be* + **adverb** and to many English sentences of the type **noun** (indefinite) + *be* + *-ing* form of **verb** + **adverb**:

A book is on the table $\Rightarrow$ *There is a book on the table.*
Students are studying in the library $\Rightarrow$ *There are students studying in the library.*

To the learner, who may equate *there* with an indication of place or direction, the English use of *there are, there is,* or the *there*-transformation may be quite confusing. The different uses of *there* can be practiced in various ways.

The adverb of location is probably practiced best in sentences contrasting *there* with *here*:

TEACHER: *Is the book here in front of me?*
STUDENT: *No, it is (over) there, on the table.*
TEACHER: *Is the chalk here in front of me?*
STUDENT: *No, it is (over) there, near the blackboard.*

The *there*-transformation can be practiced in transformation exercises:

TEACHER: *Many students are studying English.*
STUDENT: *There are many students studying English.*
TEACHER: *Many foreign students are in the U.S.A.*
STUDENT: *There are many foreign students in the U.S.A.*

Differences in meaning that result from use in different construction types can also be illustrated by instances in which separable verbs (two-part verbs) take the same outward forms as the inseparable (**verb + adverb**) combination:

*He **cheered up** his friend (he **cheered** him **up**)*   vs.   *He **cheered up**.*
*He **got off** the letter (he **got** it **off**)*   vs.   *He **got off** the train.*
*He **gave up** smoking (he **gave** it **up**)*   vs.   *He **gave up** in the last round.*
*He **passed out** propaganda literature (he **passed** it **out**)*   vs.   *He **passed out** because of the heat.*
*He **threw up** his hands (he **threw** them **up**)*   vs.   *He **threw up**.*

Obviously confusion will arise if the meaning of the one usage is mistakenly applied to the other. The different construction types must be carefully contrasted in exercises which make the meaning of each construction quite clear to the student:

*Charles **threw up** his hands in despair when he got his test back.*
*Charles **threw up** when he got sick.*

2. Similarity between English Expressions

Probably the major sources of confusion in this category are the many English two-part verbs or **verb + adverb** expressions which can be formed with the same verb. Verbs such as *bring, call, come, get,* *give*, *hold*, *keep*, *make*, *put*, *run*, *take*, *turn* can combine with a large number of prepositions or can be used with a large number of adverbials to express an astounding array of meanings:

> *He got his friend up at six (he woke him up at six).*
> *He couldn't get the medicine down (he couldn't swallow it).*
> *He couldn't get his coat on (he couldn't put it on).*
> *He got the letter off just in time (he sent it just in time).*
> *He got the book out before June (he published it before June).*
> *He tried to get his work over with (he tried to finish it).*
> *He tried to get his money back (he tried to recover it).*

Or:

> *He got up at six o'clock.*
> *He got down to breakfast at six-thirty.*
> *He got on the streetcar at eight.*
> *He got off at eight-thirty.*
> *He got to his office at nine o'clock.*
> *He tried to get on with his work.*
> *Unfortunately, he couldn't get along with his colleagues.*
> *They told him where to get off.*
> *He tried to get around them.*
> *They didn't let him get away with it.*
> *He thought he would get by with little effort.*
> *Finally he was told to get out.*
> *He never could get over this.*

The burden of various meanings carried by such words as *get*, *make*, *put* is quite formidable. Probably the best approach to the problem is to introduce various combinations of words such as *get*, *put*, *make* with prepositions and/or adverbs quite gradually and in different contexts. Only after the student has become well acquainted with such two-part verbs as *get up*, *get off*, *get on* would it be advisable to contrast these expressions in specific exercises. An early lesson based on the fifteen or twenty most common contrasting meanings of the different combinations of *get* + **preposition** (or **adverb**) would most likely create total confusion and bewilderment.

3. Similarity between English and the Foreign Language

Signifier interference due to similarity between English and the language of the learner is a special case which arises primarily with students whose native language is a Romance tongue (Spanish, French, Italian) and, to a lesser degree, with students of other European language backgrounds. Very often a word that sounds (or at least looks in spelling) like an English word is used in the student's native language with totally or partially different meanings. In many cases the word in the student's native language is a relative of the English word (goes back to, or is formed from, the same root), but the meanings in the student's language and those in English are not identical: Spanish *asistir* may mean *be present at* (not *assist*); *lectura* means *reading* (not *lecture*); *librería* means *bookstore* (not *library*); *actualmente* means *at present* (not *actually*); *atender* means *pay attention, wait on* (not *attend*); *suceder* means *happen* (not *succeed*); *conferencia* means *lecture* (usually not *conference*). In German *bekommen* means *receive* (not *become*); and *brav* usually means *well-behaved* (not *brave*). In French *deception* means *disappointment* (not *deception*); and *guarder* often has the meaning of *keep* (rather than *guard*). Examples of these so-called **false cognates** — words in which outward similarity of the foreign word to an English word is not accompanied by an overlap in meaning — could be multiplied. They do represent a fairly major problem since the student is quite naturally tempted to utilize any similarities between English and his native language in order to communicate and in order to comprehend. In many cases the similarities are, of course, not misleading and will facilitate the native Spanish speaker's (or the native French or German speaker's) acquisition of English. The false cognates are the price he must pay for the advantage he is gaining by approaching English from a cognate language background.

False cognates must be singled out for specific exercises in which both the real meaning of the English word and the correct equivalent of the similar word in the student's language are contrasted:

> *Mr. Smith is buying his books in the **bookstore**.*
> *He is borrowing some books from the **library**.*

Or:

> *Mr. Smith **attended** all the lectures.*
> *He even **assisted** Professor Jones in his experiments.*

Or:

> *What **happened** to Mr. Smith in his accident?*
> *I hope that the doctors will **succeed** in fixing up his leg.*

(C) PROBLEMS OF MEANING

Most of the student's vocabulary problems are caused not by confusion of the **signifiers** but simply by the fact that the **signified**, the
meanings of different words in different languages, rarely overlap
completely. If we picture as a field or area all the possible meanings
that can be conveyed, then English has chosen its own unique way of
cutting up the field. In most cases the student's language has opted
for different divisions.

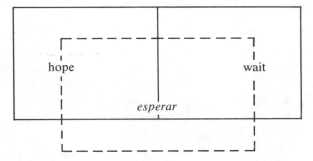

In the diagram above the divisions made by English are in solid
lines, those by Spanish in dotted lines. The fields covered by English
hope and *wait* are partly covered by Spanish *esperar*. Thus the
Spanish speaker who has learned *esperar* = *hope* or *hope for* will
also apply this equation in situations in which *esperar* is used in the
field covered by English *wait*. He might say that he is **hoping for the
bus*, while in fact he is only *waiting* for it.

In general the problems created by the lack of complete overlap
in meaning areas are of two types: (1) either the foreign language uses
two or more expressions corresponding to the area of meaning covered
by one expression in English; or (2) English uses two or more expressions for the meanings covered by one expression in the foreign language.

Situation (1) will normally result in failure to comprehend. To give
an example:

> English *for the first time* = Spanish *por primera vez*
> English *what time is it?* = Spanish *¿qué hora es?*
> English *I haven't any time* = Spanish *no tengo tiempo*

A Spanish speaker establishing the equation *time* = *vez* may completely misunderstand the English question: *what time is it?* He might
respond: *oh, it's the second time.*

Situation (2) may result in faulty expression as well as in a failure to comprehend. It can also be illustrated by the English/Spanish correspondence of *time = tiempo*.

> *I haven't any time = No tengo tiempo*
> *It's nice weather = Hace buen tiempo*

English uses two expressions (*time, weather*) corresponding to the one Spanish word (*tiempo*). Now the problem of the Spanish speaker is not so much one of misunderstanding. If he does not know the word *weather* he will simply not understand the meaning of the sentence in which it is used; but if he knows the equation *time = tiempo* he may form a sentence **it's a nice time* or **it's a good time* (intending *it's nice weather*), and he will be completely misunderstood by the native speaker of English.

Since the vocabulary problems associated with confusions of meaning are specific to the native language background of the student, we can cite only a few examples. Even though the teacher may be unfamiliar with the native language of a student, he must become sensitive to possible trouble spots—especially those instances in which one English expression is used with very different and divergent meanings or where several English expressions are used for what appear to be similar or identical concepts.

Here is an example of two English expressions, utilizing the same verb (*leave*), which have very divergent meanings:

> *I left New York at six o'clock.*
> *I left my book in the desk.*

The concept of leaving a place is very different from "leaving behind" something (perhaps forgetting it).

The verb *miss* also has divergent meanings in different English expressions:

> *I missed the train.*
> *I missed the target completely.*
> *I missed my parents very much.*

The concepts expressed by *miss* in the above sentences are totally different. A sentence such as *I missed my parents* can be totally ambiguous and may be misunderstood very easily by someone familiar with only one of the concepts expressed by *miss*.

Expressions with widely divergent meanings must be contrasted in special exercises. Restatement exercises or situational cues are appropriate:

TEACHER: (after explaining the meanings of *miss*)
Charles came to the office at six o'clock.
The professor left at two minutes before six.
STUDENT: *Charles missed the professor.*
TEACHER: *Charles was very sad because his parents were away on a trip.*
STUDENT: *Charles missed his parents.*
TEACHER: *Charles threw a dart at the target, but hit the fence instead.*
STUDENT: *Charles missed the target.*

Here is an example of two English expressions utilizing two different verbs (*make/do*) for similar or identical concepts:

*Charles **did** his homework.*
*John **made** a present for his parents.*

Many languages do not make any distinction paralleling English *make/do*. In addition to being used as an auxiliary, *do* is often used as a main verb in expressions where it implies activity: *he did his homework*; *he did some wonderful things. Make* is used in a very similar meaning; however, it refers much more directly to the process of *producing, manufacturing.* Therefore, *make* is used with concrete objects: *we make shoes, refrigerators, autos.*

The following examples show both the similar and divergent concepts of *speak/talk/say/tell*:

*Charles **speaks** French.*
*Charles **speaks** to his friends.*
*Charles **spoke** at the dinner.*
*John **talks** to his friends.*
*John **talked** after dinner.*
*John **said** that he would help us.*
*John **said**: "I am going to help you."*
*John **said** to his friends that he would help us.*
*John **said** to his friends: "I am going to help you."*
*John **told** his friends the truth.*

*John **told** the truth to his friends.*
*John **told** us that he would help us.*
*John **told** us the story.*

The above examples demonstrate that the uses of these four verbs overlap at times, while at other times they are mutually exclusive. For many students it is extremely difficult to avoid confusing them in the mutually exclusive areas, and a great many examples and a great deal of practice are needed.

A few general rules that can guide the student are:

1. *Speak* is used with languages (*speak English, French*).
2. Both *speak* and *talk* can be used without a following direct object. *Speak* often refers to formal occasions (= *giving a speech*). *Talk* refers to a less formal type of occasion (= *giving a talk*).
3. *Speak, say, talk* can be used with a prepositional phrase beginning with *to*. The phrase is not replaceable by the indirect object without preposition. *Tell* can be used with both a prepositional phrase beginning with *to* and the indirect object construction without preposition.
4. Both *say* and *tell* can be used to introduce an indirect quote (*he said that . . .*; *he told his friends . . .*). In this use *tell* normally requires an indirect object.
5. *Say* does not require a prepositional expression with *to* and is the verb normally used to introduce a direct quote.

Another common problem for foreign students concerns the use of the prepositions *in/on/at* with an expression of time:

*I met him **in** June.*
*I think it was **on** Saturday **at** six.*

To the native speaker of English it seems rather obvious that, in time designations, *on* is used with dates, days of the week, and names of holidays; *in* with months and years; *at* with hours. This distinction may prove confusing to many students, and practice may be required to avoid mistakes such as **at June, *at Saturday*. In some instances the use of prepositions with time expressions is not governed by any obvious rule and must be learned case by case: for example, *at night* vs. *in the morning*.

(D) GENERAL PROBLEMS IN TEACHING
VOCABULARY

Certain aspects of teaching meaning and vocabulary have been the perennial subject of discussions among methodologists. What words are to be taught? How is the meaning to be conveyed to the students?

The question of what words are to be taught has led to the establishment of various types of frequency lists and frequency studies. Several factors must be taken into account when considering the value of such frequency studies. First, we must keep in mind the fundamental difference between **function words** (those words which, in part at least, convey structural relationships as well as lexical meaning) and the nouns, verbs, adjectives, and adverbs which convey primarily lexical meaning. Function words are limited in number (about 160), and they are likely to appear with high frequency in any sort of English regardless of the nature of the sample. The frequency with which nouns, adverbs, adjectives, and verbs appear is largely determined by the subject matter and style of the sample.

One of the main objections raised against frequency counts is that once we go beyond the function-word-dominated range of the first few hundred words, successive samples taken from different types of speech or writing show quite divergent frequencies for the same word. From this we can draw the conclusion that the question of what words to teach should be determined by the specific needs of the student, whenever possible. No matter what his needs, he must know the function words; but once we leave the range of the few hundred most frequent words, the vocabulary taught should reflect the student's interests and needs.

Following a general classification established some thirty years ago by H. E. Palmer, we may divide frequency counts into three types: **objective**, **subjective**, and **empirical**.

The **objective** type of frequency study (of which the frequency count of English published by Edward L. Thorndike in 1924 is the most famous example) is based on counting occurrences in a random type of sample: the larger the sample the greater the confidence that we can place in the count. One refinement that can be introduced in the objective type of count is the consideration of the range of occurrence of a word. The sample can be divided into subsamples (each perhaps taken from a different type of speech or writing), and we can determine in how many of the subsamples a word occurs. Obviously a certain frequency of occurrence in only one or two of several subsamples does not have the same status as the same frequency if it is found throughout all of the subsamples.

The **subjective** approach to frequency is exemplified best by the construction of *The System of Basic English* by Charles K. Ogden. The words included are not determined by a frequency count but are those judged necessary to express essential concepts. The goal is greatest possible economy. Hence all possible synonyms are avoided, and so are expressions which can be conveniently paraphrased. The goal of *Basic English* is the creation of an international language rather than the determination of a stock of words most essential within English or for the learner of English.

The **empirical** approach is in a sense a combination of the subjective and objective approaches. The frequency list is based primarily on an objective investigation of frequency in a sample or number of samples, but the choice of sample is based on subjective judgment, and even the frequencies found in the objective counts may be subject to various manipulations according to the intention of the investigator.

The concepts of **useful meanings** and **semantic frequency** introduce a degree of subjectivity into the frequency counts; they represent a very important and pedagogically useful refinement.

It is not enough to know that a word appears with a specific frequency; it is also important to find out which are the most and least important meanings with which the word appears. To include a word in a language course because it is frequent, and then to introduce and practice it with a meaning in which it occurs only very rarely, would contradict the purpose for which the frequency list was constructed and used in the first place. Frequency counts of semantic occurrence in English were made some thirty years ago by Professors Edward L. Thorndike and Irving Lorge at Columbia University and have been utilized to varying degrees in the construction of other frequency lists and teaching materials.

Memorization of vocabulary lists of paired English and foreign words without any contextual clues is a rather poor way of going about learning the meaning of words. This kind of vocabulary learning will lend to numerous errors and confusion of the type we have described in the preceding section of this chapter.

There are a few learning situations in which the use of vocabulary lists may be justified. A student interested in reading materials in a specific technical field can be given a vocabulary list adapted to his special field of interest. Since he is interested only in passive recognition, and the concepts involved are well known and well defined, a technical vocabulary list may prove useful to him. Even in a situation where production is the primary goal, vocabulary lists associated with a specific area of experience (for example, auto racing, football, travel, etc.) may be useful. The fact that each vocabulary item on the list is associated with a specific area of experience narrows its range of meanings so that misunderstanding or misapplication is less likely to occur. English *bank* corresponds to Spanish *orilla* (*shore, bank, edge*) as well as *banco*; but in a discussion of a river there will be no confusion as to what is being referred to. The tendency of words which are used in specific contextual situations to define each other can be used in teaching their meaning.

A perennial subject of discussion among foreign language teachers is whether or not the student's native language should be employed to explain the meaning of words or at least to give the native language equivalent of the foreign word. We recommend that the native language equivalent be utilized primarily as an economy measure and only with lexical words (not function words where the establishment of equivalents between native and English words may lead to both lexical and very serious grammatical mistakes). At times, explanation within English may become quite complicated and uneconomical, and may be beyond the student's comprehension. However, in many situations in which English is taught as a foreign language, it may be impossible to give equivalents in the student's native language, either because the native language is unknown to the teacher, or because the class is made up of students of many different language backgrounds. In the latter situation it would probably be most unwise to give native language equivalents for some of the students to the exclusion of others. The only way to convey meaning to the student is then either the use of realia, or pictures, or explanation in English. Explanation in English can be given through synonyms (*little = small*; *big = great*), antonyms (*little ≠ big*; *black ≠ white*), or through definition (*a butcher shop is a place where we buy meat*). A further possibility is the establishment of meaning through examples (*if Mrs. Smith wants to buy meat for dinner, she goes to the butcher shop*).

Intimately connected with the learning of the meaning of words through realia, examples, or definitions is the problem of the cultural context and the environment in which the words function. Here the language teacher must constantly keep in mind that the student is likely to equate American or English concepts with concepts familiar to him from his own cultural environment. It is quite possible for a student to understand meanings on the structural or lexical level but to misunderstand or misinterpret them completely on the cultural level. The realia and examples used to explain meanings should preferably reflect the real cultural environment in which the language normally functions. There is an intimate and inevitable link between the study and comprehension of language and its cultural environment.

Selective Bibliography

The bibliography does not aim to be exhaustive. It lists a series of books that may serve as useful outside reading and present in greater detail some of the material dealt with in this book. With very few exceptions, the bibliography does not list periodical articles. The symbol (R) after a reference indicates that it is particularly recommended. Books marked with (R) contain either documentation or additional reading supplementing individual chapters of this text. The asterisks used with the titles are an indication of the books' level of difficulty and of the degree of technical knowledge they either presuppose or attempt to impart. Two asterisks are reserved for the most technical works, of importance only to the reader with a special interest in linguistics. Books without any marking do not presuppose a technical knowledge of linguistics and do not aim at imparting a technical knowledge beyond the minimum needed for the application of linguistics in the classroom.

For further bibliographical references the reader may consult specific bibliographies of the teaching of English as a foreign language which have appeared comparatively recently.

AARONS, A. C. "TESOL Bibliography." *TESOL News Letter* 1 (1967).

ALLEN, VIRGINIA F., and FORMAN, SIDNEY. *English as a Second Language—A Comprehensive Bibliography*. New York: Teachers College Press, 1968.

BIRKMAIER, EMMA MARIE, and LANGE, DALE L. "A Selective Bibliography on the Teaching of Foreign Languages, 1920–1966." *Foreign Language Annals* 1 (1968): 318–353.

OHANNESIAN, S. *et al.*, eds. *Reference List of Materials for English as a Second Language*. Part 1. Texts, Readers, Dictionaries, Tests. Washington: Center for Applied Linguistics, 1964.

––––– *et al.*, eds. *Reference List of Materials for English as a Second*

Language. Part 2. Background Materials, Methodology. Washington: Center for Applied Linguistics, 1966.

————, and WINEBERG, R. E., eds. *Teaching English as a Second Language in Adult Education Programs: An Annotated Bibliography*. preliminary ed. Washington: Center for Applied Linguistics, 1966.

SHEN, YAO, and CRYMES, RUTH H. *Teaching English as a Second Language: A Classified Bibliography*. Honolulu: East–West Center Press, 1965.

Because of the availability of the abovementioned comparatively recent bibliographies and the rapidly changing nature of the field it was decided not to include a bibliography of teaching materials and texts and tests in this textbook.

I. Theoretical Foundations (General Linguistics, Phonetics, Psychology)

**BACH, EMMON. *An Introduction to Transformational Grammar*. New York: Holt, Rinehart & Winston, 1964.

*BACH, EMMON and HARMS, ROBERT, eds. *Universals in Linguistic Theory*. New York: Holt, Rinehart & Winston, 1968.

BELYAYEV, B. V. *The Psychology of Teaching Foreign Languages*. Translated by Dr. R. F. Hingley. New York: Macmillan Co., 1964.

*BLOCH, BERNARD, and TRAGER, GEORGE. *Outline of Linguistic Analysis*. Baltimore: Linguistic Society of America, 1942 (reprinted in 1950).

*BLOOMFIELD, LEONARD. *Language*. New York: Henry Holt & Co., 1945.

BOLINGER, DWIGHT. *Aspects of Language*. New York: Harcourt, Bruce and World, 1968.

BURLING, ROBBINS. *Man's Many Voices: Language in its Cultural Context*. New York: Holt, Rinehart & Winston, 1970.

CARROLL, JOHN B. *The Study of Language*. Cambridge, Mass.: Harvard University Press, 1953.

————. "Research on Teaching Foreign Languages." In *Handbook of Research on Teaching*, edited by Nathaniel L. Gage, Chicago: Rand McNally & Co., 1963.

————, and SAPON, S. M. *Manual, Modern Language Aptitude Test*. New York: Psychological Corporation, 1959.

*CHAFE, WALLACE L. *Meaning and the Structure of Language*. Chicago: University of Chicago Press, 1970.

**CHOMSKY, NOAM. *Syntactic Structures*. The Hague and Paris: Mouton & Co., 1957.

————. *Aspects of the Theory of Syntax*. Cambridge, Mass.: MIT Press, 1965.

*COOK, WALTER A., S.J. *Introduction to Tagmemic Analysis*. New York: Holt, Rinehart & Winston, 1969.

DE CECCO, JOHN P. *The Psychology of Language, Thought and Instruction*. New York: Holt, Rinehart & Winston, 1967.

DINNEEN, FRANCIS P., S. J. *An Introduction to General Linguistics*. New York: Holt, Rinehart & Winston, 1967.

*EISENSON, JON. *The Psychology of Speech*. New York: Crofts, 1946.

FERGUSON, CHARLES E., supervisor. *Teaching a Second Language* (Series of five films on 1. Nature of Language, 2. The Sounds of Language, 3. Organization of Language, 4. Words and Their Meanings, 5. Modern Techniques in Language Teaching). New York: Teaching Film Custodians, 1963.

———. Teaching Manual to accompany *Teaching a Second Language*. Washington, D. C.: Center for Applied Linguistics, 1963.

*GLEASON, H. A., JR. *An Introduction to Descriptive Linguistics*. Rev. ed. New York: Holt, Rinehart & Winston, 1961.

*HAAS, WILLIAM; UITTI, KARL D.; and WELLS, RULON. *Linguistics*. Englewood Cliffs, N. J.: Prentice-Hall, 1964.

HALL, ROBERT A., JR. *Introductory Linguistics*. Philadelphia: Chilton Co., 1964.

———. *Linguistics and Your Language*. New York: Doubleday & Co., 1960.

HAMMER, JOHN H., and RICE, FRANK A., eds. *A Bibliography of Contrastive Linguistics*. Washington, D.C.: Center for Applied Linguistics, 1965.

**HARRIS, ZELLIG S. *Structural Linguistics*. Chicago: University of Chicago Press, Phoenix Books, 1963.

*HEFFNER, R.-M. S. *General Phonetics*. Madison: University of Wisconsin Press, 1949.

HERRIOT, PETER. *An Introduction to the Psychology of Language*. London: Methuen & Co., Ltd., 1970.

*HILL, ARCHIBALD A. *Introduction to Linguistic Structures*. New York: Harcourt, Brace & Co., 1958.

*HOCKETT, CHARLES F. *A Course in Modern Linguistics*. New York: Macmillan Co., 1958.

*———. *The State of the Art*. The Hague: Mouton, 1968.

HOIJER, HARRY, ed. *Language and Culture*. Conference on the Interrelations of Language and other Aspects of Culture. Chicago: University of Chicago Press, 1954.

HUGHES, JOHN P. *The Science of Language: An Introduction to Linguistics*. New York: Random House, 1962.

JAKOBOVITS, LEON A. *Foreign Language Learning: A Psycholinguistic Analysis of the Issues*. Rowley, Mass.: Newbury House, 1970.

KOUTSOUDAS, A. *Writing Transformational Grammars (An Introduction)*. New York: McGraw-Hill Book Co., 1966.

**LAKOFF, GEORGE. *Irregularity in Syntax*. New York: Holt, Rinehart & Winston, 1970.

LANGACKER, RONALD W. *Language and Its Structure*. New York: Harcourt, Brace & World, 1968.

LYONS, JOHN. *Introduction to General Linguistics*. Cambridge, England: Cambridge University Press, 1968.

MARTINET, ANDRÉ. *Elements of General Linguistics*. Chicago: University of Chicago Press, 1964.

――――. *Elements de linguistique générale*. Paris: Collection Armand Colin, 1960.

**OGDEN, C. K., and RICHARDS, I. A. *The Meaning of Meaning*. New York: Harcourt, Brace & Co., 1923.

ORNSTEIN, JACOB, and GAGE, WILLIAM. *The ABC's of Language and Linguistics*. Philadelphia: Chilton Co., 1964.

*OSGOOD, CHARLES, and SEBEOK, THOMAS, eds. *Psycholinguistics, A Survey of Theory and Research Problems*. Supplement to International Journal of American Linguistics. Baltimore: Waverley Press, 1954.

PEI, MARIO. *Invitation to Linguistics, A Basic Introduction to the Science of Language*. Garden City, N.Y.: Doubleday & Co., 1965.

**PIKE, KENNETH. *Language in Relation to a Unified Theory of the Structure of Human Behavior*. 2nd rev. ed. The Hague: Mouton & Co., 1967. Co., 1967.

**――――. *Phonemics: A Technique of Reducing Languages to Writing*. Ann Arbor: University of Michigan Press, 1947.

*――――. *Phonetics: A Critical Analysis of Phonetic Theory and a Technique for the Practical Description of Sounds*. Ann Arbor: University of Michigan Press, 1943.

*POTTER, SIMEON. *Modern Linguistics*. New York: W. W. Norton & Co., 1964.

The Principles of the International Phonetic Association, Being a Description of the International Phonetic Alphabet and the Manner of Using it. London: International Phonetic Association, 1953.

RIVERS, WILGA M. *The Psychologist and the Foreign-Language Teacher*. Chicago: University of Chicago Press, 1964. (R).

SAPIR, EDWARD. *Language: An Introduction to the Study of Speech*. New York: Harcourt, Brace & Co., 1921 (Paperback edition: Harvest Books, New York: Harcourt, Brace & World, Inc., 1949).

*SAPORTA, SOL, ed. *Psycholinguistics: A Book of Readings*. New York: Holt, Rinehart & Winston, 1961.

*SAUSSURE, FERDINAND DE. *Cours de linguistique générale*. Publié par Charles Bally et Albert Sechehaye avec la collaboration d'Albert Riedlinger. Paris: Payot, 1955.

*――――. *Course in General Linguistics*. Translated by Wade Baskin. New York: Philosophical Library, 1959.

SCHERER, GEORGE A. C., and WERTHEIMER, MICHAEL. *A Psychological Experiment in Foreign Language Teaching*. New York: McGraw-Hill Book Co., 1964.

*SKINNER, B. F. *Verbal Behavior*. New York: Appleton-Century-Crofts, 1957.

SMALLEY, WILLIAM A. *Manual of Articulatory Phonetics*. Rev. ed. 3 vols. Tarrytown, N.Y.: Division of Foreign Missions, NCCG, 1962–63.

*WEINREICH, URIEL. *Languages in Contact*. New York: Publications of the Linguistic Circle of New York, No. 1, 1953.

*WHATMOUGH, JOSHUA, *Language, A Modern Synthesis*. London: Secker and Warburg, 1956 (Paperback, New York: Mentor Books, The New American Library, 1957).

WILSON, GRAHAM, ed. *A Linguistics Reader*. New York: Harper & Row, 1967.

II. Applied Linguistics

ALLEN, HAROLD B., ed. *Readings in Applied English Linguistics*. 2nd ed. New York: Appleton-Century-Crofts, 1964. (R).

BELASCO, SIMON, ed. *Anthology for Use with a Guide for Teachers in NDEA Language Institutes*. Boston: D. C. Heath & Co., 1961.

BLOOMFIELD, LEONARD. *Outline Guide for the Practical Study of Foreign Languages*. Baltimore: Linguistic Society of America, 1942.

CORNELIUS, EDWIN T., JR. *Language Teaching (A Guide for Teachers of Foreign Languages)*. New York: Thomas Y. Crowell Co., 1953.

FERGUSON, CHARLES A., and STEWART, WILLIAM A. *Linguistic Reading Lists for Teachers of Modern Languages*. Washington, D.C.: Center for Applied Linguistics, 1963.

FRAZER, HUGH, and O'DONNELL, W. R., eds. *Applied Linguistics and the Teaching of English*. London: Longmans, Green & Co., 1969.

HALL, ROBERT A., JR. *New Ways to Learn a Foreign Language*. New York: Bantam Books, Inc., 1966.

HALLIDAY, M. A. K.; MCINTOSH, ANGUS; and STREVENS, PETER. *The Linguistic Sciences and Language Teaching*. Bloomington: Indiana University Press, 1965.

HARDING, DAVID H. *The New Patterns of Language Teaching*. London: Longmans, Green & Co., 1968.

HARSH, WAYNE. *Grammar Instruction Today*. Davis, Cal.: Davis Publications in English, No. 1, 1965.

HUGHES, JOHN P. *Linguistics and Language Teaching*. New York: Random House, 1968.

LADO, ROBERT. *Language Teaching: A Scientific Approach*. New York: McGraw-Hill Book Co., 1964. (R).

————. *Linguistics across Cultures: Applied Linguistics for Language Teachers*. Ann Arbor: University of Michigan Press, 1957. (R).

LESTER, MARK. *Readings in Applied Transformational Grammar*. New York: Holt, Rinehart & Winston, 1970.

MACKEY, WILLIAM FRANCIS. *Language Teaching Analysis*. London: Longmans, Green & Co., 1965.

MOULTON, WILLIAM G. *A Linguistic Guide to Language Learning*. New York: The Modern Language Association of America, 1970.

PEI, MARIO. *How to Learn Languages and What Languages to Learn*. New York: Harper & Row, 1966.

POLITZER, ROBERT L. *Foreign Language Learning—A Linguistic Introduction*. Englewood Cliffs, N.J.: Prentice-Hall, 1965.

SMITH, HENRY LEE, JR. *Linguistic Science and the Teaching of English*. Cambridge, Mass.: Harvard University Press, 1956.

III. General Methodology, Classroom and Laboratory Techniques

"What Do We Know about Teaching Modern Foreign Languages?" Audio Visual Instruction, vol. 4. no. 6 (September 1959). National Education Association, Department of Audio Visual Instruction.
Entire volume is devoted to language instruction, laboratory equipment, and techniques.

ABERCROMBIE, DAVID. *Problems and Principles in Language Study.* 2nd ed. London: Longmans, Green & Co., 1963.

BARRUTIA, RICHARD. *Language Learning and Machine Teaching.* Philadelphia: The Center for Curriculum Development, Inc., 1970.

BROOKS, NELSON. *Language and Language Learning: Theory and Practice.* 2nd ed. New York: Harcourt, Brace & World, 1964. (R).

CAPRETZ, PIERRE J., project director. *Audio Lingual Techniques for Teaching Foreign Languages.* Washington, D.C.: Norwood Films, 1963.

COCHRAN, ANNE. *Modern Methods of Teaching English as a Foreign Language. A Guide to Modern Materials with Particular Reference to the Far East.* Washington, D.C.: Educational Service, 1954.

CORDER, S. PIT. *The Visual Element in Language Teaching.* London: Longmans, Green & Co., 1969.

DACANAY, FE R., and BOWEN, J. DONALD. *Techniques and Procedures in Second Language Teaching.* Quezon City, Republic of the Philippines: Alemar–Phoenix Publishing House, 1963. (R).

DONOGHUE, MILDRED R. *Foreign Language and the Schools (A Book of Readings).* Dubuque, Iowa: Wm. C. Brown Co., 1967.

———. *Foreign Languages and the Elementary Schoolchild.* Dubuque, Iowa: Wm. C. Brown Co., 1968.

FINN, JAMES D., and PERRIN, DONALD G. *Teaching Machines and Programmed Learning: A Survey of the Industry—1962.* Washington, D.C.: U.S. Department of Health, Education and Welfare, Office of Education, Contract No. OE-34019, 1962.

FINOCCHIARO, MARY. *Teaching Children Foreign Languages.* New York: McGraw-Hill Book Co., 1964.

HARRIS, DAVID P. *Testing English as a Second Language.* New York: McGraw-Hill Book Co., 1969.

HIRSCH, RUTH. *Audio-Visual Aids in Language Teaching.* Monograph Series on Languages and Linguistics, No. 5. Washington, D.C.: The Institute of Languages and Linguistics, School of Foreign Service, Georgetown University, 1954.

HOCKING, ELTON. *Language Laboratory and Language Learning.* Washington, D.C.: Department of Audio-Visual Instruction, National Education Association of the United States, Monograph 2, 1964.

HOWATT, A. P. R. *Programmed Learning and the Language Teacher.* London: Longmans, Green & Co., 1969.

HUEBNER, THEODORE. *Audio-Visual Techniques in Teaching Foreign Languages: A Practical Handbook.* New York: New York University Press, 1960.

———. *How to Teach Foreign Languages Effectively.* New York: New York University Press, 1959.

HUTCHINSON, JOSEPH C. *Modern Foreign Languages in High School: The Language Laboratory.* Washington, D.C.: Office of Education, 1961.

JESPERSEN, OTTO. *How to Teach a Foreign Language.* New York: Macmillan Co., 1904.

JODICE, DON R. *Guidelines to Language Teaching in Classroom and Laboratory.* Washington, D.C.: Electronic Teaching Laboratories, 1961.

JOHNSTON, MARJORIE C., and SEERLEY, CATHERINE C. *Foreign Language Laboratories in Schools and Colleges.* Washington, D.C.: U.S. Department of Health, Education, and Welfare, bulletin 1959, no. 3.

KELLY, LOUIS G. *25 Centuries of Language Teaching.* Rowley, Mass.: Newbury House, 1969.

KONE, ELLIOT H., ed. *Language Laboratories—Modern Techniques in Teaching Foreign Languages.* New York: Bulletin of the Connecticut Audio-Visual Education Association, vol. 19, 1959–60.

LADO, ROBERT. *Language Testing: The Construction and Use of Foreign Language Tests, A Teacher's Book.* London: Longmans, Green & Co., 1961; New York: McGraw-Hill Book Co., 1964. (R).

LEE, W. R., and COPPEN, HELEN. *Simple Audio-Visual Aids to Foreign Language Teaching.* London: Oxford University Press, 1964.

MARTY, FERNAND L. *Language Laboratory Learning.* Wellesley, Mass.: Audio-Visual Publications, 1960. (R).

———. *Programming a Basic Foreign Language Course: Prospects for Self-Instruction.* Hollins, Va.: Audio-Visual Publications, 1962.

MERAS, EDMOND A. *A Language Teacher's Guide.* 2nd ed. New York: Harper & Row, 1962. (R).

MICHEL, JOSEPH, ed. *Foreign Language Teaching: An Anthology.* New York: Macmillan Co., 1967.

MORTON, R. "The Language Laboratory as a Teaching Machine." *International Journal of American Linguistics* 26 (1960): 113–166.

NEWMARK, MAXIM, ed. *Twentieth Century Modern Language Teaching.* New York: Philosophical Library, 1948.

NOSTRAND, HOWARD LEE et al. *Research on Language Teaching: An Annotated International Bibliography for 1945–1964.* 2nd ed., rev. Seattle and London: University of Washington Press, 1965.

O'CONNOR, PATRICIA. *Modern Foreign Languages in High School: Pre-reading Instruction.* Washington, D.C.: Contract No. OE-2700, bulletin 1960, no. 9.

ORNSTEIN, JACOB; EWTON, RALPH W., JR.; and MUELLER, THEODORE H. *Programmed Instruction and Educational Technology in Language Teaching.* Philadelphia: The Center for Curriculum Development, Inc., 1970.

PALMER, HAROLD E. *The Principles of Language Study.* London: Oxford University Press, 1964. (R).

POLITZER, ROBERT L. *Performance Criteria for Foreign Language Teachers.* Stanford, Calif.: Center for Research and Development in Teaching, Stanford University, 1966.

QUILTER, DANIEL E. *Do's and Don't's in Audio-Visual Teaching*. Waltham, Mass.: Blaisdell Publishing Co., 1966.

RIVERS, WILGA. *Teaching Foreign Language Skills*. Chicago: University of Chicago Press, 1968.

STACK, EDWARD M. *The Language Laboratory and Modern Language Teaching*. 2nd ed. New York: Oxford University Press, 1966. (R).

STERN, H. H., ed. *Foreign Languages in Primary Education: The Teaching of Foreign or Second Languages to Younger Children*. Hamburg, Germany: UNESCO Institute for Education, 1963.

STREVENS, PETER. *Aural Aids in Language Teaching*. London: Longmans, Green & Co., 1958.

SWEET, HENRY. *The Practical Study of Languages: A Guide for Teachers and Learners*. London: Oxford University Press, 1964.

VALETTE, REBECCA M. *Modern Language Testing*. New York: Harcourt, Brace & World, 1967.

VALDMAN, ALBERT, ed. *Trends in Language Teaching*. New York: McGraw-Hill Book Co., 1966.

WALSH, DONALD D. *What's What: A List of Useful Terms for the Teacher of Modern Languages*. New York: The Modern Language Association of America, 1963.

IV. Methodology of Teaching English as a Second Language

Teaching English as a New Language to Adults. New York: New York City Board of Education, 1964.

Visual Aids for English as a Second Language. Washington, D.C.: Center for Applied Linguistics, 1965.

ALLEN, HAROLD B., ed. *Teaching English as a Second Language: A Book of Readings*. New York: McGraw-Hill Book Co., 1965. (R).

ALLEN, VIRGINIA FRENCH, ed. *On Teaching English to Speakers of other Languages*. Papers read at the TESOL conference, May 1964. Champaign, Ill.: National Council of Teachers of English, 1965.

BUMPASS, FAYE L. *Teaching Young Students English as a Foreign Language*. New York: American Book Co., 1963. (R).

CHAPMAN, L. R. H. *Teaching English to Beginners*. London: Longmans, Green & Co., 1958.

CLOSE, Q. A. *English as a Foreign Language*. London: Allen & Unwin, 1962.

DERRICK, JUNE. *Teaching English to Immigrants*. London: Longmans, Green & Co., 1969.

DIXSON, ROBERT J. *Practical Guide to the Teaching of English as a Foreign Language*. New York: Regents Publishing Co., 1960.

FINOCCHIARO, MARY. *English as a Second Language: From Theory to Practice*. New York: Regents Publishing Co., 1964. (R).

————. *Teaching English as a Second Language*. Rev. ed. New York: Harper & Row, 1969. (R).

FRENCH, F. G. *Teaching English as an International Language*. London: Oxford University Press, 1963.

FRIES, CHARLES C. *Teaching and Learning English as a Foreign Language.* Ann Arbor: University of Michigan Press, 1945. (R).

FRISBY, A. W. *Teaching English: Notes and Comments on Teaching English Overseas.* London: Longmans, Green & Co., 1957.

GAUNTLETT, J. O. *Teaching English as a Foreign Language.* Rev. ed. London: Macmillan Co., 1961.

GURREY, P. *Teaching English as Foreign Language.* London: Longmans, Green & Co., 1955.

HORNBY, A. S. *The Teaching of Structural Words and Sentence Patterns.* 3 vols. London: Oxford University Press, 1959–62.

KREIDLER, CAROL J., ed. *On Teaching English to Speakers of Other Languages.* Papers read at the TESOL Conference, San Diego, Calif., March 1965. Champaign, Ill.: National Council of Teachers of English, 1966.

LUGTON, ROBERT C., ed. *English as a Second Language: Current Issues.* Philadelphia: The Center for Curriculum Development, Inc., 1970.

———, ed. *Preparing the EFL Teacher: A Projection for the '70's.* Philadelphia: The Center for Curriculum Development, Inc., 1970.

MILLER, P. C. *Beginning to Teach English.* London: Oxford University Press, 1963.

MORRIS, ISAAC. *The Art of Teaching English as a Living Language.* London: Macmillan Co., 1954.

PALMER, HAROLD E. *The Oral Method of Teaching Languages.* Cambridge, England: W. Heffer & Sons, Ltd., 1921.

———. *The Teaching of Oral English.* London: Longmans, Green & Co., 1940.

——— and PALMER, DOROTHÉE. *English Through Actions.* London: Longmans, Green & Co., 1959.

ROBINETT, BETTY WALLACE, ed. *On Teaching English to Speakers of Other Languages.* Papers read at the TESOL Conference in New York City, March 1966. Washington, D.C.: Teachers of English to Speakers of Other Languages, 1967.

STEVICK, EARL W. *Helping People Learn English: A Manual for Teachers of English as a Second Language.* Nashville, Tenn.: Abingdon Press, 1957.

———. *A Workbook in Language Teaching (With Special Reference to English as a Foreign Language).* Nashville, Tenn.: Abingdon Press, 1963.

WEST, M. *The Teaching of English: A Guide to the New Method Series.* London: Longmans, Green & Co., 1953.

V. English Phonetics, Teaching of Pronunciation.

ARMSTRONG, LILIAS E., and WARD, IDA C. *A Handbook of English Intonation.* 2nd ed. Cambridge, England: W. Heffer & Sons, Ltd., 1931.

ARNOLD, G. F. *Stress in English Words.* Amsterdam: North-Holland, 1957.

BRONSTEIN, ARTHUR J. *The Pronunciation of American English: An Introduction to Phonetics.* New York: Appleton-Century-Crofts, 1960.

BUCHANAN, C. D. *A Programed Introduction to Linguistics: Phonetics and Phonemics*. Boston: D. C. Heath & Co., 1963.

CATFORD, J. C., and OGDEN, C. K. *Word-Stress and Sentence-Stress*. London: Basic English Publishing Co., 1956.

CHOMSKY, NOAM, and HALLE, MORRIS. *The Sound Pattern of English*. New York: Harper & Row, 1968.

CHRISTOPHERSEN, P. *An English Phonetics Course*. London: Longmans, Green & Co., 1956.

GIMSON, A. C. *An Introduction to the Pronunciation of English*. London: Edward Arnold, 1962.

JONES, DANIEL. *Everyman's English Pronouncing Dictionary*. 12th ed. London: J. M. Dent, 1963.

———. *The Pronunciation of English*. 4th rev. ed. Cambridge, England: Cambridge University Press, 1956.

———. *An Outline of English Phonetics*. 8th ed. Cambridge, England: W. Heffer & Sons, Ltd., 1957.

KENYON, JOHN S. *American Pronunciation: A Textbook of Phonetics for Students of English*. 10th ed. Ann Arbor, Mich.: George Wahr Publishing Co., 1961.

———, and KNOTT, THOMAS A. *A Pronouncing Dictionary of American English*. 4th ed. Springfield, Mass.: G. & C. Merriam, 1953.

KING, HAROLD V. *English Phonology: Guide and Work Book*. Ann Arbor, Mich.: Ann Arbor Publishers, 1961.

KINGDON, ROGER. *The Groundwork of English Stress*. London: Longmans, Green & Co., 1958.

———. *Groundwork of English Intonation*. London: Longmans, Green & Co., 1958.

KRUISINGA, E. *An Introduction to the Study of English Sounds*. 12th ed. Groningen, The Netherlands: Noordhoff, 1960.

LEUTENEGGER, RALPH R. *The Sounds of American English: An Introduction to Phonetics*. Chicago: Scott, Foresman & Co., 1963.

PIKE, KENNETH L. *The Intonation of American English*. Ann Arbor: University of Michigan Press, 1945.

PLAISTER, TED. *English Monosyllables. A Minimal Pair Locator List for English as a Second Language*. Honolulu: East-West Center Press, 1965.

SCHUBIGER, MARIA. *English Intonation: Its Form and Function*. Tübingen, W. Germany: Max Niemeyer Verlag, 1958.

SHEN, YAO. *Articulation Diagrams of English Vowels and Consonants*. Ann Arbor: University of Michigan Press, 1958. (R).

———. *English Phonetics (Especially for Teachers of English as a Foreign Language)*. Ann Arbor, Mich.: Author, 1962. (R).

THOMAS, CHARLES KENNETH. *An Introduction to the Phonetics of American English*. 2nd ed. New York: Ronald Press, 1958.

WALLACE, B. J. *The Pronunciation of American English for Teachers of English as a Second Language*. Rev. ed. Ann Arbor, Mich.: George Wahr Publishing Co., 1957.

WARD, IDA C. *The Phonetics of English.* 4th ed. Cambridge, England: W. Heffer & Sons, Ltd., 1954.

WISE, CLAUDE MERTON. *Introduction to Phonetics.* Englewood Cliffs, N. J.: Prentice-Hall, 1958.

VI. Sound/Symbol Relation in English

ALLEN, ROBERT L.; ALLEN, VIRGINIA F.; and SHUTE, MARGARET. *English Sounds and Their Spellings.* New York: Thomas Y. Crowell Co., 1966. (R).

BLOOMFIELD, LEONARD, and BARNHART, CLARENCE L. *Let's Read: A Linguistic Approach.* Detroit: Wayne State University Press, 1961.

FRIEDRICH, WOLFGANG A. *English Pronunciation: The Relationship between Pronunciation and Orthography.* Translated by R. A. Martin. London: Longmans, Green & Co., 1958.

HALL, ROBERT A., JR. *Sounds and Spelling in English.* Philadelphia: Chilton Co., 1961.

HANNA, PAUL R.; HANNA, JEAN S.; HODGES, RICHARD E.; and RUDORF, EDWIN H., JR. *Phoneme-Grapheme Correspondence as Cues to Spelling Improvement.* Washington, D.C.: U.S. Department of Health, Education and Welfare, U.S. Office of Education, 1966.

LEFEVRE, CARL A. *Linguistics and the Teaching of Reading.* New York: McGraw-Hill Book Co., 1964. (R).

SMITH, HENRY LEE, JR. *English Morphophonics—Implications for the Teaching of Literacy.* Oswego, N.Y.: The New York State English Council, 1968.

WEIR, RUTH H., and VENEZKY, RICHARD L. *Rules to Aid in the Teaching of Reading.* Stanford, Calif.: Stanford University (Cooperative Research Project No. 2584), 1964.

WHITFORD, HAROLD C. *A Dictionary of American Homophones and Homographs.* New York: Teachers College Press, 1966.

WIJK, AXEL. *Rules of Pronunciation for the English Language (An Account of the Relationship between English Spelling and Pronunciation).* London: Oxford University Press, 1966. (R).

VII. General Works on English Structure (Morphology, Syntax)

BOLINGER, DWIGHT L. *Interrogative Structures of American English.* University: The University of Alabama Press, 1957.

BRENGELMAN, FREDERICK H. *The English Language: An Introduction for Teachers.* Englewood Cliffs, N.J.: Prentice-Hall, 1970.

CATTELL, N. R. *The New English Grammar. A Descriptive Introduction.* Cambridge, Mass., and London, England: MIT Press, 1969.

CURME, GEORGE O. *Syntax.* A Grammar of the English Language, vol. 3. Boston: D. C. Heath & Co., 1931.

———. *Parts of Speech and Accidence.* A Grammar of the English Language, vol. 2. Boston: D. C. Heath & Co., 1935.

FRANCIS, WINTHROP NELSON. *The Structure of American English.* New York: Ronald Press, 1958.

FRIEND, JOSEPH H. *An Introduction to English Linguistics.* Cleveland: World Publishing Co., 1967.

FRIES, CHARLES C. *The Structure of English: An Introduction to the Construction of English Sentences.* New York: Harcourt, Brace & World, 1952. (R).

*GLEASON, H. A., JR. *Linguistics and English Grammar.* New York: Holt, Rinehart & Winston, 1965. (R).

GREENBAUM, SIDNEY, *Studies in English Adverbial Usage.* Coral Gables, Fla.: University of Miami Press, 1970.

HATCHER, ANNA GRANVILLE. *Modern English Word Formation and Neo-Latin.* Baltimore: Johns Hopkins Press, 1951.

HATHAWAY, BAXTER. *A Transformational Syntax. The Grammar of Modern American English.* New York: Ronald Press, 1967.

HERNDON, JEANNE H. *A Survey of Modern Grammars.* New York: Holt, Rinehart & Winston, 1970.

HIRTLE, W. H. *The Simple and the Progressive Forms, An Analytical Approach.* Quebec: Les Presses de l'Université Laval, 1967.

JACOBS, RODERICK, and ROSENBAUM, PETER S. *English Transformational Grammar,* Waltham, Mass.: Blaisdell Publishing Co., 1968.

JESPERSEN, OTTO. *Essentials of English Grammar.* New York: Holt, Rinehart & Winston, 1933; University: University of Alabama Press, 1964. (R).

––––––. *A Modern English Grammar on Historical Principles.* 7 vols. London: Allen & Unwin, 1909–49.

JOOS, MARTIN. *The English Verb (Form and Meanings).* Madison and Milwaukee: The University of Wisconsin Press, 1964.

JUILLAND, A., and MACRIS, J. *The English Verb System.* The Hague: Mouton & Co., 1962.

KING, HAROLD V. *English Morphology: Guide and Workbook.* Ann Arbor, Mich.: Ann Arbor Publishers, 1961.

––––––. *Guide and Workbook in the Structure of English.* Englewood Cliffs, N.J.: Prentice-Hall, 1967.

KRUISINGA, E. *A Handbook of Present-Day English.* Part I: English Sounds, 4th ed. Utrecht: Xemink en Zoon, 1925. Part II: English Accidence and Syntax, 5th ed., 3 vols. Groningen: Noordhoff, 1931–32.

LANGENDOEN, D. TERENCE. *The Study of Syntax: The Generative–Transformational Approach to the Structure of American English.* New York: Holt, Rinehart & Winston, 1969.

*LEES, ROBERT B. *The Grammar of English Nominalizations.* 4th printing. Bloomington: Indiana University Press, 1966. (R).

LONG, RALPH B. *The Sentence and Its Parts: A Grammar of Contemporary English.* Chicago: University of Chicago Press, 1961.

*MARCHAND, HANS. *The Categories and Types of Present-Day English Word-Formation.* 2nd ed. Munich: C. H. Beck, 1969.

MARCKWARDT, ALBERT H. *American English*. New York: Oxford University Press, 1958.

MENCKEN, H. L. *The American Language: An Inquiry into the Development of English in the United States*. 4th ed. New York: Alfred A. Knopf, 1963.

NIDA, EUGENE. *A Synopsis of English Syntax*. Benjamin Elson, ed. Norman, Okla.: Summer Institute of Linguistics, 1960.

PALMER, F. R. *A Linguistic Study of the English Verb*. Coral Gables, Fla.: University of Miami Press, 1968.

PALMER, HAROLD E., and BLANDFORD, F. G. *A Grammar of Spoken English*. 3rd ed. Cambridge, England: W. Heffer & Sons, Ltd., 1969.

POUTSMA, H. *A Grammar of Late Modern English*. 5 vols. Groningen, The Netherlands: Noordhoff, 1914–29.

ROBBINS, BEVERLY L. *The Definite Article in English Transformations*. New York: Humanities Press, 1968.

ROBERTS, PAUL. *English Sentences*. 2 vols. New York: Harcourt, Brace & World, 1962. (R).

———. *English Syntax: A Book of Programed Lessons*. New York: Harcourt, Brace & World, 1964.

———. *Modern Grammar*. New York: Harcourt, Brace & World, 1968.

ROSENBAUM, PETER S. *The Grammar of English Predicate Complement Constructions*. Cambridge, Mass.: MIT Press, 1967.

SAK, F. L. *The Structure of English: A Practical Grammar for Foreign Students*. Bern: A. Francke AG, 1954.

SCHEUERWEGHS, G. *Present-Day English Syntax: A Survey of Patterns*. London: Longmans, Green & Co., 1959.

SLEDD, JAMES A. *A Short Introduction to English Grammar*. Chicago: Scott, Foresman & Co., 1959. (R).

STAGEBERG, NORMAN. *An Introductory English Grammar*. New York: Holt, Rinehart & Winston, 1965. (R).

STAUBACH, CHARLES N. *Two-Word Verbs (A Study in Idiomatic English)*. 2nd ed. Bogota, Colombia: Centro-Colombo-Americano, 1951. (R).

STRANG, BARBARA M. H. *Modern English Structure*. New York: St. Martin's Press, 1962.

THOMAS, OWEN. *Transformational Grammar and the Teacher of English*. New York: Holt, Rinehart & Winston, 1965. (R).

TRAGER, GEORGE L., and SMITH, HENRY LEE, JR. *An Outline of English Structure*. Norman, Okla.: Battenburg, 1951.

TWADDELL, W. FREEMAN. *The English Verb Auxiliaries*. 2nd rev. ed. Providence, R.I.: Brown University Press, 1963.

VALLINS, G. H. *The Patterns of English*. London: Deutsch, 1956.

VENDLER, ZENO. *Adjectives and Nominalizations*. New York: Humanities Press, 1968.

WHITEHALL, HAROLD. *Structural Essentials of English*. New York: Harcourt, Brace & World, 1956.

ZANDVOORT, REINARD W. *A Handbook of English Grammar*. London: Longmans, Green & Co., 1957.

VIII. English Vocabulary (Frequency Counts, Idioms)

BALL, W. J. *Conversational English, An Analysis of Contemporary Spoken English for Foreign Students.* London: Longmans, Green & Co., 1954.

————. *A Practical Guide to Colloquial Idiom.* London: Longmans, Green & Co., 1958.

BONGERS, HERMAN, *The History and Principles of Vocabulary Control.* Worden, Holland: Wocopi, 1947.

COLLINS, VERA H. *A Book of English Idioms.* 3rd ed. London: Longmans, Green & Co., 1958.

————. *A Second Book of English Idioms.* London: Longmans, Green & Co., 1958.

————. *A Third Book of English Idioms.* London: Longmans, Green & Co., 1960.

FRIES, CHARLES C., and TRAVER, A. AILEEN. *English Wordlists: A Study of their Adaptability for Instruction.* Ann Arbor, Mich.: George Wahr Publishing Co., 1950.

LORGE, IRVING. *The Semantic Count of the 570 Commonest English Words.* New York: Teachers College, Columbia University, 1949.

OGDEN, CHARLES K. *The System of Basic English.* 3rd ed. New York: Harcourt, Brace & World, 1944.

RICHARDS, I. A. *Basic English and Its Uses.* London: Kegan Paul, Trench, Trubner, 1943.

THORNDIKE, EDWARD L., and LORGE, IRVING. *The Teachers Wordbook of 30,000 Words.* New York: Bureau of Publications, Teachers College, Columbia University, 1944.

WEST, MICHAEL P. *A General Service List of English Words with Semantic Frequencies and Supplementary Word-List for the Writing of Popular Science and Technology.* London: Longmans, Green & Co., 1953.

WOOD, FREDERICK T. *English Verbal Idioms.* New York: Washington Square Press, 1967.

IX. Journals Dealing with Pedagogical Problems

English Language Teaching. Oxford University Press, London (The British Council).

English Teaching Abstracts. The British Council, London.

English Teaching Forum. Information Center Service of the United States Information Agency, Washington, D.C.

Foreign Language Annals. American Council on the Teaching of Foreign Languages, 62 Fifth Ave., N.Y.

Journal of English as a Second Language. American Language Institute, New York University, 1 Washington Square N., New York, N.Y.

Language Learning: A Journal of Applied Linguistics. English Language Institute, The University of Michigan, Ann Arbor, Mich.

Language Teaching Abstracts. Cambridge University Press, 32 East 57th St., N.Y.

The Linguistic Reporter (Newsletter of the Center for Applied Linguistics). 1346 Connecticut Ave., N.W., Washington, D.C.

International Review of Applied Linguistics in Language Teaching. Julius Groos Verlag, Heidelberg, W. Germany.

Tesol Newsletter. 801 N.E. 177 St., N. Miami Beach, Fla.

Tesol Quarterly (A Journal for Teachers of English to Speakers of Other Languages). Institute of Languages and Linguistics, Georgetown University, Washington, D.C.

The Modern Language Journal. National Federation of Modern Language Teachers Associations, St. Louis, Mo.

B C D E F G H I J   9 8 7 6 5 4 3